917.74
Hu   Hunt, Don
         Michigan fresh: a food-lover's guide
      to growers & bakeries. By Don and Mary
      Hunt. Albion, MI, Midwestern Guides,
      c.1992.
         288p. illus.

         ISBN:0-9623499-4-1
         1.Farm produce--Michigan--Guidebooks.
      2.Bakers and bakeries--Michigaan--Guide-
      books. 3.Wild plants, Edible--Michigan--
      Guidebooks. I.Hunt, Mary. II.Title.

MICHIGAN
·FRESH·

A food-lover's guide to growers & bakeries

DON and MARY HUNT

MIDWESTERN GUIDES
Albion, Michigan

ISBN 0-9623499-4-1

A Midwestern Guides Book

Midwestern Guides
504 Linden Avenue
Albion, Michigan 49224

Telephone:
(517) 629-4494

Printing:
Malloy Lithographing
Ann Arbor, Michigan

Photo credits: Ann Arbor Conference & Visitors Bureau, page 13.
Gregory Fox, page 233. Pat Juntti, page 287. Michigan Travel
Bureau, page 150. Midland Chamber of Commerce, page 105.
Muskegon Farmers' Market, page 115. State Archives of Michigan,
pages 14, 50, 64, 91. Ellen Weatherbee, pages 139, 146.

TABLE OF CONTENTS

WHEN THEY'RE RIPE IN MICHIGAN

FRUITS

Apples (fall) — August 25 - October 31

Apples (summer) — July 10 - August 31

Apricots — July 1 - August 15

Berries (black) — July 1 - July 10

Berries (red) — September 10 - October 1

Blueberries — July 13 - September 15

Cantaloupe — August 7 - September 20

Cherries (tart) — July 1 - August 1

Cherries (sweet) — July 1 - July 31

Grapes — September 1 - October 15

Melons — August 10 - frost

Nectarines — August 20 - September 10

Peaches — August 1 - September 20

Pears — August 20 - October 31

Plums — August 6 - September 20

Raspberries — July 1 - July 31

Raspberries — August 25 - September 30

Rhubarb — May 1 - May 31

Strawberries — June 7 - July 30

VEGETABLES

Asparagus — May 1 - June 30

Beans (snap, green) — July 1 - October 1

Broccoli — July 10 - October 15

Brussels Sprouts — October 1 - November 15

Cabbage — July 1 - October 31

Carrots — July 20 - October 31

Cauliflower — July 1 - October 31

Celery — June 15 - November 1

Corn (sweet) — August 1 - September 21
Cucumbers (for pickles) — August 1 - September
Cucumbers (salad) — July 7 - September 21
Dill — July 1 - July 31
Eggplant — July 1 - October 31
Greens (turnip, mustard, collards) — June 1 - Sept. 30
Kale — June 1 - September 30
Lettuce (head) — June 15 - September 15
Lettuce (leafy) — July 1 - September 15
Mushrooms — all year
Onions — August 25 - November 15
Onions (green) — June 15 - September 30
Parsnips — September 1 - October 15
Peas (sugar) — June 1 - June 30
Peppers — July 1 - September 30
Potatoes (white) — August 1 - October 31
Pumpkins — October 1 - October 31
Radishes — June 15 - October 31
Rutabagas — September 15 - November 30
Spinach — June 15 - October 15
Squash (summer) — July 15 - September 15
Squash (winter) — September 15 - November 30
Tomatoes (field) — August 10 - September 30
Turnips — June 10 - November 15

Farm Markets and U-Picks

Our list of farm markets includes only actual farms, where at least a good portion of the produce is grown on the premises and where the people in charge of the retail operation are farmers who know about how this produce was raised.

Differing notions of farm atmosphere

Though our criterion means the setting is rural and orchards and fields are adjacent, the atmosphere of the retail sales room may or may not be farm-like. Often the sales room is in a portion of a new metal outbuilding; it may also be a simple old wood stand, part of an old barn, or even a converted gas station.

Over the years, with the encouragement of marketing specialists at Michigan State University, some of these places have evolved into big rural destinations with bakeries, restaurants, and the like. Some have become sprawling stores; others are more like permanent, small-scale county fairs. Others try consciously to preserve the simple atmosphere of an old-fashioned family farm. We have tried to note these differences. You may want to call ahead to find more details.

By all means call ahead to be sure what is available if you're making a special trip to a farm market or U-pick. Fruits and vegetables can vary by as much as two weeks as to when they ripen. Occasionally, a freeze or hail storm will wipe out an entire crop.

Getting there

Our directions assume that you have a state of Michigan map. If you don't, they're available (in a smaller format) in travel atlases, or free at any Michigan Welcome Center at major freeway entrances to Michigan, or from the Michigan Travel Bureau (1-800-5432-YES).

A fair number of farm markets are on or near main roads, with easy-to-follow billboards and signs from major intersections. Others, however, are many miles from freeways, in often beautiful rural areas where it's surprisingly easy to get turned around or lost, even with good maps. If you enjoy backroads adventures, it doesn't hurt to have a compass in your car. And if getting lost is a frustrating ordeal rather than an adventure to you, it's smart to call ahead and get specific directions for your route, complete with landmarks.

Buying direct from farmers can be a wonderfully stabilizing ritual in this fast-changing world. That's the view of Justin Rashid, co-founder of American Spoon Foods in Petoskey. It's surprisingly refreshing to talk with hardworking, down-to-earth farm families, and to get out in the country to pick fruit. Friendly, unpretentious farm stands like Elzinga's near Torch Lake "don't just sell boxes of black cherries," says Rashid. "They sell well-being."

If you're especially economy conscious or are buying in large quantities, it pays to call around and ask for prices. We've provided the phone number for each farm market listed. They'll be happy to answer your questions.

About U-picks

Some farms have developed U-picks as a steady part of their business year after year. They need to buy extra insurance to cover U-pickers, and if their orchards and fields are extensive, they may need to hire extra people to direct customers to fields. Other farms may allow U-pick for some crops and not others, and in some years but not others. That's why our listings aren't always specific as to whether U-pick is offered. Call to find out.

The number of U-pick customers is seldom a constant. Mainstays of the business are retirees and ethnic groups who appreciate good food, buy produce at its peak of freshness, and can or freeze for winter. With them, days spent picking and canning are a rite of summer. When regional employment is high and money plentiful but time is tight, U-pick customers decline in numbers.

Tips for picking

◆ Wear sturdy shoes and clothes that can get dirty.

◆ Remember to bring hats, sunscreen, insect repellent, and gloves if necessary.

◆ A jug of water or lemonade and a picnic lunch add to your comfort and enjoyment. Many U-picks offer picnic facilities — call if it isn't mentioned. Inquire as to nearby parks with picnic areas.

SOUTHWEST MICHIGAN

Many fruit farms and blueberry farms just north of **South Haven**, around Saugatuck, Fennville, and Pullman, will be found in the West Michigan section.

▼   *The numbers before each entry are keyed to the map on p. 6.*

1   B & J Blueberry Ranch & Farm Market

(616) 423-8301.

*About 4 miles south of Decatur in the northeast corner of Cass County. On Gard's Prairie Road, south of Decatur Road. From I-94, take exit 56 to Decatur, turn left on Williams Street (Decatur Road). Also: 2 1/2 miles north of Marcellus Highway. **Open** July 1-September 7.*

U-pick and custom orders. **Blackberries, blueberries, currants, gooseberries, raspberries** (red, black, purple), plus **homemade jams and jellies**. The farm is in a beautiful area of dramatic topography where a moraine overlooks an ancient riverbed. It's not far from Russ Forest, which has virgin stands of oaks and black walnuts over 300 years old, a trout stream, hiking trails, and a pretty rustic picnic grounds with some huge tulip poplars, the giants of the eastern forest. A Michigan State Forestry research station, on Marcellus Highway 8 miles west of Marcellus.

2 Blueberry Patch

(616) 426-4521 or (616) 545-8125.

*Holloway Road, 1 mile west (toward Lake Michigan) from Sawyer in southwest Berrien County. Take I-94 exit 12. Sawyer Road crosses the Red Arrow Highway and turns into Holloway Rd. **Open** July 20th to end of August. Daily 9-6.*

Richard Soper's eight acres of blueberries include **Blue Crop** (earliest to ripen, they are large, grape-sized and easy to pick), **Ruple** (small, more tart and flavorful, good for cooking), and **Jersey** (tastiest, they ripen after August 10). Soper charges 75¢/lb. U-pick and $1/lb. ready-pick. It takes perhaps five minutes to pick a pound. Famed poet and biographer Carl Sandburg's goat farm wasn't far from here. For lots of information about nearby art galleries and food, see *Hunts' Guide to West Michigan*.

3 Calderwood Farms

(616) 471-2102.

2993 Lemon Creek Road, 2 1/2 miles west of Berrien Springs in Berrien County. From I-94 exit 16 at Bridgman, go north on the Red Arrow Highway 3 miles to Lemon Creek Road, east 8 3/4 miles. **Open** *about July 1-20 for* **cherries** *(8-7 Monday-Saturday). Peaches, pears, and apples: August 5-October 31 (10-6, Monday-Saturday).*

This big 300-acre farm is now managed by Nancy and Jim Calderwood, the fourth generation of Calderwoods to farm here. A handy cherry pitter is hand on hand to pit your ready-picked sour

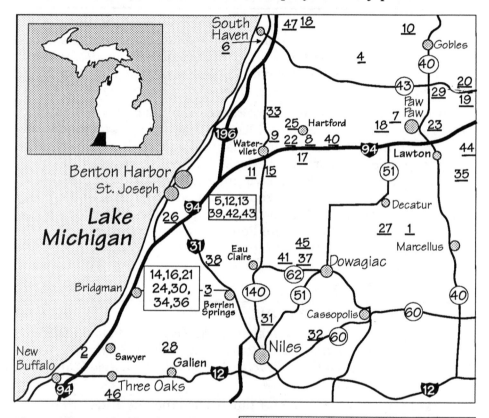

Farm Stands & U-Picks

SOUTHWEST MICHIGAN

Key

46	Farm Stand/ U Picks: pp. 5-24
🚦	Federal Highway
(140)	State Highway
●	Cities & towns

cherries (65¢/lb.). Sweet U-picked **cherries** are about $1/lb. (Remember: prices vary from season to season.)

Ten varieties of **peaches** ripen successively from about August 5 to mid-September. The key for good peaches is to buy ripe ones. Because it's important that peaches be picked immediately when they ripen, they are already picked ($14-$16/bushel). Blue (Stanley) **plums**, good for canning as well as eating, are available from late August to the first two weeks of September. **Pears** ripen about the same time. The sweet Santa Rosa plums ripen in mid-August.

U-pick is available for both **summer and fall apples**. Ready picked apples are $7 to $10 a bushel. U-pick apples are 20¢ to 25¢ a pound. **Cider** ($2.50/gallon) is pressed from the many varieties of fall apples grown here.

4 Cleveland Farms

(616) 521-4079.

In Van Buren County between Kalamazoo and South Haven. On County Road 655 halfway between Glendale (which is on M-43) and Bloomingdale. **Open** *late June to mid-September.*

U-pick **sweet cherries** (white and black) June 28-July 20. Early **McIntosh, Viking, Paula Red apples. Red plums** ripen August 25. **Stanley, Blufre prune plums** ripen September 1-15.

5 Culby's U-Pick

(616) 944-5996 or (616) 927-2315.

A few miles east of Benton Harbor. From I-94 exit 30 (Napier Rd.), go east on Napier 2 miles, then north on Blue Creek Rd. 1/2 mile. **Open** *approximately August 1-October 31, 9 am.-6 p.m. Closed Mondays.*

Pick **peaches, nectarines, sweet potatoes,** and **apples** at one of the oldest and most intensively cultivated parts of Michigan's fruit belt. Being about five miles from Lake Michigan makes this well suited to peaches; the season is typically from August 1 to September 15. Varieties, arranged from early to late, are: **Redhaven** (good for eating, freezing, canning); **Jayhaven** (also an all-around peach); **Suncrest** (multipurpose, firm flesh); **Baby Gold** (clingstone; best canning peach with an apricot flavor, also good dried); and **Goldrop** (small, all-gold, with a mild, sweet flavor).

Apple varieties are Earligold, **Jersey Mack, Empire, Akane, Ida**

Red, Connell Red, Red and Golden Delicious, Jonathan, and **Winesap.**

6 DeGrandchamp Blueberry Farm

(616) 637-3915.

14th & Blue Star Highway just south of South Haven. From I-196 take exit 18, go north on M-140, and soon turn west (left) onto 14th. **Open** *mid-July to mid-September. Monday-Thursday 8-6, Friday-Sunday 8-8.*

One of the major blueberry plantations in the nation's top blueberry state, DeGrandchamp offers you the chance to pick your own or buy picked fruit and vegetables at its farm market. You can fill a gallon container with six pounds of **blueberries** in half an hour. Throughout July you can also pick **raspberries** and in August, **blackberries**.

Visitors are invited to tour the packaging and processing plant. Fresh blueberries are shipped UPS throughout the U.S.

7 Diversity Farms

(616) 657-6283.

County Road 374 and 45th Street. A few miles west of Paw Paw on 45th St. and County Road 374 in the heart of the Fruit Belt in central Van Buren County. From Paw Paw, take the Red Arrow Highway to Lake Cora golf course, then north 1 mile, west 1/2 mile to northwest corner of 374 and 45th.

Early to late **apples,** Haven **peaches,** Bartlett and Bosc **pears,** Montmorency red **tart cherries,** Concord **grapes.**

8 Dowd's Fresh Fruit

(616) 621-3644.

Just north of I-94 exit 46 at Hartford. **Open** *9-7 in season, to 5 in winter.*

A produce store in a converted gas station on a freeway exit makes a pleasant, super-convenient highway pit stop that's far healthier than McDonald's. It's owned and operated by the Dowd family, whose orchards extend along I-94 behind it. In season, homegrown produce is featured: **strawberries, cherries, peaches, blueberries, melons, apples, cantaloupe, plums, nectarines, pears, pumpkins,** plus many kinds of vegetables, from **asparagus** to

sweet corn and tomatoes to **cabbage, squash, and pumpkins.**

The year-round grocery section offers sandwiches, produce from out of state, and a superior selection of jams, preserves, maple syrup, and other Michigan farm products.

9 Epple Orchards

(616) 463-5165.

On M-140, 1/2 mile north of Watervliet in northern Berrien County. From I-94, take Watervliet exit north. **Open** *July 1-November 1, 9-6.*

This homey, unusually attractive farm stand sells a wide variety of fruits and vegetables: **melons, apples, peaches, sweet cherries, plums, sweet corn, snap beans, tomatoes, squash,** and more.

10 Fritz Blueberries & Strawberries

(616) 521-7655.

In northeast Van Buren County 2 miles west and 1/2 mile north of Gobles on County Road 388. From I-94 at Paw Paw take M-40 north 11 miles north to Gobles, then west on 388.

Buy or pick **blueberries** and **red raspberries** in the last week of July and August. Buy or pick **strawberries** first two weeks of June.

11 Fruit Acres Farm Market

(616) 468-3668.

Northeast of Benton Harbor, off I-94 at Coloma exit, on south side. **Open** *late May through October.*

Sweet cherries are a specialty here, including U-Pick. Also an abundance of **peaches** and **apples**, plus strawberries, blueberries, cantaloupe, summer strawberry apples, and grapes. **Sweet corn** heads the list of vegetables. **Cider** available daily.

12 Gatchell's Farm Market

(616) 944-5779.

Just east of Benton Harbor. From I-94, take exit 29 (Pipestone), go east on Meadowbrook 4 miles to 5040 Meadowbrook. Or take Meadowbrook west from M-140 4 miles. **Open** *daily 9-8. Asparagus: late April to early June. Fruit: July through October.*

A simple, old-fashioned farm market sits amid an area of rolling hills and tidy fruit farms. In blossom time in early May, the views from the ridgetop here across miles of orchards would be spectacular, and you could stop here to buy fresh **asparagus**. Otherwise, Gatchell's sells fruit: **sweet and tart cherries, peaches, pears, plums, and fall apples.**

13 Higbee's Farm

(616) 926-8014.

162 S. Blue Creek Rd. just east of Benton Harbor. From I-94 exit 30 (Napier Rd.), go east on Napier 1 1/2 miles, left on Benton Center Rd. to Highland, then 1/2 mile to large sign. **Opens** *in early June.*

U-pick in a heavily agricultural area of orchards and vegetable farms. **Strawberries, sweet cherries, black and red raspberries, vegetables**, and many kinds of **peaches**, including Garnet Beauty, Red Haven, Glo Haven, Sun Crest, Crest Haven, Baby Gold, Red Skin, and Encore. Some picked fruit is also available.

14 Hillside Orchards

(616) 471-7558.

Fleisher Lane, 2 1/2 miles southeast of Baroda in central Berrien County. Take U.S. 31 to Hinchman Road, west 2 1/2 miles to Fleisher Lane (between Scottdale and Hollywood Roads), south to end of Fleisher Lane. **Open** *Monday, Wednesday, and Friday, 7:30 a.m.-6 p.m.*

You can enter the packing house of this mostly wholesale, 116-acre fruit farm to get good prices on a large variety of **apples, sweet and tart cherries, peaches, plums, nectarines,** and **apricots.**

15 Hinkelman Farms

(616) 463-3385.

On M-140, 2 1/2 miles south of the I-94 Watervliet exit (Exit 41). **Open** *June 5- July 1. Monday-Thursday, 8-8. Friday-Sunday 8-5.*

Strawberries are the big crop on this 100-acre farm. 13 acres are grown; the most popular variety is **Guardian**. U-pick costs about 55¢ a pound.

16 Johanson's Apple World

(616) 422-2426.

8700 Keehn Road, 2 1/2 miles east of Bridgman just west of Baroda. Keehn is just off Lemon Creek Road, between Holden and

Cleveland roads. From I-94 exit 16 at Bridgman, take the Red Arrow Highway north to Lemon Creek Rd., and go east 2 miles to Keehn. **Open** *August 15 to end of October. Daily 10-dusk.*

Former mechanical engineer Roy Johanson has planted 700 to 800 **apple** trees since 1975 — some 16 varieties in all. He's best known for the tasty **Mutsu**, which you can pick for $6 a half bushel. Other varieties are $5 a bushel. There's a small **gooseberry** patch in case you happen to be in the vicinity in early July. Homemade **jams** and **jellies** are also available, as is **honey**.

17 Klug Orchards

(616) 621-4037.

65980 66th Ave. a mile southwest of Hartford. From I-94 exit 46, take County Rd. 687 (it's the main north-south road) south 1/2 mile, then west a mile on 66th Ave. to 66th St., northeast corner. **Open** *mid-July through October 9-7 daily.*

Free samples of the fruits and vegetables grown on this 80-acre family farm are always available. Most produce is available picked or U-pick, except for some **older apple varieties** on trees too big to be picked without ladders. There are **tomatoes** and other vegetables,

Blueberries have become the fastest-growing and most profitable crop in Michigan. They thrive in low-lying, acidic soils unsuitable for most crops. While the legendary fruit-growing region around South Haven became famous for peaches, blueberries have become the area's biggest money-maker.

peaches, blueberries, and **apples**, starting with the Williams Red in summer. Other apple varieties are Macintosh, Jonathan, Paula Red, Delicious, and Winesap (both Turley and Stayman). **Apple cider** is pressed in nearby Hartford. There are also **pumpkins** and **squash**.

18 Lacota Depot

(616) 253-4586.

6 miles east of South Haven on Phoenix Rd. From I-196, take Phoenix east. **Open** *July through October.*

This Fruit Belt train station is conveniently surrounded by fields and orchards. Produce is available at the farm market or U-pick. Fruits: **sweet and tart cherries, apricots, raspberries, peaches, nectarines, plums, pears, melons**, and 20 varieties of **apples**. Fresh **cider** beginning in September.

The **Kal-Haven Trail** from South Haven to Kalamazoo goes right by here. A bike trail on a converted railroad bed, it offers bicyclists and hikers a delightful combination of villages and hamlets to explore and fruit farms of all kinds. For a free map and brochure, call (616) 637-2788, daytime, 7 days a week in summer.

19 Leduc Blueberry Farm

(616) 628-2769.

30th Street, 11 1/2 miles west of Kalamazoo. Take M-43 west from U.S. 131 to 30th Street, 1 mile **south. Open** *July 5-September 1, 8-8 daily. Sunday 10-6.*

Blueberries on these 170 acres can be bought picked or U-pick. Roger Leduc was one of the early growers of Michigan blueberries, the state's fastest-growing farm product. He has stuck with his U-pick operation even when prices for the berries have been high and other growers opted to shift to wholesale. Quality is a real concern of his. He grows 14 of the over 50 varieties of blueberries available.

20 Leduc Strawberry Farm

(616) 628-2769.

On 30th Street, 11 1/2 miles west of Kalamazoo. Take M-43 west from U.S. 131 to 30th Street, then 1/2 mile **north. Open** *8-8 daily during season. Sunday 10-6.*

Roger Leduc has been growing strawberries and blueberries since

1955 and has been a steady performer. His 10 to 12 acres of **strawberries** include six varieties, picked or U-pick.

21 Lemon Creek Fruit Farms & Winery

(616) 471-1321.

*533 Lemon Creek Rd. 5 miles east of Bridgman and 7 miles west of Berrien Springs. A mile east of Baroda. From I-94, take the Bridgman exit (16), go north on Red Arrow Hwy. 2 miles to Lemon Creek Rd., then east 5 miles. **Open** regularly May-December: Monday-Sat 9-6, Sun 12-6. Other times by appointment.*

The Lemon family has grown **grapes** and other fruit here, in the beautiful, rolling fruit-growing area between Baroda and Berrien Springs, since the 1850s. Between the farmhouse and orchards is a metal building housing the winery, fruit sales room, and tasting room. Visitors can **picnic** at tables outside the tasting room.

Fruits for sale (packaged or U-pick) include **raspberries**, four kinds of **sweet cherries**, **tart cherries**, three varieties of **peaches**, **nectarines**, **plums**, **pears**, and eight kinds of **apples**. The Lemons also sell all the varieties of grapes they use in making their award-winning wines. (See the chapter on wine grapes, page 132.)

In 1981, after years of falling fruit prices, many other southwest Michigan fruit farmers also replaced their orchards with wine grapes. Prices fell dramatically as a result. The Lemons, like an increasing number of fruit and vegetable producers, realized they'd be more secure financially if they marketed their own produce and added value to it in the production process. Their winery is the result. The personable Cathy Lemon is happy to give visitors an informal tour of the wine-making facilities. Just outside, you can see the vines, neatly labeled by variety, and the tall mechanical picker that straddles the rows of vines and harvests the grapes.

A June **festival** each Father's Day weekend includes hayrides, games for kids, arts and crafts booths, and live music.

22 McFarland Fruit Farm

(616) 621-4036.

*Just north of I-94 exit 46 at Hartford. Located at Shell gas station just off I-94. **Open** July 1-October 31, 9-7.*

Another gas-station freeway outlet of a family fruit farm. It sells **sweet cherries**, **blueberries**, **peaches**, **prunes**, **plums**, **raspberries**, **melons**, **apples**, **nectarines**, **tomatoes**, **grapes**.

23 Morrison's Sunnyfields Farm

(616) 657-4934.

On the Red Arrow Highway, 2 1/2 miles east of Paw Paw. Or 3 miles west of the I-94 Mattawan exit. (Go north, not into Mattawan.) **Open** *May 1 until first week in November, daily 9-6.*

This rambling but quaint farm stand under a huge tree dates from the 1930s; the farm has been in the Morrison family since 1835.

The farm is 200 acres, 130 of which are under cultivation. The season kicks off in early May with 25 acres of **asparagus**. A specialty is **peppers**; many varieties are grown. There are also **Asian vegetables**, including **eggplant** and various **greens**. Ten acres of **sweet corn** are devoted to the popular Peaches 'n' Cream variety. Other vegetables are **broccoli, beans, squash,** and **tomatoes** (the only U-pick crop).

There are also **apples, cantaloupe, cherries,** Concord and French **hybrid** (Seyvil blanc and Foch) **grapes, peaches, strawberries,** red **tart** and **sweet cherries, grapes. Cider** is made here in fall; **honey,**

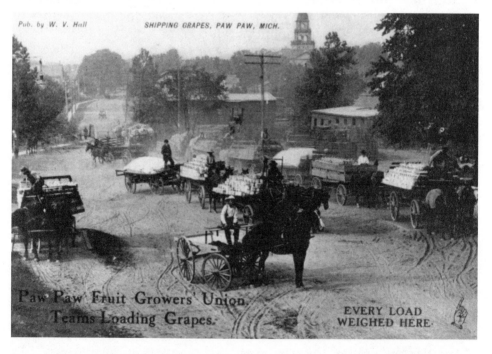

For over a hundred years, Paw Paw has been a major shipping point for fruit. In this photo taken around 1905, wagons wait for produce to be weighed and loaded onto trains. The tower of Paw Paw's splendid new courthouse is in the background.

jams and jellies, and **popcorn** are sold here, too.

Next door the current owner's Taiwanese wife runs Annly's Chow, a good Chinese restaurant that serves fresh fruit pies for dessert. (It's open year-round except January until 8 p.m.; closed Sundays and Mondays.)

There's much more to Paw Paw than the two wineries and the cluttered commercial strip between downtown and I-94. (Actually only St. Julian's still makes wine; Warner's makes juice and runs a pleasant garden restaurant.) The downtown is surprisingly lively, and the village has many old houses from its first decade of settlement in the 1830s. Seek out the post office a block north and west of the main four-corners, and you can see one of the most interesting 1930s WPA murals in Michigan. The courthouse murals are terrific, too, in a more classically voluptuous way. And don't miss Maple Lake and the Maple Lane island park, west off M-40 as you head out of town to the north.

24 Neal Nitz Farms

(616) 422-1246.

Not far south of St. Joseph. 3 miles south of Stevensville and a mile north of Baroda on Stevensville-Baroda Rd. **Open** *July-early October.*

Tart cherries, cantaloupes, and **Concord grapes** are sold at this roadside stand.

25 Nutting Family Farm

(616) 621-3062.

On 68th Street about 5 miles northeast of Watervliet in western Van Buren County. Take I-94 exit 41 (Watervliet) and go 4 miles north on M-140 to CR 376. East 3 miles to 68th Street, north 1 mile. **Open** *beginning May 5, daily 8-5.*

U-pick **asparagus, blueberries, watermelon, squash, raspberries, peppers, tomatoes, sweet corn, tart cherries, peaches, cucumbers, okra, strawberries, turnips, pumpkins, Indian corn, gourds, cabbage**, and other fruits and vegetables.

26 Nye's Apple Barn

(616) 429-0596.

Just southeast of St. Joseph and immediately north of I-94 exit 27 at Niles Ave./M-63. **Open** *daily May through October, 9-6.*

The retail sales "barn" just north of the freeway exit looks completely suburban, but the fruits, vegetables, and bedding plants sold here are actually raised quite near here, in the Nye Brothers' Orchards on Hollywood Road. Catering to St. Joseph's old-money resorters seems to be a big part of the business; **peaches** and **pears** are shipped UPS. Nye's grows hardy mums for sale for fall planting starting in mid-September; cut asters, statice, snaps, and glads are available in July and August. **Cold cider** made on the premises is available in year-round.

Fruits sold at the market include **apples, blueberries, cantaloupes, sweet cherries, grapes, peaches, pears, plums, strawberries,** and **raspberries**. As for fresh-picked vegetables, there's **asparagus, eggplant, greens, peppers, pumpkins** and **squash, sweet corn,** and **tomatoes**. And there's U-pick, too, for **raspberries, peaches, apples,** and other fruits and vegetables.

27   *Peacewood*

(616) 423-8527.

93356 36th, south of Decatur and 1 1/2 miles west of Gravel Lake in extreme southern Van Buren County. Best approached without getting lost from Marcellus Highway 4 miles west of Marcellus. At the Thompson Corners Grocery, turn north onto Lawrence Rd., go 3 1/2 miles due north. Farm is on west side of road. **Open** *daily from July through September, 10-6.*

Twelve acres of a wide variety of vegetables are raised here, according to principles of sustainable agriculture but not totally organic. (Sheep manure is the fertilizer, and spraying is avoided when possible, but chemical sprays may be used to control mildews and other diseases.)

Highlights are some two dozen kinds of **peppers**, including many hot ones suitable for drying; many kinds of **green and yellow beans;** **sweet corn; tomatoes**, including Roma tomatoes for making sauces, and **melons (cantaloupe** and **yellow and pink watermelons)**. Also: **beets, eggplants,** a big representation from the **cabbage** family, and many **winter squash**, plus **pumpkins, gourds,** and decorative corn. Cut flowers and tomatoes are U-pick, everything else is picked.

The attractive farm is in a remote and beautiful part of southwestern Michigan, where ancient riverbeds contrast with high moraines and enough mature forest to support a hardwood logging industry. Nearby Russ Forest (see page 5) offers picnic spots and

Farmer Darlene Rhodes, along with husband Gene, grows 200 tons of pumpkins and 50 tons of squash. They sell it all from their farm stand. There's a huge variety to choose from. The Rhodeses call themselves "the pumpkin people" and reflect this theme with orange clothes, orange vehicles, an orange tractor, and lots more. Darlene puts out a terrific cookbook of pumpkin and winter squash recipes which she gives away to customers.

hiking trails through a virgin forest with spectacular black walnuts and tulip poplars, and oaks that are probably over 300 years old.

In 1969 farmers John and Judy Yaeger left the University of Chicago for country living with a big measure of physical work. Most of Peacewood's customers are local people and cottagers at nearby lakes. The Yeagers are happy to provide suggestions on how to use and preserve their produce; their recipes highlight salsas and things they've grown a lot of. (Judith, incidentally, has returned to academe but says that working on the farm is a life-enhancing antidote to the craziness of academic politics.)

28 Phillippi Fruit Farm & Cider Mill

(616) 422-1700.

On Cleveland Ave. 1/4 mile south of Glendora and about 5 miles east of Sawyer in southern Berrien County. You could take Cleveland south from St. Joseph or north from Galien and U.S. 12, or take Sawyer and Glendora roads east from Sawyer to Cleveland, then south (right). **Open** *daily May thru mid-November, 9-6.*

U-pick fruits: **sour cherries** (pitting available), **Concord grapes,
apples.** Picked fruits: **strawberries, sweet cherries, pears,
melons, peaches, plums, apples. Apple cider** and **grape juice** are
pressed here.

Vegetables: **asparagus, peppers, squash, pumpkins, tomatoes,
turnips, turnip greens, cabbage, sweet corn, beans, potatoes,
cucumbers, eggplant, cauliflower.**

29 The Pumpkin People

(616) 668-2952.

On M-43, 6 miles west of Kalamazoo. Look for the pumpkin mailbox.
Open *September 15 to mid November. Daily 10-8.*

Gene and Darlene Rhodes grow 200 tons of **pumpkins** and 50
tons of **squash** on the 140-acre centennial farm. Unlike most farm
operations, the Rhodeses don't do any wholesale business at all.
Everything they grow they sell at their farm stand, where they price
their vegetables in a relaxed subjective fashion rather than by the
pound. Each pumpkin is viewed in terms of size and quality before a
price (normally quite reasonable) is assigned. "A whole lot depends
of the buyer's attitude," explains Gene.

There are lots of varieties of squash available: **Butternut, Acorn,
Silver Hubbard, Golden Hubbard, Green Hubbard, Buttercup,
Golden Buttercup, Sweetmeat, Sweet Potato, Sweet Dumpling**,
and occasionally **Golden Nugget**.

Pumpkins range from miniature decorative varieties that are
edible but can fit in the palm of your hand to ones weighing over
100 pounds. Some are best suited for jack-o-lanterns. Varieties good
for baking include New England and Cushaw.

You can also buy **sunflower heads** from the Rhodeses, as well as
Indian corn, corn shocks, straw, and **hay**.

30 Quint's Fruit Farm

(616) 422-1375.

*497 E. Shawnee Road, 5 1/2 miles east of Bridgman, 5 1/2 miles
west of Berrien Springs. From I-94 take Exit 16 (Bridgman). Go north
on Red Arrow Highway to first stoplight (Lake Street), turn right. Lake
Street becomes Shawnee Road.* **Open** *July through September.*

At Quint's you can get picked or U-pick **peaches, grapes,** and
apples in season. **Cider** is also on hand.

31 Radewald Farms

(616) 683-4194.

2580 Pucker St., 5 miles north of Niles. Pucker runs parallel to M-140 between it and M-51 and M-140. From either state highway it's reached from Ullery Rd. on the south or Pokagon Rd. on the north. **Open** *approximately June 10-25.*

U-pick **strawberries**.

32 Roseland Farms Market

(616) 445-8987.

M-60 near corner of Dailey Road, 5 miles west of Cassopolis, 6 miles east of Niles. **Open** *daily 9-5.*

This serious organic farming venture features some **fruits** and **vegetables, wild apple juice,** and organic **grains** and **meats**. You can buy organically grown beef and pork, sold by halves, quarters, and individual cuts, as well as chicken and turkey.

33 Sarno's Farm Market

(616) 764-1721.

On M-140, 7 miles north of Watervliet. Or: on M-140 5 miles south of I-196 near South Haven. **Open** *July 20-November 5.*

Peaches, apples, nectarines, plums, pears, and **grapes**, plus **tomatoes, sweet corn,** and most other vegetables.

34 Schmidt's Blueberries

(616) 465-5206.

On North Gast Rd. just east of Bridgman Take I-94 to Exit 16 (Bridgman). Turn north on Red Arrow Highway to stoplight. Turn east at light, continue 1 mile, turn north onto North Gast Road. **Open** *daily, July 15-Labor Day, 9-8.*

Schmidt's sells **blueberries** either picked or U-pick. **Peaches** are sold ready-picked only. Unlike some huge blueberry plantations farther north, the setting here has a pleasantly intimate rural feel.

35 Schultz's Fruitridge Farms

(616) 668-3724.

On County Road 652 1 1/2 miles south of Mattawan. (Mattawan is between Paw Paw and Kalamazoo a mile south of I-94. Take Mattawan exit 66 south to Mattawan; main street becomes 652 and leads to farm. **Open** *August 1- October 31.*

Peaches, apples, plums.

36 Shafer Orchards

(616) 422-1972.

About 6 miles southeast of Bridgman and I-94 in west central Berrien County. Take I-94 Exit 16 (Bridgman). Turn north onto Red Arrow Hwy., east at light onto Lake St. which becomes Shawnee Rd. Go 5 miles to Hills Road, south 3/4 mile to Shafer Road.

Shafer sells **vegetables** as well as U-pick **apples, grapes, nectarines, peaches,** and **plums.** Cut flowers are also available.

37 Sprague's Old Orchard

(616) 782-2058 or (616) 782-8578.

1 mile north of Indian Lake between Eau Claire and Dowagiac on 33085 Middle Crossing Rd. at Indian Lake Rd. From M-62 between Eau Claire and Dowagiac, go north on Indian Lake Rd. to farm. **Open** *daily except Sunday July-December, 8 a.m.-6 p.m.*

This exceptionally beautiful old farm and orchard has been farmed by the same family since 1868. It has a Civil War-era house and big trees. Antique farm implements are displayed by the sales barn. Most fruit is sold picked only. U-pick or picked: **apples,** sometimes **peaches** and **plums.** Sold in packages only: cherries, raspberries, blueberries. Also for sale: **sweet corn, fall squash** and **pumpkins,** Indian corn, gourds, and dried flowers (both loose and in arrangements). Ten to twelve varieties of **apples** are grown here, and all are used in making **cider** with a rack and cloth press.

38 Stover's U-Pick & Farm Market

(616) 471-1401.

On U.S. 31, 3 1/2 miles north of Berrien Springs. Take I-94 to exit 28, go south on U.S. 31 8 miles. From South Bend, go north on U.S. 31 24 miles. **Open** *June-November, 8-8, closed Sunday.*

Picked or U-pick **strawberries, sweet and tart cherries, red** and **black raspberries, blackberries, blueberries, peaches, plums, grapes, nectarines, apples, pumpkins, apricots.** Also vegetables.

39 Sunrise Farms

(616) 944-1457.

On Hillandale Road just east of Benton Harbor. From I-94 take Exit 30, east on Napier 2.6 miles. **Open** *June 5-October 15, 9-6.*

This big (200-acre), attractive family farm, run by Jim Culby and his sons Larry and Mike, makes a wonderful picking destination for people who like authentic farm atmosphere without entertainment. A good deal of its business is wholesale, so there are lots of big crates around. The drive is dirt, wetted to keep the dust down, and the buildings predate World War II. (The picturesque farmhouse was built by talented designer-builders from the legendary House of David religious community in Benton Harbor.) An 1835 log cabin has been moved to the site and furnished by Jim's late wife to look pretty much as it did in pioneer days. It's open to visitors. They are welcome to use shady picnic tables and a barbecue grill.

You can buy picked or U-pick **blueberries, red raspberries, nectarines, sweet** and **tart cherries,** and 11 varieties of **peaches.** (Early peaches make the best eating.) **Peppers** are another specialty here; they come sweet and hot, in green and red. Other vegetables for sale are **sweet potatoes, cucumbers,** and **tomatoes,** including Roma tomatoes for sauces and canning.

40 Sunshower

(616) 674-3103.

48548 60th Avenue 2 1/4 miles east of Lawrence to 48th, 1 mile south to 60th, 1/4 mile. **Open** *year-round.*

Organic pears and **apples,** and many organic **vegetables. Apple cider.** Fresh and frozen **apple cider, pear cider,** tart **cherry juice** and many variations of **blended juices, apple and pear butter,** also **maple syrup** and occasionally chestnuts. U-pick by arrangement.

41 Tree-Mendus Fruit Farm

(616) 782-7101.

Summer ripe & ready report: (616) 461-4187. On East Eureka Road, off M-62, 2 miles due east of Eau Claire and 5 miles northwest of Berrien Springs. From I-94, take M-140 (Watervliet exit 41) south about 14 miles to M-62, go east 1/4 mile and look for signs. **Open** *last week in June into October. To Labor Day daily except Tuesday 10-6. After Labor Day through 3rd week in October Friday-Monday 10-6.*

Canning may not be as delightful as this idealized illustration in a 1920s women's magazine suggests, but it is a satisfying way to capture "summer in a jar," in the words of songwriter Greg Brown. Canned jams and fruit compotes in liqueur made wonderful gifts, too. Some advantages of buying from farmers rather than raising your own: you can get the produce all at once, rather than harvesting it gradually, and you can choose a cooler day to buy it and can it.

Cherries ripen in July, followed by **apricots, peaches, plums, nectarines, apples, pears**, and **pumpkins**. All are grown on the farm and sold U-pick or picked. Recently the Teichmans have gotten into **experimental vegetables**, traditional and exotic, for sale when available.

Beginning in the 1960s, fruit farmers have found it difficult to make a profit selling their fruit wholesale. Trucking strikes, farm labor boycotts, and erratic prices led far sighted growers to think about diversifying. In this challenging new economic environment, many successful growers have succeeded by combining direct-to-consumer sales with recreation.

No one has done this better than Herb Teichman of Tree-Mendus Fruit. He has transformed his father's Skyline Orchards, tucked away on a scenic, hilly road west of Indian Lake, into a well-organized, attractive visitor destination, aggressively promoted while still personal and low-key.

Tree-Mendus Fruit artfully provides a pleasant day in the country for a generation of Americans who no longer have relatives down on the farm. In addition to 560 acres of U-pick orchards, there's a big **picnic area** and 120-acre **nature park** with **hiking trails** through wooded wildlife areas with ponds. Visitors can fill **water jugs** at a deep well.

Teichman manages to focus on fruit and teach visitors a lot about it. He loves to talk to customers when time permits. His outstanding

orchard tours cover the evolution of fruit varieties, samples of antique apples, and a first-hand look at cultivation techniques from grafting and pruning to harvesting, depending on the season. **One-hour tours** (from $3 to $5/person, depending on options, with a $40 minimum) are given by appointment, on short notice when possible. On the weekend of the Cherry Pit Spitting Championship, and on Saturdays and Sundays after Labor Day, musicians and comic characters circulate in the orchard, and an orchard admission fee ($4/adult, $2/child) is charged, which includes a narrated orchard tour by wagon. The fee is credited toward purchase of fruit.

Teichman's **"old-time apple museum"** has grown from a few dozen antique apple trees to a remarkable collection of over 300 varieties from around the world. Here you can taste the Spitzbergen (Thomas Jefferson's favorite), the Westfield Seek-No-Further, and the tasty, tart, crisp Calville Blanc, which goes back to 1627. Modern marketing demands apples that look uniform and attractive, ship well, and can be picked at once. Such requirements have eliminated many old favorites. About 50 antique varieties are for sale here.

Apples you pick yourself cost 38¢ a pound, while antique and unusual varieties are more like a dollar. Jams, apple butter, frozen peaches and cherries, homemade cherry topping, and the farm's distinctive varieties of cider and cherry cider are for sale in the **Tree House Country Store.** Waffle boat desserts, cooked while you wait, have peaches, cherries, or apples in season and lots of whipped cream. On crisp fall days, pickers and hikers can warm themselves by the big fireplace.

42 Vineyard View Farms

(616) 927-3216.

Corner of Yore and Snyder roads east of Benton Harbor. Take I-94 to Exit 30, turn east on Napier Ave. to Yore Ave. South 1 1/2 miles to farm. Open August 15-October 15. Monday-Saturday, 10-7. Closed Sunday.

U-pick **blueberries, grapes, peaches.**

43 Weckwerth Orchards/ Stan & Steve's Farm Stand

(616) 944-5862.

On Territorial Road, 5 miles south of Watervliet at the east edge of Berrien County. Take I-94 to Watervliet exit, go 5 miles south on

M-140 to northwest corner of Territorial. First farm on right. **Open** *July 10-October 31.*

Summer and fall **apples, pears, peaches, sweet corn, tart** and **sweet cherries, grapes**.

44 Westview Farm

(616) 668-3603.

On County Road 652, about 1 1/2 miles south of Mattawan. Mattawan is between Paw Paw and Kalamazoo. From I-94, take exit 66 south through Mattawan. Main St. becomes 652. **Open** *July 1-November 15, 8:30-8 daily.*

Picked or U-pick **sweet and tart cherries, peaches, pears, apples, grapes,** and **pumpkins. Apple cider**.

45 Wicks Apple House

(616) 782-7306.

52281 Indian Lake Rd. north of Indian Lake between Eau Claire and Dowagiac. From I-94 Watervliet exit, go south 10 miles on M-140, turn left onto Columbia Rd. Where it ends, turn left onto Indian Lake Rd. **Open** *Mem. Day through October, 8-6. Closed Mon. except holiday weekends.*

This farm market has grown into a cider mill, bakery, gift shop, and a very pleasant, informal restaurant for breakfast and lunch — all without losing too much of the flavor of the family farm it remains. Three generations of Wickses help grow the **asparagus, tart cherries, Stanley plums, apples,** and **Concord grapes** that are sold here, along with other Michigan produce whenever possible. No U-pick, but customers can select their own apples from big orchard-run crates.

46 Williams Orchard

(616) 756-9417.

18967 Three Oaks Rd. south of Three Oaks (7 miles east of New Buffalo) and almost in Indiana. **Open** *July 20 through November.*

Nectarines, peaches, cider and **honey**. U-pick **apples** and peaches. See also page 166.

47 Z Z Ranch

(616) 253-4344.

6 miles east of South Haven, just inside the Allegan County line near Lacota. Take Phoenix east to 62nd, go north 2 1/2 miles to farm. **Open** *May-November when produce is in season.*

Bedding plants and vegetable seedlings, plus **beans, broccoli, cabbage, cauliflower,** and **pumpkins.**

WEST MID-MICHIGAN

See also Southwest Michigan section for many fruit and vegetable farms in the South Haven area within Van Buren County.

▼ *The numbers before each entry are keyed to the map on p. 26.*

1 Aussicker's Blueberries

(616) 399-6267.

3 miles north and 4 miles west of Holland at O-15985 Quincy. Go north from Holland or Zeeland on most any street to Quincy, west to 160th Avenue, 1 1/2 miles east of Lake Michigan. Look for the gold barn on northeast corner. **Open** *in July to Labor Day until sunset,*

This 27-acre blueberry patch grows over 10 varieties, extending the normal season from about July 10 to Labor Day. U-pick **blueberries** sell for about 65¢ a pound.

2 Beard's Produce

(616) 896-8296.

3 miles north of Allegan and about 25 miles southwest of Grand Rapids. From U.S. 131, take Dorr exit to 142nd Ave., 7 miles west, 1 mile south, 1/2 mile west to farm at 2763 140th Ave. Or take 30th St. (County Rd. 37) from Allegan. **Open:** *U-pick strawberries June 10-July 1, 8-8. Asparagus available in May, 9-6. U-pick blueberries July 20-September 1, Hours 8-5,Tuesday & Thursday to 8, Saturday until 3. Closed Sun.*

Otto Beard runs this 100-acre farm which his dad began farming 25 years ago. The 11 acres of **asparagus** are picked by locals; you're best advised to place orders ahead of time. They'll keep about a week in the refrigerator. The **Early Glo** and larger **Guardian strawberries** are best picked earliest in the season.

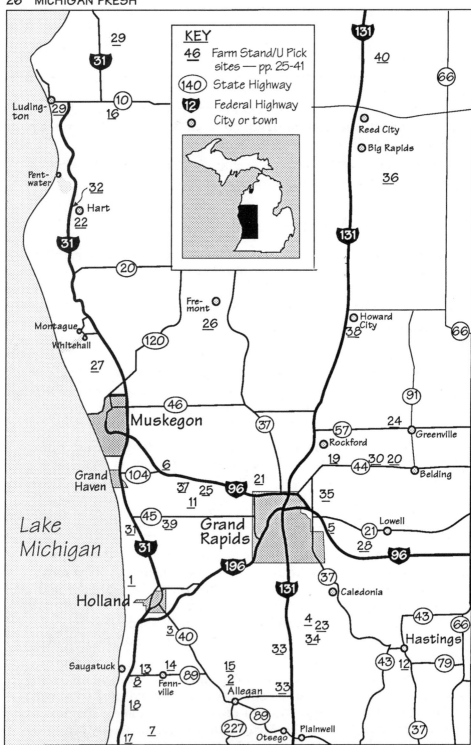

KEY

46   Farm Stand/U Pick sites — pp. 25-41

(140)   State Highway

12   Federal Highway

○   City or town

Farm Stands & U-Picks WEST MID-MICHIGAN

3 Big Blueberry Farm

(616) 396-3185.

3 miles south of Holland at 84303 52nd, just off M-40. From I-196, take exit 49, turn south on to M-40, go 1 1/2 miles, follow signs. **Open** *July 1-September 1, daily 8-6.*

This 96-acre farm, run by Juliann Cook, has 30 acres of **blueberries**, which you can buy U-pick (60¢/lb.)or ready-pick ($12 for 10 pounds). Five varieties of blueberries are grown here. **Jerseys**, ripe the first week of August, are the all-around favorites for their sweet taste. Also sweet are the season's first variety, the **Early Blues**. **Blue Rays** have a fuller flavor which some connoisseurs prefer. They're usually ready the last two weeks of July, the same time the tart **Blue Crops** ripen. **Rubels**, available in late July or early August, are preferred for pies.

4 Bin-An-Oan Orchards

(616) 455-4278.

12 miles south of Grand Rapids at the corner 84th and South Division. From U.S.-131 take exit 74 at 84th Street. East on 84th. First farm on left. **Open** *July through December, Monday-Saturday 9-6.*

The 14 acres here provide a full-time occupation for former biology teacher Abe Moerland. Here he grows **apples, pears, peaches, plums, pumpkins**, and some **vegetables**. Northern Spies are a favorite of the 20 to 25 apple varieties grown. A rack and cloth cider press makes fall **cider**, accompanied by fresh doughnuts.

"Bin-An-Oan" means "garden of peace" in Chinese. It's a legacy of Mrs. Moerland's parents, who were missionaries in China.

5 William Bos Greenhouse and Farms

(616) 949-5685.

5 miles east of Grand Rapids on Spalding Ave. From I-96, take exit 43B (Cascade Rd.). Go east on Cascade Road about 1 mile to Spaulding, turn right. Go south 1/2 mile. **Open:** *May hours Monday-Friday 9-3, Saturday to 5. June -October: Monday-Friday 9-6, Saturday 9-5.*

Along with bedding plants, Bos sells **sweet corn, beans, broccoli, summer and fall squash, cucumbers, raspberries, tomatoes, potatoes**, and **peppers**, plus **honey** and **pumpkins**.

6 Vince Brown Farms

(616) 899-2333.

7 miles east of Coopersville between Grand Rapids and Muskegon. On 8th Ave. 4 1/2 miles north of I-96. Take I-96 to exit 25, then north 4 1/2 miles on 8th Ave. From Grand Haven, take 104 east to Nunica. At Nunica, take Cleveland east to 8th Ave., go north 1 1/2 miles on 8th Ave. to farm. **Open** *June-November. June-October: Monday, Wednesday, and Friday 7 a.m.-8 p.m., Saturday 7-5. In November, Monday and Saturday 9-6.*

U-pick **strawberries, red raspberries, tart cherries, blueberries, peaches, apples, tomatoes, pumpkins, broccoli, grapes, nectarines**. Picked **sweet cherries, peaches, prunes, apples, grapes, cabbage, broccoli, tomatoes, sweet corn, squash, pumpkins, cider**.

7 Ronald Brush Farm

(616) 637-5368.

788 66th St., east of South Haven. From I-196 exit 26 (Pullman exit), go east 2 miles to 66th, turn south 1/2 mile to farm on right side of road. **Open** *mid-July to mid-November.*

This 490-acre farm uses half its acreage to grow fruits and vegetables. Because most of the produce here is sold wholesale through brokers to major supermarket chains, visitors get to see big-time farming up close. Brush started the retail operation when the severe freeze of 1968 just about wiped out his peach crop.

The retail stand is located in a small part of the packing shed. Migrant families from Texas and Florida come up here and live during the picking season.

While you can get **peaches** in July, the specialty here is cole crops: **brussels sprouts, broccoli,** five kinds of **squash, cabbage, cauliflower,** and **apples.** You buy brussels sprouts by the stalk ($1); a good stalk yields about three pints. Broccoli is 50¢/lb. There are even better buys on seconds.

8 Conifer Lane Farm Market

(616) 561-2524.

On M-89 about 6 miles southeast of Saugatuck and 3 miles west of Fennville. Turn east onto M-89 from I-196 exit 34 or the far more scenic Blue Star Highway south of Saugatuck. **Open** *from mid-July through October, 9-6.*

This large produce market looks so spiffy and slick, you might not realize that most of the produce is grown in orchards right here or at the Ed Raak family's other farm closer to South Haven. A wide variety of fruits and vegetables are available U-pick or picked. Also on hand: **cider**, specialty cheeses, and free recipes.

11 Cook's Produce

(616) 837-8764.

*Between Grand Rapids and Grand Haven. On 60th Ave., between the villages of Eastmanville and Lamont. From I-96, take Eastmanville exit, go south on 68th Ave. to village, then east (right) on Leonard to 60th, south following signs to farm. Or take Leonard Street from Grand Rapids or Spring Lake to 60th Ave. **Open** June-October, 8-5.*

U-pick **strawberries, tomatoes**. Picked **beans, squash, peppers**. Leonard Street is an exceptionally pretty country road paralleling the Grand River and connecting three quaint river towns on its way from Grand Rapids to Spring Lake. Ask for directions to a nearby park across the Grand towards Grand Haven, in an area of bayous and wildlife.

12 Cotant's Farm Market

(616) 945-4180.

*Just south of Hastings about 25 miles southeast of Grand Rapids. On M-37 1 1/2 miles south of Hastings, and half a mile north of the M-79 intersection. **Open** mid-April-Halloween, Monday-Saturday, 9-6. Closed Sunday.*

Cotant's sells **apples, sweet corn**, and **bedding plants**. You can pick your own **strawberries** and **blueberries. Baked goods** and fresh pressed **cider** also for sale.

13 Crane Orchards and Cider Mill

(616) 561-5126.

*Southeast of Saugatuck and 1 1/2 miles west of Fennville on the north side of M-89. From I-196 exit 34, go east on M-89. **U-pick** (on north side of M-89) **open** beginning in late July daily 9 a.m.-6 p.m. Hours of **Crane's Pie Pantry** and restaurant (south side): **open** year-round. May-October: open daily 10-5 except Sunday 11-5. Nov.-March: Tuesday-Saturday 10-5, Sunday 11-5, closed Monday. April: open weekends only*

U-pick **apples** and **peaches** are the big draw at the Gary Crane Farm on the north side of M-89. The season begins with transparent apples in late July. Red Haven peaches start in early August, followed by Glo Haven, Loring, and Red Skin through the first week of September. Fall apples start with Gala in early September, followed by Empire, McIntosh, Cortland, Jonathan, Red Delicious, Golden Delicious, Ida Red, and Rome. Most trees are dwarf trees, which makes for easy picking.

The Crane family, which has been growing fruit here for six generations, has also developed one of Michigan's pleasantest and most successful agri-tourism spots on the old family homestead. Next door, surrounded by orchards, is the Crane House bed and breakfast, fetchingly furnished with farmy, primitive antiques. Across the road on the south side of M-89 is **Crane's Pie Pantry** and Restaurant in the lower level of an old barn. It's a cheerful, homey hodgepodge of interesting farm artifacts, where visitors can eat plump apple pies (also available frozen), soups, and sandwiches — all very tasty and satisfyingly prepared. **Cider** is available by the glass or jug, fresh in season and frozen the year 'round. More kinds of **picked apples** are for sale here, along with some **raspberries** in season. Cold storage facilities at big producers like Crane's insure that apples stay crisp through winter.

14 Dalton Farm

(616) 561-2210.

On 55th at M-89, just east of Fennville. From I-196 exit 34, go east on M-89. **Open:** *no hours; someone's always on hand in season.*

You can buy or pick your own **peaches**, **raspberries**, **nectarines**, or **apricots** here, but the biggest crop is **apples**. There are 18 varieties, beginning with Early Blaze in the last half of August. Granny Smiths are a major variety grown at Dalton's. **Antique apples** include the legendary **Tolman Sweet**, once the country's leading sweet apple and still favored by the local Dutch population. It ripens in October. Also on hand are the now-rare Opalescent apples, one of the most beautiful-looking apples. It ripens in late fall to a dark red, almost purplish shade and has the reputation as a fine baking apple. Opalescents were first discovered in Barry County, Michigan.

Fennville is famous for its fall Goose Festival, held on the third weekend of October. It's also the home of Su Casa, an excellent Mexican restaurant, run primarily for the many Mexican-Americans who came to the area first to work as pickers and then to take full-time jobs in canneries in Fennville and Holland. Su Casa is open daily for breakfast, lunch, and dinner. It occupies the rear room of a Mexican grocery store at 306 Main, just west of the Shell station.

15 Dendel Orchard

(616) 793-7255.

On 127th Ave., Six miles north of Allegan and some 23 miles southwest of Grand Rapids. Take A-37 (a major north-south road between Allegan and Hudsonville) to 127th Ave., then 3/4 mile east. **Open** *June 20-October 31.*

U-pick sweet **cherries** are usually ripe here from June 20 through July 5. **Peaches** are on sale from July 25 through October. There are also **plums, pears,** and **apples,** all available picked or U-pick.

Apple varieties include Red Free (like a Jonathan but ripens early and keeps better than most early apples), Transparent, Grimes Golden, King, Paula Red, Ida Red, Spy, McIntosh, Jonathan, and Red and Golden Delicious. A continuous-belt cider press produces **cider** in quantity that's treated with preservatives and sold at Meijer and Harding stores.

16 Dolson's Sugar Ridge Orchards

(616) 757-3552.

About 7 miles east of Ludington. From Ludington or U.S. 31, take U.S. 10/31 east to Scottville, then take Scottville Rd. south from the town center 1 1/2 miles. Go east on Conrad Rd. 1 mile, then south on Darr Rd. less than a mile to 1688 Darr. **Open** *summer and fall, daily 10-7.*

Sweet and **tart cherries** are available U-pick or picked. Dolson's also grows and sells **peaches** (mainly freestone, but also cling), **nectarines,** and **apples**. Harmony and Harbrite peaches have been in demand lately; they come into season when Red Havens, the best-known freestone, are gone. The Harmony peach is quite large.

17 Dutch Farm Market

(616) 637-8334.

7 miles north of South Haven on 109th Ave., just east off I-196, exit 26. **Open** *daily May 15-November 1, 8-7.*

Peaches, grown in almost every variety suited to Michigan, are the mainstay of the fruit farm here, along with **cherries** and **apples**.

But the highway produce stand also carries home-grown **apricots** and **plums**, plus other produce purchased elsewhere: **vegetables**, **cider**, specialty **cheeses**, **sausages**, **doughnuts**. No U-pick here, but most of these fruits are available U-pick at Conifer Lane on M-89 west of nearby Fennville, owned by the same family.

18 Earl's Berry Farm

(616) 543-4255.

8 miles south of Saugatuck on 118th Ave., 1 1/4 miles east of the Blue Star Highway. From I-196, take exit 34 (Fennville/M-89), go east 1/4 mile to Blue Star Highway, south 3 miles to 118th Ave., then east to farm. **Open** *approximately June 10 to July 15, 8 a.m.-7 p.m.*

Strawberries and **raspberries** can be picked here from about the last half of June through the first half of July.

Farm markets range from huge theme-park extravaganzas to simple tables set up in a front yard like Plummer's asparagus stand south of Saugatuck. A charming aspect of these small operations is the honor system. A small cash box is left to help customers make change.

19 Grass Lake Orchards & Farm Market

(616) 874-7194.

About 8 miles northeast of Grand Rapids and 4 miles southeast of Rockford on M-44 (also known as Belding Rd.), just across from Lake Bella Vista. 1 1/2 miles east of Beltline/Wolverine Dr. Open May to mid-December, Tuesday-Saturday 9-6. Also open Sundays noon-5 in October only.

A big variety of homegrown produce is for sale. Vegetables: **asparagus, green and yellow beans, sweet and hot peppers, potatoes, sweet corn, summer squash, and tomatoes**. Fruit: **sweet cherries, red and black raspberries, strawberries, blueberries, cantaloupe, watermelon, peaches, Stanley plums, pumpkins**, and **apples**. Other farm products are for sale: cut glads, zinnias, and baby's breath; maple syrup; comb honey; pickles; and decorative corn stalks. Country crafts are made by the owner's daughter.

To eat on the spot or take home: fresh **cider** (pressed elsewhere) and apple doughnuts and caramel apples made on the premises. Homemade pies ($6 and $7) can be baked to order.

Apple varieties include: Ida Red, Early McIntosh, Empire, Fuji, McIntosh, Red and Yellow Delicious, Northern Spies, Rome, and Jonathan. Apple gift boxes are a big deal here at the holidays. (Controlled-atmosphere storage keeps apples fresh.) Extra fall attractions include straw for kids to play in, a cornstalk archway, and special events like a rabbit show.

20 Hall's Farm Market

(616) 794-0146.

About 20 miles northeast of Grand Rapids and a mile west of Belding on M-44, a quarter-mile west of the M-91 intersection. Open May -October. Open daily 9-7 in summer, 9-6 in fall. Sundays 11-5.

This 120-acre farm starts producing in May with asparagus and bedding plants. It grows and sells all sorts of vegetables and fruits, including 11 varieties of apples and kinds of peaches. It's known for its abundant crops of sweet crops, grown over 50-70 acres and ripening between the 2nd week of July and September 10. There are U-pick and ready-picked **strawberries** and **raspberries**.

Drives to Greenville or Lowell, crossing the Flat River and its tributaries, are beautiful in fall. Between Belding and Lowell, White's Bridge Road leads to a lovely area highlighted by an old covered bridge, dam, and pretty riverside park.

21 Happy Apple

(616) 784-0864.

On the northwest outskirts of Grand Rapids at 2390 Four Mile Road NW. From I-196, take Walker exit, go north on Walker, then right (east) on Four Mile Rd. **Open** *July-November, Monday-Saturday, 9-6.*

This 200 acre-farm includes a big 30-acre blueberry patch. Of the four kinds of **blueberries** grown, the Blue Crop, ripening in mid-July, taste best. Also grown are apples, peaches, pears, sweet corn, and other **vegetables**. **Cider** is made and sold, too.

22 Hill Crest Fruit Farm

(616) 861-2955.

Between Muskegon and Ludington, 2 miles north of Shelby and 3 miles south of Hart. Take Oceana Dr. north of Shelby, turn west at the Oceana Golf Course; orchard is first farm past it. **Open** *year-round.*

Cherries, peaches, pears, plums, and **apples.** No U-pick, and no cider, either. "We don't want to mess with lower-quality apples for cider," says the owner. "We try to raise sharp-looking apples." Many varieties of each fruit are grown, some old and some new. Apple varieties, for instance, include McIntosh, Cortland, Spy, Winter Banana, Baldwin, Hubbardston, Mutsu, Ida Red, Wealthy, Grimes Golden — "most everything but Empires."

The **Hart-Montague Trail**, once a railroad line, now a bike/hiking/cross-country ski trail, runs right near here through the pretty, rolling orchard country between Montague and Hart. For more information, call the chamber of commerce at Silver Lake (616-873-5048) or White Lake (616-893-4585).

23 Hilton's Apple Acres

(616) 891-8019.

About 12 miles south of Grand Rapids and 4 miles southwest of Caledonia, on 108th St. 4 1/2 miles west of M-37. (108th St. is the southern county line of Kent County.) From U.S. 131, take the Caledonia exit, go east 2 miles on 100th St., then south on Kalamazoo Ave. 1 mile to 108th St. and east 3/4 mile to farm. **Open** *July 1-Dec. 24. Monday-Sat 9-6 Open Sundays 1-5 in October only. Opens Memorial Day to July 1, Friday and Saturday 9-6 for winter apples and country crafts.*

This multifaceted country destination offers a picnic area, farm animals to pet, and hayrides and orchard tours by appointment. There's U-pick for **Red Haven peaches** and **pumpkins**. Other homegrown produce for sale includes **apples, pears, sweet corn,** and many other vegetables. **Cider** and caramel apples in season. Also, doughnuts, honey, jams, maple syrup. Country crafts and gifts.

24 Klackle Orchards

(616) 754-8632.

2 miles west of Greenville and about 25 miles northeast of Grand Rapids on 11466 West Carson City Rd. (M-57). From U.S. 131, take the Greenville/M-57 exit, go about 15 miles east. **Open** *July-October, daily 10-6.*

Apples, peaches, pumpkins, squash, honey. U-pick **apples,** summer and fall red **raspberries**. Fresh-pressed **cider** and **doughnuts**.

25 Langeland Farms

(616) 837-8951.

15 miles west of Grand Rapids and 15 miles east of Grand Haven. On Garfield Rd. overlooking I-96. From I-96, take the eastern Coopersville exit (Exit 19), go south on 48th, west on Garfield. First farm on right (overlooking expressway). **Open** *daily year-round except Sundays.*

This 2,000-acre dairy farm also has 150,000 white leghorn chickens. In a little unmanned stand by the road you can pick up strictly **fresh eggs** for 80¢ a dozen. Some city folk will buy 20 or 30 dozen at a time for themselves and neighbors. Sales average 100 dozen a day. Poultry has been a big business in Ottawa County for generations. Some family operations have grown much bigger than this. In tiny Borculo, north of Zeeland, for instance, there's Bil-Mar, the second-largest maker of turkey products in the U.S.

26 Maxson's Blueberry Farm

(616) 924-0229.

5 1/2 miles south of Fremont, about 25 miles northwest of Grand Rapids and 15 miles northeast of Muskegon. On 92nd Street, 5 1/2 miles south of Fremont. From downtown Fremont, go south on Warner (it starts as M-82) 5 1/2 miles, turn west on 92nd St. 1 1/4 miles to farm. **Open** *July-August. Monday-Friday 8-8, Saturday 8-5.*

U-pick **blueberries** near the Baby Food Capitol of the World. Gerber has discontinued its wonderful tours, but has an elaborate visitor center open weekdays.

27 Mork's Blueberries

(616) 766-2200.

Between Muskegon and Whitehall at 4139 Whitehall Rd. From U.S. 31, take North Muskegon exit (M-120) west into North Muskegon, turn north onto Whitehall Rd. Farm is 4 1/2 miles north. **Open** *mid-July to mid-September.*

U-pick **blueberries** in a very pretty area. Ask for directions to Duck Lake State Park, which has a picnic grounds overlooking peaceful Duck Lake, and separate Lake Michigan beachfront. (See *Hunts' Highlights of Michigan* and *Hunts' Guide to West Michigan*.)

One of our favorite farm stands is this quaint egg stand on Langeland Farms between Grand Rapids and Muskegon. It's a self-serve operation, but still sells 100 dozen fresh eggs a day.

28 Orchard Hill Apple and Angus Farm

(616) 868-7229.

About 15 miles southeast of Grand Rapids on Cascade Rd., 5 1/2 miles east of the village of Cascade, between I-96 and the Grand River. From I-96 take Lowell exit, 1/2 mile north to blinker, turn west on Cascade Road. 2 1/2 miles from blinker. **Open** *through December daily 9-6.*

U-pick and picked **cherries**. For sale picked: **apples, plums, pears, pumpkins**, and **vegetables**. Many extras make this a rural destination: a bakery, farm animal exhibit, demonstration beehive, and maple syrup display.

For a nearby scenic drive that's especially nice in fall, take M-21 from Lowell to Ada. Two covered bridges are in beautiful spots near here: the Fallasburg Bridge on Flat River north of Lowell and another one across the Thornapple River in the center of Ada. Small parks are by both.

29 Orchard Market

(616) 464-5534.

2 locations in Mason County. **Ludington:** *1 block south of the light at the U.S.10/U.S. 31 intersection.* **Freesoil:** *corner of U.S. 31 and Freesoil Road.* **Open** *May to mid-November. May-August: 8-7 daily. September to mid-November: 8-6.*

Fruits grown and sold at these popular, well-regarded markets include **strawberries, cherries, peaches, plums**, and **apples**. Homegrown vegetables include **asparagus, sweet corn, potatoes, cabbage, broccoli, cauliflower**, and more. Also: jams, honey, maple syrup, baked goods from nearby Amish farms.

30 Paulson's Pumpkin Patch

(616) 451-6595.

20 miles northeast of Grand Rapids, 3 miles west of Belding on M-44. **Open** *August-October, daily 9 a.m.-dark.*

Sweet corn, watermelons, apples, winter **squash, pumpkins, Indian corn**. See page 33 for notes on scenery around Belding.

31 Reenders Blueberry Farms

(616) 842-5238 or 842-6675.

5 miles south of Grand Haven and about 10 miles north of Holland on West Olive Rd. at U.S. 31, 1 1/2 miles south of M-45. **Open** *July 4-September 20, daily except Sunday.*

Blueberries, picked and U-pick, at a large blueberry plantation along U.S. 31. A display of antique farm equipment is a new attraction.

32 Rennhack Orchards

(616) 873-4582.

In Hart, between Muskegon and Ludington. From the U.S. 31 Hart exit, go 1 mile east on Polk Road. On the south side of the road, across from Hansen Foods. **Open** *July 4-Labor Day. Monday-Saturday 9-6.*

Sweet and tart cherries, peaches, apricots, plums, apples, nectarines, and **melons,** plus **sweet corn** and other **vegetables**.

33 Brown's Ridge View Fruit Farm

(616) 672-5245.

About 25 miles south of Grand Rapids and about 2 miles due west of Martin on 116th Ave. (M-222). From U.S. 131, go less than a mile west on M-222 at Martin exit. **Open** *June- October. Summer hours: Monday through Saturday, 8-8. After Labor Day: Monday through Saturday 9-6.*

An unusual combination of topography — hilly uplands, wooded in part, and bits of muckland — makes for a more varied and interesting landscape and variety of fruit than at many fruit farms. Blueberries love the acid muck. **Strawberries** in June are followed by **sweet cherries, blueberries, black and red raspberries, summer apples, Bosc and Bartlett pears,** and fall **apples** (Red and Golden Delicious, McIntosh, Ida Red, Empire, and Gala). Everything is available picked or U-pick, and the savings can be substantial. Most trees were planted in 1955 by Jeff Brown's grandfather, as suburbanization was encroaching on his old orchard in Byron Center.

In fall, cider is pressed with a rack and cloth press. An increasing number of special weekend attractions include horse-drawn wagon rides and a haunted house. But this farm still feels like a farm and not an overgrown retail store and amusement park. If you drive west on M-222, you may glimpse next door some of the Arabian race horses Nicole Brown trains. Horses started out as a hobby but have become her profession; last year, her Bristol Breeze had the second-highest earnings of any filly in the nation.

34 Ritz Farm Market

(616) 877-4732.

10-15 miles south of Grand Rapids and a mile east of the village of Moline and A-45. At the corner of 9th and 144th. From U.S. 131, take Dorr exit (or Caledonia exit), go east to A-45, then north (or south) to Moline, and a mile east on 144th. **Open** *July through February.*

U-pick **cherries**. Other fruit, for sale only picked, includes **apples, grapes, peaches, pears, plums**. Also, **cider, doughnuts, honey**, and **popcorn**.

35 Sietsema Orchards and Cider Mill

(616) 363-0698.

On the northeast side of Grand Rapids, north of where I-196 turns west from I-96. From I-96, take the East Beltline exit, go 2 miles north on Beltline to Knapp Rd., east on Knapp 300 ft. **Open** *July-May 8 a.m.-6 p.m.*

Apples, pears, grapes, cherries, and **peaches** are grown at this diversified fruit farm that goes back over 50 years. There's U-pick only for **grapes**. Also for sale: **cider** (made here with a rack and cloth press), **doughnuts, caramel apples, popcorn**, and **honey**. Some 25 kinds of apples include Spies (the world's best pie apple because it holds its shape), Rome Beauties, and Mutsu, which marketers are starting to rename "Crispin." Unlike many urban fruit farms that make cider, this still feels like a farm.

36 D & D Stout Orchards

(616) 823-2119.

About 15 miles southeast of Big Rapids and 35 miles north of Grand Rapids. From U.S. 131, take Stanwood exit, go east into Stanwood. Take Pierce Rd. east to 135th Ave., south for 7/10 mile. **Open** *June-October, Monday-Saturday, 9-7.*

This big fruit farm grows **strawberries, red** and **black raspberries, sweet** and **tart cherries, melons, peaches, nectarines,**

pears, plums, apples, and **grapes,** along with **sweet corn, tomatoes, squash,** and **pumpkins. Cider,** too.

37 VenRoy Blueberries

(616) 837-6482.

Between Grand Rapids and Grand Haven, 2 miles northwest of Eastmanville on 84th Ave. From I-96 take exit 16 (68th Ave.) south 3 miles to Eastmanville (exit 16). At the 4-way stop, turn west on Leonard, go 2 miles to 84th Ave., north a mile on 84th. **Open** *July 15-August 15. Monday-Friday, 8 a.m.-dusk. Saturday 8-5. Closed Sunday.*

U-pick and picked **blueberries**. Picnic area, refreshment stand. It's a beautiful backroads drive along the Grand River out Leonard

The Blue Star Highway between Saugatuck and South Haven is dotted with old-timey farm stands and odd little stores geared to visitors. Driving along it is a lot like going back to the 1940s and 1950s, when tourism was on a more casual, ma-and-pa scale. Radseck's Farm Market a few miles south of Saugatuck is among the larger of such businesses.

from Grand Rapids, with many attractive old farms and idyllic-looking preindustrial villages built as river ports, then bypassed by railroads.

38 Watts Orchard

(616) 937-4094.

At the southwest edge of Howard City, about 30 miles north of Grand Rapids and 15 miles south of Big Rapids. On Washburn Road, at the southwest corner of the Howard City village limits. From U.S. 131, take Big Rapids exit (18), go east to second road, south to orchard signs. Or take old U.S. 131 out of Howard City to Washburn Road, west to sign. **Open** *July 2 or 3 until first week of November.*

Tart and sweet **cherries, peaches, apples, plums, pears, apricots**. Also, **vegetables** and **cider**.

39 Weippert's Blue Valley

(616) 842-2682.

About 13 miles north of Holland and 9-10 miles south of Grand Haven, about 2 miles east of U.S. 31 and 1 mile south of M-45 (Lake Michigan Rd.) which goes west from Grand Rapids and Allendale. From M-45, go south onto 144th, right (west) to Pierce Road. Farm is on right side. **Open** *mid-July to mid-September.*

U-pick and picked **blueberries**. No pesticides used.

40 Will-lane Farm and Orchards

(616) 768-4305.

About 10 miles south of Cadillac, 20 miles north of Big Rapids, and a mile north of LeRoy. From U.S. 131, take Mackinaw Trail into LeRoy, continue north on Mackinaw Trail a mile to 17 Mile Rd. Go west on 17 Mile half a mile, look for sign to orchard on corner of 17 Mile Road. **Open:** *call ahead for times.*

Apple, peaches, pumpkins, and **cider** are produced on this working farm with animals. Some U-pick. Horse-drawn hayrides to the orchard and pumpkin patch are free in the fall.

NORTHERN LOWER PENINSULA

▼ *The numbers before each entry are keyed to the map on p. 43.*

1 Amon Orchards and U-Pick

(616) 938-9160 or (800) 937-1644.

Just east of Traverse City overlooking the East Arm of Grand Traverse Bay. On the east side of U.S. 31, 2 1/2 miles north of where it intersects with M-72 in Acme by the Grand Traverse Resort. Open January-April: Saturday 10-5. May-October: daily 9-6. November & December: Saturday 10-5.

Here around Traverse City, in the center of U.S. tart cherry production, overproduction perennially depresses wholesale cherry prices. It has been a continuing battle for most cherry farmers to stay profitable and avoid having to sell out to developers. Fruit farmers in general are notoriously poor marketers. But cherry farmer Dave Amon (pronounced AM-uhn) has successfully reoriented his family's business to tourism while retaining its pleasantly farmy flavor.

That's one good reason why this is the best cherry farm to tour. Another is the farm's splendid view of the East Arm of Grand Traverse Bay. Astonishingly blue in the distance, it reminds one of Traverse City's claim to be "A Great Lakes Paradise."

Family-run, Amon's is less slick than the area's other heavily-advertised orchard. Plenty of knowledgeable people are around the sales room to field questions about cherry cookery and cherry agriculture. Half-hour horse-drawn **trolley tours** by employees cover area cherry history and how cherries are grown and marketed. There's also a **petting zoo** of common farm animals kids can feed.

In the summer, Amon's usually offers U-pick and picked **sweet** and **tart cherries, red** and **black raspberries, thornless blackberries, nectarines, grapes, apricots, peaches.** In the fall: **raspberries, apples, plums, peaches, pumpkins, cider** and **doughnuts.** You can also press (with a hand crank) your own apple cider. Prices on picked fruit are lower at small front-yard stands along U.S. 41 from here almost to Charlevoix. But Amon's gives a lot of entertainment for your money. And there are free samples of an interesting variety of homemade cherry products, from barbecue sauce to cherry cider and the best-selling cherry fudge sauce.

Lake
Michigan

Cross
Village

31

119

5

Harbor
Springs

14

12 Petoskey

Charlevoix

31   66   Boyne
City

8

East
Jordan

131

10   32

88

3

Northport

4 1/2

22   22

7→

Leland

9

Suttons
Bay

Old
Mission

22

Elk
Rapids

22

Empire

72   11   13   1   72

Kalkaska

Traverse
City

22

131

31   Interlochen

Frank-   Beulah
fort   Elberta Benzonia

37

113

6

Arcadia

72

31

2

Onekama

Kaleva

Manis-
tee

KEY

4   Farm Stand/U Pick site — see pp. 42-52
140   State Highway
12   Federal Highway
⊗   City or town

Farm Stands & U-Picks
NORTHERN LOWER PENINSULA

Cherries and cherry products can be shipped UPS.

Fruit farming goes back in some families for many generations, but not here. Dave's father started the orchard in 1947, when he quit his job as a GM accountant to come up north. His first year turned out to coincide with the best cherry crop ever. It paid off the whole farm, with enough left over for a down payment on a second farm.

2 Apple Valley Orchards

(616) 889-4343.

*About 15 miles north of Manistee and 15 miles south of Frankfurt at 11240 Milarch Rd., between Onekama and Bear Lake. From U.S. 31 3 miles north of Onekama, turn west onto Hwy. 600 at the Blarney Castle gas station. In 1 1/4 miles, take a left at the Y. Follow sign to Apple Valley, look for the two-story red farmhouse. **Open**: May-December. No set hours. Leave money in jar if no one's there.*

In the Meister family of German farmers who first settled Onekama and founded the town's first church, the sons went downstate, got educated, worked, but eventually all returned. Now a second generation of college-educated sons has come back to the family farm up north. **Asparagus, apricots, sweet** and **tart cherries, peaches, nectarines,** and **apples** are the crops of this big fruit farm, which also sells to Mrs. Smith's Pies.

There's no U-pick here, but plenty of tips and advice from Mrs. I. R. Meister if you catch her in. For instance, she says the best apple pies combine different kinds of apples. And Michigan apples taste better than the ones grown in Pennsylvania. That's why fruit buyers for Mrs. Smith's Pie comes all the way up here to buy pie apples. Mrs. Meister was shocked to realize that Mrs. Smith's frozen pies tasted better than her own, until she asked the corporate apple-buyer for their secret: mix varieties. They use Golden and Red Delicious, Spies, and Jonathans. Despite their reputation for blandness, Delicious make good pie apples, I. R. says, because they're not too acid. Even better for pies she likes the tangier Spy Golden, her favorite of the 15 apple varieties grown here.

Another tip: if you've missed the really delicious local asparagus in season, you can stop by the frozen food plant at Bear Lake and buy it direct from them in bulk, along with other frozen local vegetables.

Yet another tip: peaches are best canned with no extra sugar.

And a final tip: Cortland apples make the best Waldorf salad. The bright red skins look terrific, they're nice and tart and crisp, and the flesh doesn't turn brown.

The best cherry farm tour is at Amon Orchard just east of Traverse City. Dave Amon, pictured with some younger Amons, has managed to create an interesting destination for visitors without making it into too commercially slick an operation. His father gave up an accounting job at G.M. back in 1947 to start cherry farming.

If you're headed downstate after a stop here, consider a final stop in the interesting town of **Kaleva** (pronounced KA-le-va) about 10 miles east of here. An unscrupulous land developer lured Finnish settlers to these pine barrens, in part by naming the town after the Finnish national epic, Kalevala. Through a lot of very hard work, they succeeded in making a pleasant town here. Their story is reflected in a most interesting **Kaleva Historical Museum** in the famous **bottle house**, a trim bungalow made of some 60,000 pop bottles by a retired bottling plant owner. Actor James Earl Jones grew up a few miles south of here, in an even more unpromising place. He credits his high school English teacher in Kaleva as a major factor in his success. A book of the teacher's enjoyable poetic observations on the life around him is for sale at the museum. The museum is open Saturdays in summer from noon to 4, or call (616) 362-2080 to arrange a tour. Be sure to ask good directions on going southeast from Kaleva without getting lost.

3 Bells of Christmas

(616) 386-5909.

1 mile north of Northport at the tip of the Leelanau Peninsula on M-201. **Open** *daily June through December.*

The main business here is wreaths and roping for Christmas, but **fruits** and **vegetables** are also sold in the summer and fall. Some of the vegetables are grown in a small garden right here: **potatoes**, **green beans**, **carrots**, and **radishes**. The rest are bought from area farmers: **tomatoes**, **sweet corn**, **cherries**, **peaches**, **apricots**, **apples**, **syrup**, and **honey**.

The drive out M-201 to the pleasantly rustic Leelanau State Park is one of the most delightful in Michigan. Especially memorable are the park's rocky beaches, hiking trails through low dunes, and lighthouse museum with tower views across to the Fox and Manitou islands. For details, see *Hunts' Highlights of Michigan.*

4 Bill's Farm Market

(313) 347-6735.

445 Mitchell Rd., up the hill about 3 miles east of the high school. Mitchell is Petoskey's main retail street; it extends east-west up the hill from its intersection with U.S. 31 downtown.

Open June 15-December 20. Monday through Saturday 9-6, Sunday 12-5.

People in Petoskey who care about good food and the simple pleasures of the land around them come to Bill's to sample the best offerings of the seasons. He stays in touch with other high-quality, small-scale local producers for tree fruit, berries, and other things he doesn't grow.

It's all imaginatively displayed in a simple old frame building up on the hill, with a splendid site overlooking town and bay. "Bill really takes you through the seasons," says Justin Rashid, co-founder of American Spoon Foods, based down the hill in Petoskey. "In fall, Bill creates an incredible pumpkin place. Then it's full of Christmas greenery, with wreaths and more."

Rashid has been Bill's friend and admirer since the beginning, when Bill's mom, who as a girl peddled vegetables with her brothers, was telling him to give up the produce business he started in high school at the local farmers' market and go to college to become a CPA instead. (For decades, societal attitudes toward farming and manual work put pressure on farmers' kids to "make more of themselves." High school counselors in the 1960s and 1970s actively steered bright kids away from agriculture.) Rashid urged him, "They're not making any more great farmers," and said that if he stuck with his farm market idea, by the time he was 35 he'd be richly rewarded with success in doing what he loves best.

Now Bill's has the kind of loyal and discriminating clientele you'd expect to find in a resort area like Petoskey. With customers like Stafford's inns and the celebrated Tapawingo restaurant in Ellsworth, it makes sense to grow three acres of cut flowers; **pearl onions, tiny zucchini**, and other **miniature vegetables**; and 25 kinds of **squash** and **pumpkins**, including the delicious Sweet Dumpling squash, Bill's favorite. Another novelty is **mini sweet corn**, finger-size ears of regular sweet corn picked at just the right stage, where kernels have developed but the entire cob is still edible raw. Bill's may have fancy vegetables like these, popular on the West Coast, but prices on more typical Midwestern vegetables are quite reasonable enough for it to be a regular summer stop for budget-conscious home cooks.

Spinach and **strawberries** kick off Bill's produce season. Five kinds of **lettuce** are available all season long; so is **sweet corn** from mid July to frost. Many kinds of **peppers** and **tomatoes** are another summer specialty.

4 1/2 Blueberry Forest Farm

(616) 584-3443.

Between Gaylord and Mancelona, 2 miles east of Alba. Alba is on U.S. 131 between Mancelona and Petoskey. From U.S. 131 in Alba, take C-42 2 miles east to Tobias Rd., then 1/2 mile north to farm. **Open** *daily from mid-July to mid-September. 8:30-8, except Friday it closes at 5:30.*

Buy or U-pick **blueberries** are grown on new, half-high bushes that are easier to pick from. Be sure to bring containers.

5 Bluff Gardens

(616) 526-5571.

On the northwest edge of Harbor Springs at 721 W. Lake. From downtown, take State west up the hill to West Bluff (M-119). In about a mile, turn right onto Peffer, then left onto Lake. **Open** *year-round. Hours change with resort season. From Memorial Day through Christmas, open daily except Sunday, 9-5 at least. Winter: open Friday and Saturday 12-5. May: open afternoons only.*

This glorified produce stand caters to the entertaining needs of resorters in the exclusive cottage enclaves of this most elegant and private of Midwestern resorts. It's come a long, long way from a simple front-yard produce stand, and it merits inclusion in this book more as a curiosity than a normal farm market for regular folks.

The tiny **carrots, beets**, and **potatoes** for which Bluff Gardens is famous are displayed like crown jewels in the carpeted sales room, alongside costly housemade jams, dressings, and relishes (about $4 for an 8-ounce jar). These make popular holiday gifts, shipped with a touch of the glamor of Harbor Springs and the magic of Northern Michigan. There are no homey country crafts here; the big gift sideline is Quimper, French earthenware famous for its peasanty motifs in blue, yellow, and red-orange.

Bluff Gardens does remain a real garden, producing **asparagus, strawberries, radishes, onions**, and **spinach** in spring; **sweet corn, tomatoes**, and other summer vegetables; and **squash**. Some produce from other area growers is also sold here.

6 Brookside Berry Farm

(616) 882-4630.

6 miles south of Benzonia and about 10 miles southeast of Frankfurt, on Joyfield Rd. west of U.S. 31. Or, for a pretty drive from Frankfurt and Elberta, go 6 miles south on M-22 to Joyfield Road. Follow signs east to Brookside. **Open** *June 20-September 1, 9-5.*

A small brook flows through the middle of this 215-acre farm. The main crop is wholesale apples, grown on 50 acres. But there are two acres of **strawberries**, two acres of **raspberries**, and half an acre of **blackberries** available for retail customers. All are U-pick. Most notable are the hard-to-find **black raspberries**, which ripen sooner (about the 10th of July) and have a different flavor from red raspberries. Both types are about $1.10 a pound. U-pick strawberries are about 55¢ a pound.

7 Cripps Fruit Farm and Market

(517) 727-2005.

About 15 miles southwest of Alpena, not far from M-65 and Hubbard Lake. Call for directions. **Open** *mid-June through October.*

The fruits grown here, picked or U-pick, are **strawberries, tart cherries, apples**, and above all, **pumpkins**. In addition, a farm market handles produce grown elsewhere. From the first weekend in October through Halloween, the pumpkin fantasyland takes over, supplemented by hayrides to the pumpkin patch, fresh cider, and doughnuts.

8 Elzinga's Farm Market

(616) 599-2604.

10 miles south of Charlevoix or half a mile north of Atwood on U.S. 31. **Open** *mid-June-December 20.*

A homey, general-purpose farm stand, Elzinga's sells **sweet** and **tart cherries, apples, pears, peaches**, and most of the vegetables of the season. It's a favorite stop of American Spoon Food's Justin Rashid on his way to Traverse City, because he can sit in the lunchroom, enjoy a quick sandwich, coffee, and a piece of good fruit pie, and look out and watch the workings of the farm, as lugs of cherries are brought in from the orchards. Baked goods and local hand-crafted country gifts are for sale here.

9 Flying Scotts Farm

(616) 271-3871.

Just west of Suttons Bay mid-way up the Leelanau Peninsula. It's the first farm out of Suttons Bay off M-204. A quarter-mile past the intersection with M-22, turn right onto a dirt road, go to the end. Watch for signs. **Open** *daily, approximately July 10-August 5, 8-dark.*

Sweet and **tart cherries** are sold from a farm that enjoys one of the best views of all on the beautiful Leelanau Peninsula. Ask to walk up into the orchard at the top of the hill. In one direction you can look down over the town of Suttons Bay across to Stony Point and the Old Mission Peninsula. Turn around, and you can see Lake Michigan, its dunes, and the Manitou Islands. Retired engineer-turned-cherry farmer Jerry Scott and his wife, Jackie, refused offers to sell out to a huge resort project that wanted to build ski runs, several golf courses, and 180 condos here. (They're both aviators;

hence the "Flying Scotts" name.)

This cherry farm is one of the few left on the Leelanau Peninsula to use professional Mexican-American pickers. Fruit on a tree doesn't ripen at once. When the fruit at the top is ripe, the cherries on the inside are still greenish. Mechanical pickers that shake the tree "get everything — overripe fruit, green fruit, bird's nests," Jerry says. Bruised by picking, mechanically harvested cherries are fit only for canning. Most of the fruit sold fresh at farm stands has been picked by hand. By relying on these labor-saving devices to avoid the cost and hassle of hired help, Jerry complains, "Michigan cherry farmers are content to be second-class. They don't want to go for an 'A,'" — like their counterparts in California.

There's no U-pick any more — too many people picked all over, emptying the trees reserved for hired pickers.

Migrant Mexican-American cherry-pickers were regular summer residents of Suttons Bay until mechanical pickers put them out of work in the 1960s. The photo above shows some migrant workers in 1949. Mechanical pickers shake the trees, causing ripe cherries as well as debris to fall out, and bruising some cherries in the process. Hand-picked cherries are in better condition. In fruit-growing regions with more jobs in canning factories and other industries, onetime migrants have become important permanent parts of communities like Holland, Paw Paw, Hartford, and Fennville.

10 Friske Orchards

(616) 588-6185.

*South of Charlevoix and north of Torch Lake. From U.S. 31 10 miles south of Charlevoix, turn east onto County Road 48 at the north end of the village of Atwood. Go east 2 miles and turn north at the sign onto Docter Rd. **Open** year-round. Monday through Saturday 9-5, to 6 in July and August.*

Sweet and tart cherries (U-pick or picked) are grown at this large, 250-acre fruit farm, plus **peaches, nectarines, apricots, pears, plums**, and 20 kinds of **apples**. Quite a bit of this fruit shows up in seasonal dishes prepared at nearby Tapawingo, the celebrated restaurant four miles away at Ellsworth. (See page 51 for more on the apples and cider.) They also collect and sell their own honey and produce jams and jellies.

Apple butter, sweetened only with that honey, and cooked until it's thick, has been a big seller, to the general public and to Stafford's inns. Now it's joined by other cherry products (cherry butter, cherry mustard, and a pepper jelly) and by quick-frozen cherries in one- and two-pound bags, so you can take a single frozen cherry out of the freezer and pop it in your mouth. This handy, consumer-size package has many people around here excited, because it promises to finally provide a new and improved market for tart cherries, above and beyond the traditional canned pie fillings and frozen pies.

Cherry farming and the politics of land development are hot topics everywhere up here. Falling prices and low demand for cherries mean it's a constant temptation for cherry farmers to sell off their beautiful orchards to developers. Yet most cherry farmers haven't cooperated or invested in new ways of storing and selling cherries; their wholesaling setup remains wedded to bulk packaging for commercial makers of food products.

That's why buying, eating, and promoting new uses for cherries is the patriotic thing to do up here in Cherryland. The Friske brothers' quick-freezing process means their cherries hold up to canning better, without becoming mushy once they're in jars and thawed. The Friskes hope their new quick-frozen cherries, preserved in cider and used in sauces and toppings, will become a popular gift item.

11 Gallagher's Farm Market

(616) 947-1689.

On M-72, 3 1/2 miles west of Traverse City. **Open** *June-October.*

Sweet cherries, both picked and U-pick. Other fruits and **vegetables.** Home-baked goods, jams and jellies, honey, and maple syrup.

12 Hinkley Produce

(616) 348-2551.

On the southwest edge of Petoskey on West Sheridan Rd., 1/2 mile west of U.S. 131 as it descends the hill into town. **Open** *July 5 to October or first frost. 9:30-5:30. Closed Sunday.*

This fourth-generation truck farm offers 11 varieties of **sweet corn,** ripening between mid-July and October. Another specialty is **lettuce:** bibb, Romaine, and leaf, selling for $1/lb. You can pick your own **tomatoes.** Also grown are **carrots, beets, broccoli, asparagus, squash, pumpkins, peppers,** and **spinach.** Though it's close to Petoskey's booming motel strip, Hinkley's remains quite a farmy place. Their peppers and little squashes especially stand out.

13 Underwood Orchards

(616) 947-8799.

On Old Mission Peninsula just north of Traverse City. 2 1/2 miles out Center Road, turn right on McKinley Road. **Open** *mid-June to December 23, daily 9-6.*

The retail outlet of this large apple and cherry orchard has been slicked-up and gentrified in suburban style, befitting the suburban character of the southern part of the beautiful Old Mission Peninsula. Homegrown summer produce includes U-pick or picked **sweet cherries,** plus **vegetables** and more **fruit.** In the fall: **apple cider, cherry-apple cider, pumpkins,** and **apples.** Fresh fruit pies and good cinnamon rolls are specialties of the **bakery.**

MID-MICHIGAN

▼   *The numbers before each entry are keyed to the map on page 54.*

1 Andy T's Farms

(517) 224-7674.

1 mile south of St. Johns and 18 minutes north of Lansing. On U. S. 27, east side of road. **Open** *daily May -December 24. May-October 8 a.m.-9 p.m.. November-December 9 a.m.-8 p.m.*

Twenty kinds of **squash** are grown for this farm stand, along with **sweet corn** and other **fruits** and **vegetables**. Also, Amish **baked goods** and a variety of pickles.

2 Ashton Orchards and Cider Mill

(313) 627-6671.

South of Ortonville, at the north edge of Oakland County. 3925 Seymour Lake Rd., 1/8 mile west of Sashabaw Rd. From I-75 at Clarkston, take Sashabaw Rd. (exit 89) 5 miles north to Seymour Lake Rd., then west 1/8 mile. From Genesee County (Davison & Flint), take M-15 south thru Ortonville, turn left onto Seymour where M-15 goes right onto Ortonville Rd. toward Clarkston. **Open** *August-March 1.*

Fruit: **peaches, apples, pears, plums**. Also, **sweet corn**, popcorn, honey, doughnuts. In fall, **pumpkins** and **cider**.

In a pretty area of glacial lakes and hills. Quite close to Independence Oaks County Park, and not far from the Ortonville State Recreation area.

3 Balzer's Blueberries of Onondaga

(517) 628-2370.

Between Eaton Rapids and Leslie about 13 miles south of Lansing. 2784 South Aurelius Rd., 2 1/4 miles south of Aurelius Center. Take Aurelius Rd. south from East Lansing and Holt, or take U.S. 127 Barnes Rd. exit between Leslie and Mason, go west on Barnes, then south onto Aurelius at Aurelius Center. **Opens** *usually in mid-July. Monday-Friday 12-9, Saturday and Sunday 8-8.*

U-pick or picked **blueberries**.

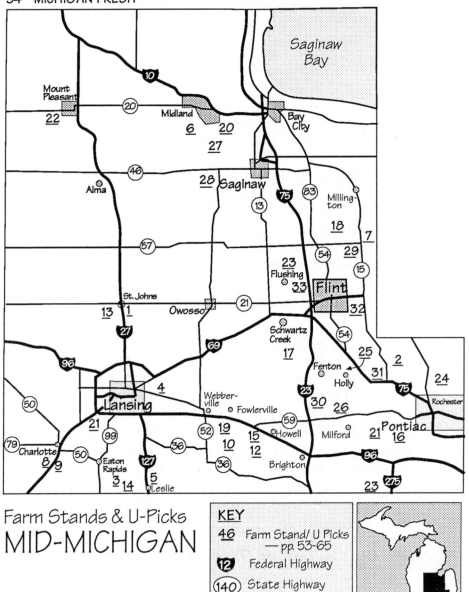

Farm Stands & U-Picks
MID-MICHIGAN

4 **Bird Strawberry Farm**

(517) 339-2934.

East of Haslett, which is about 3 miles east of East Lansing. On Piper Rd. Call for directions. **Open** *around June 10, daily 8-8 in season.*

Picked and U-pick **strawberries**, **blueberries**, and **pumpkins**. Not far from a popular swimming beach at Lake Lansing.

5 Blossom Orchard

(517) 589-8251.

*Between Lansing and Jackson on east side of U.S. 127, north of Leslie. **Open** August-December. Tuesday-Sunday 9-5:30.*

U-pick **apples**. Also **peaches, pears, plums,** and **pumpkins,** along with **honey** and **popcorn**.

6 Blueberry Acres

(517) 642-8403.

About 8 miles south of Midland at 2070 Tittabawassee Rd. (which is the Midland-Saginaw county line), between Patterson and Badour roads. From I-675 just north of Saginaw, take exit 6 (Tittabawassee Rd.) west 19 miles. From M-46 at Hemlock (between Saginaw and Alma), go north 4 1/2 miles on Hemlock Rd. to Tittabawassee, then 2 1/2 miles west.

70 acres of high-bush **blueberries**, U-picked or picked. This is a new operation; the owner may also grow vegetables.

7 Blueberry Lane Plantation

(313) 793-4590.

*About 12 miles northeast of Flint and 12 miles northwest of Lapeer. 1/2 mile west and 1/2 mile south of the village of Otter Lake at 13370 Blueberry Lane. From M-15 3 miles north of Otisville, turn east onto Lake Rd. In 2 1/2 miles, turn south onto Blueberry Lane. **Open** late July-Labor Day, daily 8-6. Call ahead.*

U-pick **blueberries**. Restrooms, picnic area.

8 Cook's Berry Farm

(517) 543-4558.

*Near Charlotte, about 15 miles southwest of Lansing at 3534 West Kalamo Hwy. **Open** July 15-Labor Day. Closed Sunday. Phone ahead for picking hours and directions.*

U-pick **blueberries**.

9 Warren Cook Family Farm

(517) 543-0111.

South of Charlotte and about 15 miles southwest of Lansing at 680 East Five-Point Highway. Take Exit 57 off I-69.

U-pick **strawberries, red** and **black raspberries, blueberries, blackberries, peaches**. Also **tree fruits, flowers**, and **herbs**. Ready-cut **asparagus**.

10 DeGroot's Strawberries

(517) 223-3508.

Midway between Lansing and Ann Arbor, about 7 miles northeast of Stockbridge and 6 miles north of Gregory at 4232 Bull Run Rd. From I-96, take the Fowlerville exit, go south on Fowlerville Road to Howell-Mason Rd., west to Bull Run Rd, 4 miles south. Call for directions from the south and southeast. **Open** *June 8-8.*

The DeGroots run an exclusively U-pick **strawberry** operation. It's family-oriented, with a play area provided for children. Well-behaved children can also pick with their parents.

There are 12 acres of strawberries in all. Sweetest, earliest, and reddest are the Earli Glow. They tend to be ripe by June 5. Then comes the Guardians and the Red Chiefs.

South of here, a scenic east-west route is along M-36, a very old road with many Greek Revival farmhouses. Just south of it is the beautiful Pinckney Recreation Area. A network of unusually varied and beautiful hiking trails extends west from the popular no-wake swimming area at Silver Lake. (Ask for good directions; it's easy to get lost in this crazy-quilt area of glacial hills and lakes.)

11 Diederich's Berry Barn

(517) 521-3415.

20 miles east of Lansing and 2 miles north of Webberville at the corner of Morrice and Allen roads. From I-96, take Webberville exit north to Webberville, go east (right) downtown onto Grand River Ave., turn north (left) onto Morrice Rd. at the edge of town. **Open** *around June 10, 7-7.*

Four acres of U-pick and picked **strawberries**.

12 Dinkelville Melons

(517) 546-4838.

6 miles south of Howell midway between Detroit and Lansing at 945 West Schafer Rd. From downtown Howell at the main corners — or from the main Howell exit (NOT the M-59 exit) — go 6 miles south on Pinckney Rd., then west 1 mile on West Schafer Rd. **Open** *from mid- or* *late July and August, daylight to dark.*

Muskmelons, sweet corn, squash, peppers, green beans, and **tomatoes** are for sale here, already picked. **Howell melons** have been celebrated for the past half century, ever since a plant breeder at Schroeder's Greenhouse developed a new strain of cantaloupe (muskmelons and cantaloupe are one and the same) and, somewhat later, Dr. May, the local family doctor, started the Howell Melon Festival, held each year in August. (Call 517-546-3920 for details.) Melons require good drainage on sandy or gravelly soil, provided by the glacial soils of high ground around Howell.

Nowadays the big seed companies have developed melons of comparable excellence, and the pressures of the uncertain agricultural economy, real estate development, and taxes have combined to steer most of the children of old-time melon farmers away from following in their parents' footsteps. Melons have to be shipped in for the Melon Festival. Alan and Audrey Dinkel are among

Faced with low wholesale prices, more and more farmers are seeking to sell fruits and produce directly to the public. Increasingly elaborate theme-park-like farm stands are one marketing strategy. Cripp's Fruit Farm, west of Alpena, makes big pumpkin displays each fall to lure customers.

the very few melon-growers left around Howell. Alan Dinkel is also a homebuilder. In the 1950s, he put up the ranch houses around the melon farm. Residents dubbed the subdivision "Dinkelville," a name the Dinkels enjoy using for their business.

Michigan melons are vine-ripened, in contrast to earlier melons grown in Florida and elsewhere, which are picked early for shipping. (Howell melons last 5 to 7 days in the refrigerator.) Dinkelville's retail customers buy these melons by the case to give to their friends and neighbors. People have been known to ship a case of melons to Florida. Howell melons are especially popular among salesmen, who are always on the lookout for little gifts for their customers' VIPs and their secretaries.

Melons are a very demanding and expensive crop to raise, says Audrey Dinkel. That's why they cost a lot — at the store or here. (Small melons run $14 a case, for 19 or so. Premium giant melons are $25 a case.) The Dinkels grow 20,000 to 40,000 melon plants from seed in their greenhouse, then raise them on 30 acres. They use five miles of plastic to boost soil temperature and keep weeds down. Weeding between rows of plastic is still necessary. So is irrigating.

When the melons ripen, they are picked — 400 to 500 cases a day, with 12 to 19 melons a case, is typical — and refrigerated immediately.

Immediately east of here on Schafer Road., in this belt of glacial lakes and hills, is the scenic Brighton State Recreation Area, with trails, picnic areas, and swimming beaches. If you enjoy beautifully restored historic buildings, it's well worth checking out two in Howell, right downtown on Grand RiverAvenue: the courthouse (closed weekends) and the Carnegie Library a few blocks west of it.

13 Enright's Orchard and Greenhouse

(517) 224-2002.

2 1/2 miles west of St. Johns and some 15 miles north of Lansing. From U.S. 27 and the center of St. Johns, take M-21 west 2 1/2 miles. **Open** *daily mid-August to November 1.*

A wide assortment of fruits and vegetables can be bought at this seasonal market and greenhouse. Along with bedding plants, hanging baskets, flower boxes, you can find homegrown **popcorn**, sand-grown **potatoes**, fall **gourds**, and **apple cider**.

14 Don Gibbs Farm

(517) 628-2663.

Between Lansing and Jackson in the southwest corner of Ingham County, 1 1/2 miles south of the hamlet of Onondaga at 5428 Onondaga Rd. (the north-south road through Onondaga that ends at M-50 and begins west of Holt). From U.S. 27, take Leslie exit, go west on Bellevue Rd. 6 miles to Onondaga Rd, south 2 miles to farm. **Open:** *call ahead for hours.*

Picked **asparagus**. U-pick and picked **strawberries, blueberries,** fall **raspberries, apples**.

15 Art Hazen's Blueberries

(517) 548-1841.
1144 Peavy Road, Howell. West on Mason Road to Peavy Road, Turn south to farm. **Open** *mid-July.*

Blueberries.

16 Hazen's Blueberry Farm

(313) 363-4072.

Wise Road (north side) between Carrol Lake and Bogie Lake Roads near Milford in western Oakland County. Call for directions. **Open:***season begins approximately July 4. 8-8 on selected U-pick days.*

Picked **blueberries** arranged by pre-order. Call for U-pick days.

17 Houghton's U-Pick

(313) 635-9872.

About 10 miles southwest of Flint and 3 miles south of Swartz Creek at the corner of Morrish and Grand Blanc roads. From U.S. 23, take Grand Blanc exit, go 5 miles west. Call for directions from I-69 and I-75. **Open** *June-July, Monday-Saturday 8-7, Sunday 10-7.*

Strawberries picked and U-pick. Call for picking conditions.

18 I & J Wolverton Nursery

(517) 871-2325.

6197 East Lake Road, Millington. Take I-75 Clio exit, go 10-11 miles, through Clio and to Belsay Rd., then 2 miles north on Belsay to

*Lake Rd. Farm is 1/ mile east on Lake Rd. **Open** April-July.*

U-pick or picked **asparagus** is ready in April and May. U-pick **strawberries** is the big draw, usually ready from around June 10 to July 4. **Red and purple raspberries**, July 4-18. Fall **red raspberries** in September and October. Berries are available picked and U-pick. A wide variety of **garden vegetables,** from spring **spinach** and **radishes** through **sweet corn, carrots, broccoli,** and **cauliflower,** is sold mostly at the Flint Farmers' Market and also here at the farm. Fresh flowers can be cut to order. This is mainly a nursery focused on trees and shrubs. Because it's a farming area where most everybody has a big garden, non-U-pick retail sales are not a big part of the business.

19 Kern Road Farm

(517) 223-8457.

*About 6 miles south of Fowlerville, which is about 25 miles east of Lansing. On Kern Road. Take I-96 to Fowlerville exit, south on Fowlerville Rd. to Mason Rd., east 3/4 mile to Kern Rd. South 1 mile. **Open** July through fall, 9 a.m.-dark.*

U-pick thornless **raspberries** in July. U-pick fall **raspberries, pumpkins, squash, gourds,** and fall **ornamental weeds**.

20 Leaman's Green Applebarn

(517) 695-9228 (home), 695-2465 (business).

*475 North River near Freeland between Saginaw and Midland. Call for directions. **Open** year-round.*

Rhubarb, apples, pears, cider. U-pick **raspberries** and **blackberries**. Also, flowers, both air-dried and freeze-dried.

21 Long Family Orchard & Farm

(313) 360-3774.

*4 miles east of Milford and just west of Farmington Hills on Commerce Rd., 1/3 mile west of Bogie Lake Rd., north of Huron Valley Hospital. From the north, take M-59 to Bogie Lake Rd. (near Alpine Valley Ski Resort), south to light and west 1/3 mile. From the south, take Haggerty north to end. **Open** May-October. Call for hours.*

Asparagus in May. U-pick or picked **strawberries** in June. U-pick **tart cherries** in July. In September and October, U-pick or picked **apples**, along with **cider** and **caramel apples**. In October, **pumpkins**, **gourds**, **squash**, decorative **cornstalks**.

22 McIntosh Orchard

(517) 773-7330.

5 1/2 miles west of Mt. Pleasant at 1731 West Remus Road (M-20), south side of highway. **Open:** *Mid-July-March. Closed Sundays.*

A variety of fruit trees grow on this 60-acre farm. U-pick **sweet cherries** are available in mid-July. U-pick **plums** are ready in early September. The farm market is open September-March for **apples** (8 varieties), **pears**, and **cider**.

23 Meyer Berry Farm

(313) 349-0289.

48080 West Eight Mile Rd. northwest of Northville in the southwest corner of Oakland County. Two miles west of Sheldon Road on north side of Eight Mile Road (near Maybury State Park). From M-14 just west of I-96, take Beck Rd. exit north to Eight Mile, then west (left). **Open** *in June and October.*

In September and October, attention turns to busy work and school schedules, to football and apple cider. It's easy to forget that harvest's bounty in Michigan lasts through September and well into October.

U-pick **strawberries** in June, **pumpkins** on October. The working farm at Maybury State Park on the other side of Eight Mile is a real delight — an authentic, unfussy farm run the way it would have been in the 1930s and early 1940s, in the last days of draft horses. The barns are nearly always open, and if you're lucky, you can see the big Belgians at work in the fields. For more on the interesting history of Northville and Plymouth and Henry Ford's Rouge River Parkway, see *Hunts' Guide to Southeast Michigan.*

24 Middleton Berry Farm

(313) 693-6018 or 693-6124.

2 1/2 miles east of Lake Orion and 6 miles north of Rochester in northeastern Oakland County at 2120 Stoney Creek Rd. From Rochester go north on Rochester Rd. to Stoney Creek, then 2 1/2 miles west. **Open** *mid-June-Halloween.*

U-pick **strawberries, vegetables, raspberries, fall raspberries, pumpkins**.

25 Mitchell Farm

(313) 634-4753.

3 miles north of Holly at North Holly Road and Mitchell Road, about 10 miles south of Flint. From I-75, exit 108, go south on Holly Road 3 miles. **Open** *late April-July 1 & late July-Nov. 1. Daily 10-6.*

In late July on into September, the Mitchell Farm sells their **sweet corn, tomatoes, peppers**, and **cucumbers**. In September and October, there are **apples, cabbage, ear corn, Indian corn, popcorn, broom corn, pumpkins**, 12 kinds of **squash**, and **gourds**. On October weekends, you can pick your own pumpkins.

26 Ridgemere Berry Farm

(313) 887-5976.

3 miles northwest of Highland in far western Oakland County at 2824 Clyde Rd., 1/8 mile east of Hickory Ridge Rd. From U.S. 23, take the Clyde Rd. exit about 5 miles east; or, from M-59, take Hickory Ridge Rd. 3 miles north, then east on Clyde. **Open:** *Mid-June and September-October.*

U-pick **strawberries** in mid-June, fall **raspberries** in September and October. U-pick **pumpkins**, hayrides in October. Just a few miles southeast of here is the Highland State Recreation Area —

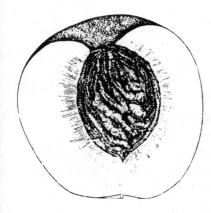

Before South Haven became known for blueberries, its fruit-growing fame derived from the development there of the Haven Peach, the first popular peach to be eaten fresh. (Before the Haven, peaches were usually only cooked or canned.) For canning, non-Haven clingstone varieties like the Baby Gold hold their shape better.

5,500 acres of strikingly hilly terrain with several fishing lakes, over 12 miles of trails, and two swimming beaches. It's remarkably uncrowded, considering how close it is to Detroit's booming northwest suburbs.

27 Russell Blueberry Farm and Nursery

(517) 339-2422 (office), 781-2859 (farm)

7 miles west of Saginaw and 11 miles south of Midland at 11895 Frost Rd. From the M-46 and M-52 junction, go 2 miles north on Graham Rd. (the northern extension of M-52) and half a mile west on Frost. **Open** *July 15-October 1.*

U-pick **blueberries,** and **blueberry plants** for sale.

28 Schantz's Blueberries

(517) 642-8892.

About 8-9 miles west of Saginaw at 3540 South Gleaner Rd. From M-46, go 1 mile west of M-52 to Gleaner Rd., go south on Gleaner 3 1/2 miles to farm. **Open** *July-September, 7:30 a.m.-8 p.m. daily.*

Blueberries, U-pick or picked. Children welcome. Bring your own containers.

29 Smith's Berry Farm

(313) 653-6187.

About 10 miles northeast of Flint —7 miles east of Mt. Morris at 7242 East Mt. Morris Road **Open** *June-July.*

U-pick **strawberries.**

30 Spicer Orchards Farm Market

(313) 632-7692.

About 20 miles south of Flint and 10 miles north of Brighton. 1/4 mile east of U.S. 23. and 3 miles north of M-59 on Clyde Rd. Just east of the Clyde Rd. exit. **Open** *year-round 9-6.*

Buy or U-pick **raspberries, apples, peaches, plums, pears, sweet and tart cherries,** and **blueberries.** Picnic tables enjoy a sweeping long view to the south; the orchard sits atop a long glacial moraine. The pleasant sales room sells **cider, doughnuts, honey, preserves,** and baked goods from the **bakery** on the premises.

31 Vallee of Pines Fruit Farm

(313) 625-3027.

Between Clarkston and Holly in northwest Oakland County at 9500 Bridgelake Rd. Take Dixie Highway (U.S. 24) 3-4 miles north of I-75 Clarkston interchange to Rattalee Lake Rd., 1 1/2 miles east to Bridgelake Rd., north to farm. **Open** *in season.*

Strawberries, raspberries, sweet and **tart cherries, blueberries, apricots, nectarines, peaches, pears, plums, apples** and **cider, grapes.** No U-pick.

32 Walker Farm and Market

(313) 743-0260.

2 miles east of Flint and 4 miles north of Grand Blanc at 5253 East Atherton Rd., 1/4 mile east of Genesee Rd. Atherton Rd. is a major east-west artery on Flint's south side. **Open** *May-November 1.*

The Walker family raises a whopping 150 acres of **vegetables** on their 200-acre farm, everything from squash and beans to peppers and greens. In May and June, U-pick **strawberries** are available.

33 McCarron's Orchards

(313) 659-3813,

7456 West Carpenter Rd., 1/2 mile off Elm's Road, Flushing. Call for directions. Flushing is about 10 miles northwest of Flint. **Open** *August-May.*

Apples, asparagus, sweet corn, peaches, pears, plums, squash, cider, honey, baked goods.

FROM MACOMB COUNTY TO THE THUMB

▼ *The numbers before each entry are keyed to the map on p. 66.*

1 Altermatt's Berry & Vegetable Farm

313) 781-3428.

About 8 miles northwest of Mt. Clemens and 5 miles southeast of Washington at 16580 25 Mile Rd., corner of Romeo Plank Road. Washington. 4 1/2 miles east of VanDyke (M-53). **Open** *May 1-November 1.*

U-pick **strawberries,** spring **raspberries, tomatoes, peppers.** Roadside market has **corn, tomatoes, cucumbers, cauliflower, melons, cantaloupe, cabbage, pumpkins, squash, brussels sprouts.**

2 Bigelow Berry Farm

(313) 688-2181.

About 10 miles northeast of Lapeer on Lake Pleasant Rd. Take M-21 (Imlay City Rd.) straight east from Lapeer for 7 1/2 miles. Turn north on Lake Pleasant Road. Farm is 8.7 miles north of M-21. **Open** *May 1-July.*

Ready-picked **strawberries** in June and July. U-pick **raspberries** in July. The Bigelows also raise bedding plants and vegetable seedlings for sale in their greenhouse.

3 Blake's Big Apple Orchard

(313) 784-9710.

1 mile south of downtown Armada at North Ave. and 33 Mile Rd. in northern Macomb County. From the main four-corners, take North Ave. south one mile. **Open** *May-December.*

A big selection of U-pick fruits and vegetables are grown on this 90-acre farm: **apples, pears, strawberries, peaches, pumpkins, tomatoes,** usually 20% below market price. One of the few places with U-pick peaches. Because pickers must be careful to pick only the ripe peaches, most peach farmers don't let the public near their trees.

An animal farm, wagon rides and pony rides are extra family attractions.

Port Austin

(25) (53)

Caseville
10

Harbor Beach

Pigeon
(142) Elkton   Bad Axe   (142)

Sebewaing

(53)

*Lake
Huron*

(25) (138)

(81)   Cass
City

(19)

Caro

12
(46)

Sandusky   Port Sanilac
11

Vassar

Marlette   Croswell   21
8

(15)

Millington   North
Branch   (90)   Lexington

(90)   18
2   (25)

Lapeer   15   Lakeport
Port
Huron

(136)

Imlay City   Capac   14
(69)

(24)   19   53
13   Almont   19

7

4   22
3   Richmond   St. Clair

Key

46   Farm Stand/ U Picks:
see pp. 65-74   Romeo   5,7,17,20
23.24   New
Haven   94   Marine
City

(140)   State Highway   1,6
9,16   (29)   Lake
St. Clair   (29)   *Canada*

12   Federal Highway   Utica   (59)   Algonac

City or town   Mt. Clemens

Farm Stands & U-picks
MACOMB COUNTY & THE THUMB

4 Blake's Orchard and Cider Mill

(313) 784-5343.

17985 Armada Center Rd., 3 miles west of Armada in northern Macomb County. **Open** *June 1-December 23.*

Run by the same family as the Big Apple Orchard, this 400-acre farm is more entertainment-oriented, but it also features a full season of U-pick fruits and vegetables, starting with **strawberries**, followed by **raspberries** and **tomatoes**, **pears**, **apples**, and **pumpkins**. 30 varieties of apples, including the venerable Northern Spy and the up-and-coming Empire, make for good **cider**.

For visitors there are 20-minute tours of the 150-acre orchard on a tractor-train/trolley ($1), an animal petting farm, and demonstrations of pressing apple cider (a 45-minute operation).

5 Bowerman's Westview Orchards

(313) 752-3123.

65075 Van Dyke (M-53) at 30 Mile Rd., 2 miles south of Romeo. From M-53/Van Dyke, take Romeo exit, follow signs to Orchards, Downtown to old part of the road. **Open** *July-April, Monday-Sun. 8-7.*

Sweet and tart **cherries** are available U-pick or picked. Other fruits are sold already picked: **peaches, nectarines, pears, plums,** and **apples**. Vegetables include **sweet corn, broccoli, squash, onions,** and winter **cabbage**. Also **sweet cider** and **honey**.

Romeo is an especially old country town, settled in the early 1820s, known for its beautiful historic houses.

6 Boyka's

(313) 286-1886.

About 7 miles northwest of Mt. Clemens on 23 Mile Road between Romeo Plank and Card roads, on north side. Take 23 Mile Rd. exit from Van Dyke (M-53) and go 5 miles east, or from I-94 and go 5 miles west. **Open** *mid-July through October, daily 10-6.*

A father and his three sons runs this ambitious produce and fruit stand, growing most of what is sold on 120 acres out back. The Boykas strive to provide their customers a lot of varieties to choose from. The 60 acres devoted to **sweet corn** yields a whopping 35 to 40 different varieties. There are six or seven kinds of **peppers** and lots of **lettuces**. There are also lots of **green beans, cauliflower, melons, tomatoes,** other fruit and vegetables.

7 Coon Creek Orchard and Cider Mill

(313) 784-5062.

78777 Coon Creek Rd., 4 miles northwest of Armada in northwestern Macomb County. Call for directions. **Open** *daily July-November.*

U-pick **sweet** and **tart cherries, seedless grapes, peaches, nectarines, raspberries, apricots, pears, plums, apples,** and **pumpkins**. Also, petting farm, hayride, and **cider**.

8 Croswell Berry Farm Market

(313) 679-3273.

33 Black River Rd. in Croswell, about 20 miles northwest of Port Huron and 5 miles west of Lexington. From Detroit area: go east on I-94 to Port Huron, take U.S. 25 to Lexington, west on M-90 (Peck Rd.) to North Black River Rd., then right (north) 1 city block past the Corner Market. **Open** *June 1-December 23. Weekdays 8-6, Sunday and holidays 8-4.*

U-pick or picked **strawberries**. Summer and fall **raspberries, blueberries, blackberries**. Frozen berries for sale. **Bakery** on the premises with ethnic specialties from Germany, Poland, Greece, and the owner's mother country, Italy. Homemade jams and jellies, with and without sugar. Gift shop. **Christmas trees**, wreaths, centerpieces.

Lunch is served daily in summer on a deck overlooking land-scaped gardens and farm fields. Ice cream parlor.

M-25 along Lake Huron is studded with swimming beaches and pretty small towns like Lexington and Port Sanilac, developed as lake ports. Once rail lines were extended into the Thumb's interior, opening up its rich soil to commercial agriculture after the lumber was cut, the lake ports were eclipsed by farm towns with big elevators and rail connections. With no development pressure, their historic homes are well preserved. The Sanilac Historical Museum, in a wonderful old Italianate farmhouse, is an especially interesting local museum, open in summer Thursday through Sunday afternoons. For swimming near Croswell, there are Lakeport State Park's beach just south of Lakeport, and the Lexington County Park north of Lexington.

9 Deneweth's Greenhouses & Pick-Your-Own Strawberry Farm

(313) 247-5533.

In central Macomb County 2 miles north of Lakeside Mall at 16125 22 Mile Road, 2 1/2 miles east of Van Dyke (M-53) and half a mile east of Hayes Rd. **Open** *June and July for strawberries.*

U-pick **strawberries**.

10 Depner's Pumpkin Patch

(517) 856-2615.

Just west of the tip of the Thumb, between Caseville and Sleeper State Park. From M-25 at the entrance to Sleeper, turn south (opposite the entrance) onto State Park Rd. At the first right, in about a mile, turn right (west) onto Conkey Rd. Pumpkin Patch will be evident in season. **Open** *from mid-September (or whenever the pumpkins are mature) through the end of October.*

Pumpkins, squash, gourds, dried flowers, and Indian corn have been sold at this fall farm stand and U-pick pumpkin field for years. But it wasn't until rather recently, when Ivoughn Depner was a college student, that she started embellishing her parents' fall business with painted pumpkins and front-yard scenes of pumpkin

Growing fruit was and is a family affair. This family posed with its apple crop in 1891. Today it's typical for fruit-farming families up and down West Michigan's fruit belt to work closely (and for the children to play) with the families of Chicano pickers. Many U-pick farm operations have been in the same family for five and more generations, sometimes ever since the land was settled.

figures in cornstalk settings. Now it's all taken on a life of its own;
each year, the Depners say, may well be their last. They don't want
the pumpkin patch to outgrow its country charm.

Halloween is definitely not the theme here; Rather, it's "Fall in
the Country," focused on rustic characters in overalls, pumpkin
pigs, and such. "We dwell on the harvest, and not the wicked
witch," says the artist's mother. Some figures have painted burlap
faces. Kids are still encouraged to go out and pick their pumpkins in
the field. The centerpieces have become Ivoughn's painted
pumpkins, decorated with country scenes. (It sounds like a
contemporary folk-art genre akin to painting on crosscut saws.)
Uncarved, the pumpkins last until Christmas. "They're like the
Christmas tree, beautiful for their season," says Mrs. Depner.

11 Green Thumb Blueberries

(313) 648-2974.

*Halfway up the Thumb on its east side, 2 miles east of Sandusky and
14 miles west of Port Sanilac at 455 South Stringer Rd. See directions
for Croswell Berry Farm but continue north on M-25 to Port Sanilac,
then west on M-46 14 miles to Stringer, then south 3/4 mile.* **Open**
mid-July to frost, daily 8:30-5.

U-pick **blueberries** only. For more about the Thumb, see notes
after the Croswell Berry Farm Market, above.

12 Hill's Orchards

(517) 673-6894.

*Some 18 miles east of Saginaw and 25 miles northeast of Flint,
about 6 miles southwest of Caro. At M-81 and Fenner Rd., a mile east
of Watrousville.* **Open** *daily year-round, except major holidays, 9-6.*

A big produce market at an 80-year-old fruit farm features apples
grown here and local produce in season. It's supplemented by
California produce in winter. Cider is made from some half-dozen
apple varieties as long as the supply of apples lasts, usually into early
summer, and there are 25 flavors of ice cream.

13 HoneyFlow Farm

(313) 796-2344.

*In the southwest corner of Lapeer County, midway between Flint
and Port Huron and 25-30 miles from each. 4 miles west of Almont and*

2 1/2 miles due south of Dryden at 4939 Mill Rd. **Open** *from September through mid-October, Thursday through Sunday.*

Pick 20 varieties of **grapes**, including **red and white seedless grapes** and **wine grapes**, also red and white. **Grape juice** is also for sale. The best deal of all is **honey** filled in your own containers. Honey is also sold in the comb, liquid, or creamed.

14 Jeffrey's Blueberries

(313) 324-2874.

8 miles west of Port Huron at 3805 Cribbins Rd. Take M-21 (Lapeer Rd.) west from Port Huron, then 1 1/2 miles north on Cribbins. Or, from I-69, take the Barth Rd. exit some 5 miles west of I-94, go north on Barth to M-21, then west a little over 2 miles to Cribbins, then north. **Open** *Monday-Saturday 10-7, Sunday 12-5.*

U-pick or picked **blueberries**.

15 McCallum Orchard

(313) 327-6394.

About 13 miles northwest of Port Huron and 4 miles northwest of Lakeport. From M-25 about a mile north of Lakeport State Park, go west on Harris Rd. 3 miles. **Open** *May-December, 8-6 daily.*

U-pick **asparagus, strawberries, cherries, raspberries, plums, peaches, pears, grapes, apples, pumpkins, squash.** (All this is also available picked.) **Mums.** Also for sale: **cider** and **doughnuts**, plus **jam, apple butter, popcorn, honey,** and gifts. This is quite a rural place, not a suburbanized farm destination.

16 Olejnik Farms

(313) 598-7708.

About 8 miles due west of New Baltimore and 8 miles east of Rochester Hills on 23 Mile Road. From I-94, take the Algonac-New Baltimore exit, go about 4 miles west. **Open,** *May-October, daily 9-6.*

Fresh corn picked daily, and an extensive variety of fresh **homegrown vegetables**.

17 Rapp Orchards

(313) 752-2117.

*63545 Van Dyke Rd. between 29 and 30 Mile roads, less than 4 miles south of Romeo and 10 miles northeast of Rochester. West side of road. From M-53/Van Dyke, take Romeo exit, follow signs to Orchards, Downtown to old part of the road. **Open** year-round.*

U-pick **cherries** and **pumpkins**. Vegetables, and many other fruits, are available picked: **pears, cherries, plums, peaches**, and **apples** (Red and Golden Delicious, McIntosh, Jonathans, Empire, Red Gold, Ida Red, Paula Red, Fuji, and Mutsu). **Jams** and **honey**. Fresh **cider** is available in season. (It's pressed elsewhere, from their own apples, on a rack-and-cloth press.) Sandwiches and cheese are for sale at a deli counter; a picnic area may be installed soon.

Picking your own raspberries and blackberries is by far the best and most economical way to acquire these delectable berries, so easily bruised they are quite costly at the supermarket. Summer and fall raspberries mean the season is in July and also late August and the first half of September.

18 Reynolds Berry Farm

(313) 688-3559.

*5861 Cedar Creek Road, 3 miles southeast of North Branch and about 12 miles northeast of Lapeer. Take M-90 from North Branch 2 miles east, then 1 3/4 miles south on Cedar Creek Rd. **Open** daily May-October.*

The Reynoldses are best known for their **strawberries**. They grow four varieties on 10 acres and charge 55¢ a pound U-pick. Best bets are the Earli Glo and the Honey Eye. Their four acres of **asparagus** are usually ready by May 1. U-pick **red raspberries** are $1.50 a quart, $1.50 a pint ready-picked. There are also 700 **peach trees**, in four varieties, and six to eight kinds of **apples** for sale each year.

19 Rheaume Orchards

(313) 796-3382.

*In the southwest corner of Lapeer County, midway between Flint and Port Huron (25-30 miles from each), 18 miles northwest of Rochester, 2 miles south of Dryden. At 5436 Casey Rd. 4 miles west and 1 mile north of Almont. **Open** July through September.*

In July you can pick your own **cherries**, sweet or tart. U-pick **peaches** in August, U-pick **raspberries** in September.

20 Southview Orchards

(313) 752-2512.

*2 1/2 miles south of Romeo at 63910 Van Dyke Rd. (M-53). From M-53/Van Dyke, take Romeo exit, follow signs to Orchards, Downtown to old part of the road. **Open** August-February, 8:30-6:30.*

Over 40 acres here produce **peaches, pears, plums**, and **apples**. The peaches ripen toward the end of July. Over 15 varieties of apples include the legendary Golden Russet and the flavorful Mutsu. Bushels of apples start at $8. **Cider** is made beginning October 1, when the apples are mature enough to make to make a good drink.

21 Tringali Orchards

(313) 359-8158.

*4 miles north of Lexington and 24 miles north of Port Huron at the base of the Thumb. 3457 Lakeshore Rd. (M-25). **Open** year-round 10-6, daily except Wednesday.*

Year-round produce and fruit market with cold storage for homegrown **potatoes, onions, squash**, etc. **Peaches** in season (no U-pick). U-pick or picked **apples** and **pears**. In fall, **cider**.

Also, **herbs** and **spices, eggs, honey**, and **popcorn**.

22 George & Judith VanHoutte Farm

(313) 784-5680.

Van Dyke (M-53) at 35 Mile Road, 3 miles north of Romeo in the northwest corner of Macomb County. **Open** *daily mid-July to October 31.*

Tomatoes, super-**sweet corn, honeyrocks, watermelon, potatoes, broccoli, cabbage, cauliflower, peppers, squash, peaches**. U-pick **pumpkins**.

23 Van's Valley Produce

(313) 781-8488.

66745 Van Dyke (M-53), 1 mile south of Romeo, just south of 31 Mile Road across from Wendy's. From M-53/Van Dyke, take Romeo exit, follow signs to Orchards, Downtown to old part of the road. **Open** *May-first weekend November, 8-8.*

Strawberries by the case or quart. Fresh-picked bicolor **sweet corn, tomatoes, honeyrocks, peppers, beans, cauliflower, cabbage. Peaches, apples, squash**, and **pumpkins**.

24 Verellen Orchards & Cider Mill

(313) 752-2989.

63260 Van Dyke (M-53), 3 miles south of Romeo. From M-53/Van Dyke, take Romeo exit, follow signs to Orchards, Downtown to old part of the road. **Open** *July-May.*

U-pick **cherries, strawberries**. Homegrown fruit for sale picked: **peaches, apples, plums, pears, grapes**. Fresh **doughnuts** daily. **Cider** in season.

Also for sale: **honey, eggs, potatoes, jams** and **jellies**.

SOUTHEAST MICHIGAN

▼   *The numbers before each entry are keyed to the map on page 76.*

1 Girard's Produce Farm

(313) 697-1685.

West Huron River Drive. I-94 to exit 187 (Rawsonville Road). Go south 1 mile to West Huron River Drive, turn left. Farm is 1 1/2 miles on right. **Open** *mid-July through September and into October. Daily 8-7, Sunday 8-6.*

Retail and U-pick produce includes **asparagus**, many **bean** varieties, **greens, peppers, lima beans, okra**, and **tomatoes**. At the big farm market you can buy homegrown **sweet corn, cantaloupes** and several kinds of **watermelons**, and many other fruits and vegetables, many grown right here, and some things like bananas bought at Detroit's Eastern Market. Owned and operated by the same people who have Rowe's farm market (see page 75), Girard's offers the same variety of **beans** (U-pick and picked) and **peas** (here picked only; the fields are at Rowe's nearby).

2 Hideaway Orchard

(517) 263-0060.

On M-52, 3 miles south of Adrian. 8 miles north of the Ohio-Michigan border. **Open** *end of June through January, 9-5. Closed Mondays.*

Homegrown fruits for sale include **sweet** and **tart cherries, plums, nectarines, peaches**, and **apples**. These can be made up into fruit baskets. Fresh **cider** in fall. Vegetables include **squash, peppers, tomatoes**, and **pumpkins**. Also for sale: jams, jellies, maple syrup, honey.

3 Kapnick Orchards

(517) 423-7419.

4 miles southeast of Tecumseh. From M-50 less than a mile east of Tecumseh, go 4 miles south on Rogers Hwy. **Open** *year-round. Monday-Saturday 8-8, Sunday 10-8.*

This big operation buys its vegetables from other area farmers (and from California in the winter) and grows its own fruits on 140 acres. There are over 20 varieties of **apples**. Also available are

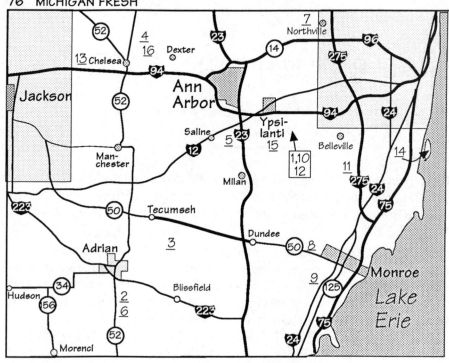

Farm Stands & U-Picks
SOUTHEASTERN
MICHIGAN

KEY

<u>4</u> Farm Stand/ U Picks, pp. 75-82

(140) State Highway

(12) Federal Highway

⊙ ▨ Towns and cities

---

peaches, **pears**, **plums**, and **nectarines**. You can pick your own **cherries**, **strawberries**, **raspberries**, and **blueberries**. The Kapnicks press their own **cider**, and have a **bakery** which makes fresh **doughnuts**.

A festival is held here the second weekend of each October. The entertainment, food and drink, and activities draw some 10,000 visitors a day.

Nearby Tecumseh has a remarkable stock of unusual 19th-century homes (many are right on Chicago Boulevard/U.S. 12) and a lively downtown oriented to antiques and country or Victorian gift shops. In Adrian's old Carnegie Library, the Lenawee County Historical Museum is an unusually interesting local museum. It's on the business routes of M-52 and M-223 northbound; and it's open

Tuesday through Saturday 1-5. Ask about Adrian's good Mexican restaurants, too. A few miles west of Tecumseh on M-50, Hidden Lake Gardens, a Michigan State University extension facility, is a delightful arboretum, conservatory, and natural area with trails and fantastic spring-flowering shrubs.

4 Lesser Farms

(313) 426-8009.

On Island Lake Road, 5 miles west of Dexter and about 12 miles northwest of Ann Arbor. From I-94, take the Baker Rd. exit, north on Baker to Dexter, west on Main Street to Y at Huron River. Take right fork under bridge. At the next Y (soon), take left fork onto Island Lake Rd. **Open** *summer and fall: Monday-Saturday 9-6, Sundays 1-6.*

This 450-acre farm primarily raises hogs and cattle, but it also has an orchard. **Red Haven peaches** sell for $12 per 3/4 bushel. They're in short supply, so order ahead. There are plenty of **prune plums** and a 7-acre apple orchard. Varieties include **Northern Spy** and go for $9 a bushel. Lesser also sells **honey** from his hundred beehives: for $3.50 for 3 pounds or $6 for 6 pounds.

Island Lake Road is an especially scenic country road (partly dirt) that leads into a band of glacial lakes. Many are part of the beautiful Pinckney Recreation Area. There's also a commercial trout farm on the road. On the way to Lesser Farms, about three miles west of the second Y, Dexter Townhall Road leads north to the beautiful and popular Silver Lake swimming beach and many miles of hiking trails through dense upland forests and wetlands full of wildlife.

5 Makielski Berry Farms and Nursery

(313) 434-3673 or (313) 572-0060.

7130 Platt Rd. just south of southeast Ann Arbor. 1 mile south of U.S. 12 and half a mile west of the U.S. 23/U.S. 12 interchange. From Ann Arbor, you can simply take Platt Road south from Washtenaw Ave., Huron Parkway (it ends at Platt), or Packard. **Open** *8 a.m.-9 p.m. in season.*

The delectable berries available here (U-pick only) include summer and fall **raspberries**, red and black **currants**, and **gooseberries**. These berries really reward people who take the time to pick them. Since they are highly perishable, they're costly when they are available at all in supermarkets. Yet they freeze well, providing a healthy and luxurious wintertime treat.

Scandinavians prize black currants for their tart flavor (sweetening is always required) and high vitamin C content. They enjoy currant jam and also use currants as a base for fruit drinks and as a medical elixir. Gooseberries are likewise valued in many European countries for jams. Green and streaked, they have the highest pectin content and the tartest flavor. When they turn purple, they're sweeter.

All the berries grown here are also for sale as nursery plants, held in cold storage under winter-like conditions until just before planting. That way, you aren't buying plants that have sat around on nursery lots for weeks and longer before being planted.

6 Marvin's Fairfield Orchard

(517) 436-3378.

On M-52 4 1/2 miles south of Adrian and the M-52/U.S. 223 intersection and 7 miles north of Ohio state line. **Open** *August-December daily 9-6, Sunday 12-6.*

This 70-year-old orchard grows **peaches, pears, plums,** and **apples** on 20 acres. Some antique apple varieties are here which you won't easily find elsewhere. The Red Astrachan came originally from Russia in 1835. It's an early summer apple that's good for applesauce and pies. The Black Arkansas, a hard apple that ripens late in the season, is a good keeper. There are also Russets and Transparents. A newer variety worth asking for is the Golden Blushing, an attractive cross between Yellow Delicious and Jonathan.

There's also a **cider mill** here, and Mrs. Marvin, a schoolteacher, is famous for the **doughnuts** she makes on fall weekends, several batches a day.

7 Meyer Berry Farm

(313) 349-0289.

48080 West Eight Mile Rd. northwest of Northville in the southwest corner of Oakland County. Two miles west of Sheldon Road on north side of Eight Mile Road (near Maybury State Park). From M-14 just west of I-96, take Beck Rd. exit north to Eight Mile, then west (left). **Open** *in June and October.*

U-pick **strawberries** in June, U-pick **pumpkins** in October. The working farm at Maybury State Park on the other side of Eight Mile is a real delight — an authentic, unfussy farm run the way it would have been in the 1930s and early 1940s, in the last days of draft horses. The barns are nearly always open, and if you're lucky, you can see the big Belgians at work in the fields.

8 Navarre Farm

(313) 241-0723.

*Just west of Monroe north of the River Raisin at 1485 Bates Lane, 2 miles west of Telegraph Rd. (U.S. 24). Take North Custer Rd. west from Telegraph, turn north onto Bates Lane. **Open** June-September.*

U-pick **strawberries, raspberries, asparagus** in one of the oldest settled parts of Michigan. Many stately farmhouses are along North Custer Road, renamed for General George Armstrong Custer, the pride of Monroe.

Well before 1776, French-Canadian *habitants* moved from Detroit to Monroe (then called Frenchtown) after the British took over the fort and town at Detroit. Quite near the Navarre Farm is the Navarre-Anderson Trading Post, a three-building complex operated by Monroe's outstanding county historical museum. Open summer weekends, it includes what's quite possibly the oldest surviving house in Michigan, built by fur trader François Navarre in 1789. Call (313) 243-7137 for more details. The main museum in downtown Monroe includes a wealth of material on Custer and a smorgasbord of other interesting artifacts. For more on Monroe, see *Hunts' Guide to Southeast Michigan.*

9 Rauch's Berry Farm

(313) 242-5272.

*About 5 miles southwest of Monroe at 2196 West Stein Road, From Telegraph (US-24), go west on Stein 1 1/21 miles. **Open** June, July, September, October.*

U-pick **strawberries, raspberries.**

10 Glenn Rowe Produce Farm and Market

(313) 482-8538.

*Southeast of Ypsilanti and just north of Willis at the far eastern side of Washtenaw County at 10570 Martz Rd. Take I-94 to exit 187 (Rawsonville Rd.), go south 2 1/2 miles on Rawsonville to Martz, then west (right). **Strawberry season**: open 7 a.m.-8 p.m. daily. Farm market and other U-pick open from July into October.*

This 100-acre farm allows U-pick **strawberries, okra, peppers, tomatoes**, and many varieties of **peas** and **beans** — for instance, shelling peas, edible-podded sugar peas and Chinese peas, purple and silver crowder peas (a great favorite with the many Kentuckians who have lived here in Ypsilanti Township ever since the Willow Run Bomber Plant was built during World War II). Bean varieties include Italian, yellow, stringless, Kentucky Wonder, lima, baby lima, and speckled beans. At the big farm market you can buy homegrown **sweet corn, cantaloupes** and several kinds of **watermelons**, and many other fruits and vegetables, many grown right here, and some things like bananas bought at Detroit's Eastern Market.

11 Sandy Acres Blueberry Farm

(313) 753-9969.

In southwestern Wayne County, about 6 miles southwest of Metro Airport and a mile south of New Boston at 8093 Judd Road. Go 4 miles south of I-94 on I-275 to Sibley Rd. (exit 13). West on Sibley 1/2 mile to Huron River Dr. in New Boston. then south (left) 1 mile to Judd Rd., 1/3 mile west to farm, on left. **Open** *about July 4- September 1. Monday-Saturday 8-6, Sundays 10-6. Phone for picking dates.*

U-pick **blueberries**. Children allowed only with parental supervision.

12 Raymond Schultz Farm

(313) 483-1370.

10090 Martz Rd., Ypsilanti. Exit from I-94 at exit 187 (Rawsonville Rd.). Go south 2 1/2 miles to Martz Rd., right 3/4 mile to second strawberry farm on left. **Open** *June 5-July 5.*

U-pick **strawberries**.

13 Sylvan Orchard

(313) 4475-1943.

On Cavanaugh Lake Road west of Chelsea. 1 mile north of I-94 between Kalmbach Road (exit 156) and Pierce Road (exit 157). **Open** *end of July-August.*

U-pick and picked **peaches**. Cavanaugh Lake Road skirts the south edge of the Waterloo Recreation Area, a sprawling patchwork of lakes, wetlands, steep-sided glacial hills, and hunting lands, with many hiking trails. Call headquarters at (313) 475-8307 for a map of trails, or stop at the Gerald Eddy Geology Center off Bush Road, which begins at the north end of Pierce Road. It's open daily, and it's at the hub of the most interesting nature trails. The nearest swimming is at Clear Lake County Park, on Clear Lake Road about 3 miles north of the I-94 Clear Lake Road exit (exit 155).

14 Westcroft Gardens

(313) 676-2444.

West River Road on Grosse Ile, downriver from Detroit off Jefferson/ Biddle Ave. From Grosse Ile County Bridge, turn immediately right on ramp to West River Road; turn north 2 miles. Or: from Grosse Ile Toll Bridge, take first right at blinking light (Meridian Road) to second blinking light, turn right (Horsemill Road becomes West River). About 1 mile south. Call for freeway instructions. **Open:** *retail store open year-round on complex schedule that changes with the seasons. Call first. Raspberries usually available from mid-August to October 15 (or first hard frost).*

U-pick red **raspberries** are the only edible food grown at this fabulous Grosse Ile garden, famous for developing and selling azaleas and rhododendrons that are guaranteed winter-hardy in southern Michigan. With four acres of display gardens that include wildflowers, ground covers, perennials, and water plants in a pond, there's a lot to see here throughout the growing season. Some herbs are on hand, too. The nursery is open year-round. Call for hours.

15 Wiard's Orchards

(313) 482-7744.

Take I-94 to Huron St. (exit 183) at Ypsilanti, then go south 4 miles. Follow the signs. **Open** *year-round, 10-6 daily.*

From a farm established in 1853, Wiard's has grown into a veritable circus of attractions. The centerpiece remains the **apples**. Nine varieties are grown on 200 acres. The rack and cloth press blends as many of the nine as are ripe, with the peak number in the first or second week of October. You can pick your own apples, **peaches**, and pears in the fall, as well as **asparagus, strawberries, cherries, pears,** and **peaches** earlier in the season.

This is a fun place to take kids, but if you like your farm stands and U-picks pure and simple, it's not the place for you. The

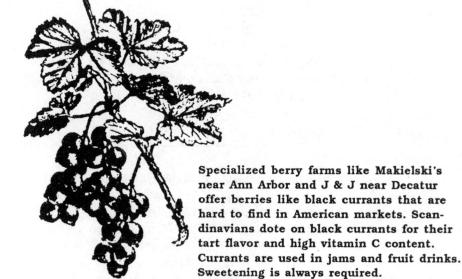

Specialized berry farms like Makielski's near Ann Arbor and J & J near Decatur offer berries like black currants that are hard to find in American markets. Scandinavians dote on black currants for their tart flavor and high vitamin C content. Currants are used in jams and fruit drinks. Sweetening is always required.

atmosphere is more like a country fair. Tour busses lumber down the dirt road to U.S. 23. There's live country music every weekend in September and October from noon to 6. There are fire engine rides, train rides, wagon rides, pony rides, a petting farm, a haunted barn, orchard tours, apple butter-making demonstrations, face painting, candle making, and even a straw maze for kids.

Along with fresh produce and fruit purchased at the Eastern Market, there's plenty else to eat coming from a full-line bakery and butcher shop. Hot dogs, caramel apples, candies, and nuts are also for sale.

16 Zabinsky Blueberry Farms

(313) 426-2900.

About 10 miles west of Ann Arbor between Dexter and Chelsea on Beach Rd. between Dancer and Lima Center roads, a mile north of the Dexter-Chelsea Rd. From I-94, take the Fletcher Rd. exit, go north on Fletcher to T intersection, then right on Dexter-Chelsea Rd. less than a mile, left onto Lima Center Rd., and first right onto Beach. **Open** *mid-July to mid-September.*

Blueberries.

SOUTHERN MICHIGAN

▼ *The numbers before each entry are keyed to the map on page 84.*

1 Eicher's Blueberry Patch

(616) 651-2433.

About 20 miles west of Coldwater and 8 miles north of Sturgis. From M-66, which extends from Sturgis north to Mendon and Battle Creek, turn east onto Findley Rd. about 8-9 miles south of M-60 and about 7 miles north of Sturgis. Go east on Findley 1 1/2 miles. **Open** *daily except Sunday 8-6 August-September.*

U-pick or picked **blueberries**.

This farm is in a very interesting area of St. Joseph County, where a big underground aquifer supports a considerable seed corn industry. (Raising seed corn is so labor-intensive, farmers can't afford the risk of dry summers; irrigation is essential.) Also, St. Joseph County has an unusual number of towns and villages that haven't changed in size for over a hundred years; only Three Rivers and Sturgis really saw any kind of industrialization that affected town development. In recent decades, increasing numbers of Amish from the densely populated home settlement in nearby northern Indiana have moved into the county. (The ice cream parlor in nearby Nottawa is a popular meeting place for Amish families.) Amish farms are diversified, with lots of animals to see. It all makes for an unusually interesting area for backroads explorations, with some beautiful old farmhouses in a landscape that's often little changed from a hundred years ago.

2 Glei's Orchards and Greenhouses

(517) 437-4495

Northeast of Hillsdale and east of Jonesville at 3500 Milnes Rd. From U.S. 12 between Moscow and Jonesville, turn south at the flasher light onto Milnes Rd., go south 4 miles. **Open** *year-round, Monday through Saturday 8-6.*

There's a lot going on all year at this diversified grower of field vegetables (25 acres), bedding plants, herbs, and perennials (2 acres of greenhouse), fruits (pears, plums, and some 25 kinds of apples), and Christmas trees (sold cut and in pots). There's no U-pick.

The farm market features homegrown vegetables in season

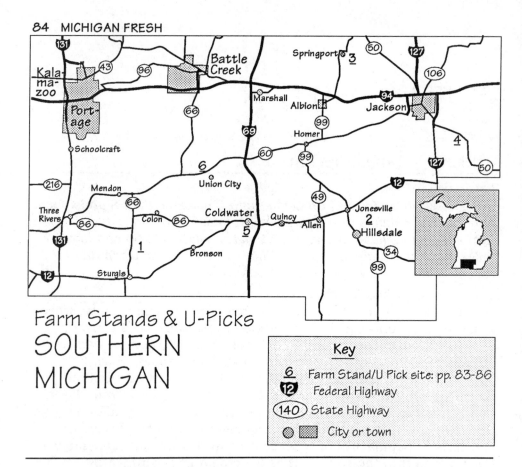

Farm Stands & U-Picks
SOUTHERN
MICHIGAN

Key

6   Farm Stand/U Pick site: pp. 83-86
12   Federal Highway
140   State Highway
   City or town

(**tomatoes, melons, cukes, peppers, sweet corn, cabbage, broccoli, cauliflower**, and **squash**), supplemented by tropical fruit and produce bought at the big Detroit markets in the off-season. Controlled-atmosphere storage keeps apples fresh and crisp all year. Varieties include the crunchy, flavorful Gala, the Jonagold (today the #2 apple in Europe), and, coming into production in 1992, the Fuji, which co-owner David Glei says "has an excellent flavor but looks like trash."

Glei's grows some 600 kinds of plants, the largest selection in the south-central part of the state, and sells them at very competitive prices. Don't wait long after April 15 to get just the kind of ground cover you want; specific varieties are likely to sell out for big landscaping jobs.

U.S. 12 from Clinton to Jonesville and Allen is dotted with interesting summer destinations, from the engaging Southern Michigan Railroad that runs between Clinton and Tecumseh (weekends only, summer and fall), the historic Walker Tavern, Ike's Presidential railroad car, and St. Joseph's shrine in the Irish Hills,

Stagecoach Stop (an exceptionally entertaining family-run make-believe village, worth an all-day excursion), and the Grosvenor House in Jonesville, a historic house museum that's the apogee of Gilded Age splendor (open weekends, 2-5, June through September). Finally, in Michigan's self-proclaimed antiques capital of Allen, there's the Green Top Antique Mall (a charmingly quirky collection of buildings just west of town) and many other antique shops. For more on the area, see *Hunts' Highlights of Michigan.*

3 The Log Cabin

(517) 857-3628.

11 miles north of Albion and about 15 miles northwest of Jackson. From I-94 just east of Albion, take M-99 north about 9 miles through the village of Springport. The cabin is on Mock Road, 1 mile east of Springport just off M-99. Look for sign. **Open** *May 1-December 23. Daily 11-4.*

An old log cabin is the centerpiece of this charming country spot. The big garden around and behind the little cabin produces **sweet corn, tomatoes, peppers, cucumbers, cabbage, squash,** and other vegetables. Fresh **herbs** and **fresh flowers** are also for sale, along with bedding plants in May and June. The herbs and everlastings are started here; owner Ilene Moss uses them in her wreaths, and to fill the handmade baskets that hang everywhere inside. Moss teaches basket-making in the winter; one of her baskets was featured in *Country Living,* to her surprise.

4 Makielski Berry Farm

(517) 536-4092.

6 miles southeast of Jackson and about 3 miles west of Napoleon. Take U.S. 127 south to M-50, go east on M-50 5 miles to Wheaton Rd., turn right (south) and find the red metal barn at 6461 Wheaton Rd. **Open** *July and August, 8-8.*

The Makielskis, longtime operators of an Ann Arbor berry farm, now have retail U-pick sales here at their old nursery. There are 5 acres of **blueberries,** 2 1/2 acres of **purple raspberries,** and 15 acres of **black raspberries.** Their red and black **currants** ripen in July, along with the blackberries and blueberries. Scandinavians especially prize the black currants, which are high in vitamin C. For more on Makielski's and sales of their plants, see page 77.

5   Pleasant Acres Farms

(517) 278-8689.

1 1/2 miles south of Coldwater on Old U.S. 27. From I-69, take the first exit south of Coldwater, follow Business Route 69 signs toward town. **Open** *from mid-May through Thanksgiving, depending on weather. 10-5:30 Monday through Saturday at least. In season (July into October) open daily 9-6.*

This farm stand sells its own produce in season, supplemented by wholesalers. **Apples, peaches, pears,** and **plums** are grown here, along with **asparagus, strawberries, sweet corn, tomatoes, melons**, and many other vegetables. **Cider** is made in fall.

6   Weirich's Pineview Farm Market

(517) 741-7495.

On M-60, west of Union City 1 mile. Union City is about 8 miles west of I-69, midway between the Marshall and Coldwater exits. **Open** *May-August 9-8:30. Open September and October 10-6.*

This large and classy farm market offers much homegrown produce picked or U-pick: **strawberries, raspberries, blueberries, green beans**, and many kinds of **peppers,** sweet and hot. More is for sale already picked: **watermelon, cantaloupe, sweet corn, cabbage, broccoli, pumpkins, squash**, and more. The bakery has more sophisticated offerings than you'd expect to find in this rather remote part of southern Michigan. Bedding plants and hanging plants are sold in spring and early summer.

Farms with shocks of corn and teams of horses can be seen even today on the back roads of St. Joseph County, in south-central Michigan, where an increasing number of Amish families have settled. Eicher's Blueberry Patch is a U-pick farm in this area, near Colon.

UPPER PENINSULA

Upper Peninsula U-pick operations are generally much smaller than ones closer to large urban areas. Especially with strawberries, it's always best to call ahead to reserve a place in line and be sure there will be ripe berries when you come.

SAULT STE. MARIE AREA

1 Carley Farm

(906) 632-8330.
About 8 miles southeast of Sault Ste. Marie on Nicolet Road at 7 Mile Road. Open from around the first of July for 3-4 weeks.

U-pick **strawberries.**

MANISTIQUE/GARDEN PENINSULA AREA

2 Garden Orchards

(906) 644-2140.
In the village of Garden on the Garden Peninsula. From U.S. 2 16 miles west of Manistique and 23 miles east of Rapid River, turn south onto State Highway 183. Sales building is a former elementary school on the north edge of Garden. **Open** *from cherry season (about July 10) to Christmas.*

The late Ed Mawby, a fruit farmer originally from Grand Rapids, established this orchard in 1978-79 when he saw that the fruit farm he and his son, winemaker Larry Mawby, had on the Leelanau Peninsula was subject to the same development pressure and escalating land values that made him leave Grand Rapids for the Leelanau Peninsula in the 1960s. The Mawbys planted 5,000 trees on the Garden Peninsula, so named because the surrounding waters of Lake Michigan moderate the temperature so it's more like that of mid-Michigan 200 miles to the south.

Sweet and **tart cherries** and **apricots** are grown here, but the big crop here is **apples**, some 50 kinds. Nine-tenths are sold direct to individual buyers; there's also a big business with holiday gift boxes. The biggest seller is the good-looking Spartan, which tastes like a McIntosh with firmer flesh. (The name seems to help sell it, what

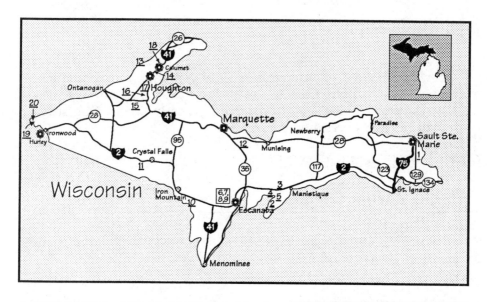

UPPER PENINSULA
Farm Stands, U-Picks
& Farmers' Markets

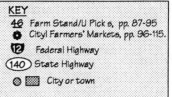

KEY
46 Farm Stand/U Pick s, pp. 87-95
⚙ Cityl Farmers' Markets, pp. 96-115.
12 Federal Highway
140 State Highway
⚙ ▦ City or town

with all the Michigan State alums.) The Connell Red, developed in Minnesota, gets attention because of its size — up to two pounds. But the apple repeat customers line up for is the Honey Gold, a very tasty apple high in sugar, with one major marketing limitation. Its skin is so sensitive that it requires extremely careful handling. The fingerprints of apple pickers stay on it to market; on the grading belt it bruises. So here it's picked and handled by gloved workers.

Despite the unusual varieties of apples, prices are not fancy here. Utilily grade apples are $7 a bushel, top grade are typically $10-11. In addition, **cider** is made on the premises, along with **jam** and **honey**. Some neighbors on the Garden Peninsula sell smoked fish; ask for directions. Closer to the peninsula's tip are the two sections of Fayette State Park, one the townsite of an interesting 19th-century charcoal iron furnace, the other the campground and beach.

3 Hepker Farm

(906) 341-6543.

5 miles northwest of Manistique. From the west side of Manistique and U.S. 2, take M-94 north 4 miles to Indian Lake Road, then 1 mile west to farm. Call ahead. July-November.

Strawberries (picked or U-pick) are ripe for about three weeks from the first of July. **Potatoes**, hand-dug and thus free from bruises, are available from the first of August through November. As the Schoolcraft County extension agent, Al Hepker is setting a good example in promoting area farmers to take up potato farming again.

4 Al-O-Ray Motel

(906) 341-2479.

Six miles west of Manistique in Thompson, on U.S. 2. **Open** *most of the time in blueberry and pumpkin season. Call to insure availability.*

During the Depression, Pete Hoholik picked wild blueberries for a living, and he still enjoys it. Smaller and sweeter than cultivated blueberries, they're considered a delicacy. "But they're hard to pick," says Pete's wife, Gert. "People think he's crazy. But he was raised on a farm. It never leaves them." The motel property, which the Hoholiks have owned for 36 years, includes 70 acres of land.

In season, from the first part of July into early August, **wild blueberries** are sold here for $3 a quart. In late September and October, **pumpkins** are for sale, U-pick or picked. After frost flattens the leafy vines, the pumpkin patch by the motel is a striking sight.

5 Rondeau Farm

(906) 644-2777.

Near Cooks, at the base of the Garden Peninsula. From U.S. 2, take M-442 north through Cooks, turn left at the first opportunity north of the hamlet, onto Spielmacher Road. Farm is in 12 mile. Call ahead; picking by reservation preferred.

Gradually this abandoned potato farm is being built up and developed into a diverse operation, with both picked and U-pick berries. **Strawberries** usually come in early July and last 2 1/2 weeks, followed by three varieties of **raspberries** from mid-July into August. **Potatoes** and, for hunters, **sugar beets** are fall crops.

ESCANABA AREA

6 Chenier Farm

(906) 786-7879
About 10 miles west of both Gladstone and Escanaba. From U.S.
2/U.S. 42 between Escanaba and Gladstone, turn north onto County
Road 426 on the west side of the Escanaba River. In 3 miles, turn west
onto County Road 416. Farm is in 2 1/4 miles, at 4200 CR 416, near
the hamlet of Flat Rock.

Raspberries, U-pick or ready picked, at Frank and Nancy
Chenier's farm. Usually ready from the second week of July through
the first week of August. Next-door neighbors are Fruit Full Acres.

7 Fruit Full Acres

(906) 786-3899.
See directions to Chenier Farm. Next door at 4166 CR 416.
Season *runs from after July 4 into late October. Open Monday*
through Saturday 8-8. Call first to be sure of availability.

Downstaters Larry and Linda Klope love the U.P. but were disap-
pointed by the quality of fruit they found when they moved here.
Inspired by trips to the Yates Cider Mill in Rochester and Uncle
John's in St. Johns, Larry intends to open a farm market and eventually a cider mill with an old-fashioned rack-and-cloth press.   The
1,200 fruit trees the Klopes planted in 1986 are just coming into
production. They chose varieties of **tart** and **sweet cherries,
plums, pears,** and **apples** that he expects to be reliable in this
northerly latitude; the **peaches** and **apricots** are more experimental, he says. Everything is for sale either picked or U-pick.
Blueberries may also be available. The market will eventually feature
muffins, pies, and other baked goods using homegrown fruit.

8 Ledvina Farm

(906) 786-3614.
West of Gladstone and north of Escanaba at 7772 County Road
426. From U.S. 41/U.S. 2, turn north onto CR 426 along the west
bank of the Escanaba River. Farm is about 2 miles northwest of the big
Mead paper mill. Open from late June into around July 20. Call first.

Strawberries, U-pick or already picked.

9   Don Pellegrini Farm

(906) 786-9084.

About 10 miles west of Escanaba on County Road 537. From U.S. 2/U.S. 41 west of Escanaba, look for sign at the hamlet of Hyde. **Open** *late June-mid or late July for strawberries; mid-September for deer feed.*

Strawberries, picked or U-pick. In fall, **cabbage**, **rutabagas**, and **beets** are sold mostly to deer hunters.

10   Roger Pellegrini Farm

(906) 563-8577.

Near Vulcan, a few miles east of Norway and Iron Mountain. From U.S. 2 between Loretto and West Vulcan, turn south onto County Road 577 (River Road). Farm is in 1 mile. **Open** *from the end of June or so through fall.*

Some of the best potato land in the United States is the flat, sandy loam of Schoolcraft County, around Manistique. The area was a big producer until after World War II. Potato farms like this one, photographed in 1940, were common. Then longtime potato farmers reached retirement age and their sons, returning from war, had far more opportunities in the wider world. Also, new farming technology required greater investment.

So much potato land went into the soil bank program (whereby farmers are paid not to farm), that 2,000 potato acres had dwindled to nothing by 1972. Today potato production is up to 600 acres, thanks to contracts with the potato chip industry and Ore-Ida frozen potato processors.

Strawberries, picked or U-pick, usually are available from late June through mid-July, followed by **raspberries** and then by **rutabagas** and **cabbage** (mainly for hunters) and **cauliflower**.

CRYSTAL FALLS/IRON RIVER/IRON MOUNTAIN AREA

11 Idlewild Farms

(906) 875-3777 or (906) 875-3300.
About 5 miles southwest of Crystal Falls, northwest of Alpha. Call for directions and availability.

U-pick **strawberries** are a sideline of this potato farm. The season usually starts just after July 4 and lasts two or three weeks.

MARQUETTE AREA

12 Johnson's Berry Farm

(906) 942-7558.
*In Skandia, off U.S. 41 about 20 miles southeast of Marquette. At U.S. 41 and Dalton Road, in the center of what little there is in Skandia, go east on Dalton a very short ways, under 1/4 mile, then turn north onto Ingalls Road. Farm is in 12 mile. **Open** usually from late June for 2-3 weeks into July, daily from 8 a.m.*

There are lots more customers than **strawberries** at the only strawberry farm in Marquette County, what with the U.P.'s biggest town and K. I. Sawyer Air Force Base next door. Come early, or that day's ripe berries will all be gone. U-pick and ready-picked berries.

KEWEENAW PENINSULA
13 Randy Grego Farm

(906) 482-6929.
Between Houghton and Freda south of the Portage Canal. Open 3 p.m.-9 p.m. in season.

Organic farm stand on the way to a popular restaurant in Freda. See the organic chapter, page 131, for details. Specializes in warm-weather vegetables — tomatoes, okra, cukes, peppers, and such.

14 Hughes Organic Farm

(906) 337-5185.

Between Calumet and Hubbel on Calumet Golf Course Road.
Open *in strawberry season and from late July into October. 11-6,
closed Friday and Sunday.*

Organic strawberries and vegetables, including nice tomatoes. See page 131 for details.

15 Hulkonen Farm

(906) 338-2792.
*At the base of the Keewenaw Peninsula, about 12 miles west of
Baraga a little south of M-38. From M-38 in the hamlet of Nisula, turn
south onto Hulkonen Road. Farm is at end of road.* **Open** *year-round,
in berry time from 8 a.m. until it's picked over. Come early.*

Fresh eggs are sold year-round at the poultry farm of the
Hulkonen brothers and their sons. It also features strawberries in
season (U-pick or picked) and an assortment of fresh vegetables
that usually includes **beans, peas, sweet corn, squash**, and
tomatoes.

16 Keweenaw Berry Farm

(906) 523-6181.
*On U.S. 41 some 18 or so miles north of Baraga and south of
Houghton and Chassel.* **Open** *May-October, Monday-Saturday 7 a.m.-9
p.m., Sunday 8 a.m.-9 p.m.*

The Upper Peninsula's only large farm market-turned-visitor
attraction is probably the prettiest in the entire state. **Strawberries**
come on toward the end of June, followed by **blueberries** from mid-
July into early August, and **raspberries** beginning in early August. All
are available picked or U-pick.

To get the full effect of this delightful place, walk behind the large
retail building through the grounds, colorful with flowers. There's
no admission charge to the big, attractive landscaped area for small
animals. Most farmyard favorites are here: pigs wallowing in the
mud, big-eyed Jersey cows, goats, ponies, turkeys, chickens, and
colorful guinea hens — along with llamas, wallabies, and buffalo.
Little kids are out in force on weekends, feeding animals apples and
chatting away with them.

The full-menu **restaurant** is open for breakfast and lunch. In addition to daily specials, it offers pasties made in the in-house **bak-**

Upper Peninsula strawberries have the reputation for being sweeter and more flavorful than strawberries from lower latitudes. The colder climate, tempered by the Great Lakes, lets the berry develop more slowly, producing more sugars. Rain is ample, and the longer summer daylight hours have an effect, too. At most berry farms, picking begins at 8 a.m. It pays to come early to be sure of having enough ripe berries to pick.

ery. Everything's made from scratch there, including four breads baked fresh each day (whole wheat, rye, white, and a sourdough rye) and used for *nisu* toast — a Finnish cinnamon toast also flavored with cardamom.

17 Kim and Linda Sohlden Farm

(906) 523-4779.
  4 miles south of Chassel and a half mile west off U.S. 41 on Klingville Road. Open in August.
  Blueberries, picked or U-pick.

18 Martin Sotala Farm

(906) 482-3879.
*U.S. 41 opposite Hancock Airport, turn west onto Boston Road. Farm is in less than a mile. **Open** from around July 4 through Halloween. Call first for U-pick. Vegetables ready after mid-August. Farm stand hours: Sunday, Monday, Tuesday Thursday 11-7.*

U-pick **strawberries** come on around July 4 for two or three weeks, followed by **raspberries** around the end of July for another two or three weeks. Truck farm features many vegetables — **sweet corn, green beans, cole crops** — but tomatoes are an uncertain crop.

IRONWOOD AREA

19 Jopac Farm

(715) 893-2278.

Near Saxon, Wisconsin, about 15 miles west of Ironwood, Michigan, and Hurley, Wisconsin. On U.S. 2 about 2 1/2 miles west of the County Trunk 122 intersection. Open from early May to Halloween, 9 a.m. to dusk.

Joe and Pat Cattelino have turned their onetime dairy farm into a very pleasant farm market and truck garden. Almost everything is grown by them or by their neighbors, from spring **asparagus** to fall **pumpkins**. A single exception is fall **apples** and **cider** from nearby Bayfield, near the Apostle Islands. Everything's grown here that an old-fashioned farm garden would produce: **rhubarb, peas, beans,** and most kinds of summer **vegetables**. Specialties include a thin-hulled **white popcorn** (many customers buy 10 pounds at a time, for gifts) and **maple syrup**. Some country crafts made in the neighbor-hood are also on hand.

20 Kauppi's Strawberry Farm

For readiness report, call the owner (906-932-4791) or, if not in, call either nearby bar (715-893-2242 or 715-893-2450).

Near Saxon Harbor, Wisconsin, about 18 miles west of Ironwood, Michigan, and Hurley, Wisconsin. From U.S. 2, go west from Hurley 11 miles to County Trunk 122 at Saxon. Turn north (toward Saxon Harbor). Farm is in 3 miles.

The biggest **strawberry** farm in the area now has a new owner; next year, summer **raspberries** will be in production, too. A nice, sandy Lake Superior Beach is two miles away at Saxon Harbor. Strawberries usually peak around the Fourth of July and last two to three weeks. Raspberries follow.

Farmers' Markets

Farmers' markets can offer the very best selection of the freshest fruits and vegetables, along with the spectacle of a scene not unlike the throngs on market days in medieval times. You can often pick and choose among far greater varieties of than would be found in a supermarket. At some you'll find over 30 varieties of tomatoes or squash and a dozen kinds of sweet corn.

Adrian

Downtown in a parking lot behind Croswell Opera House. Lot is on Toledo Street, between Broad & Main streets. Open June-October 31, Saturday 8-noon. Contact Liza Zubke at City Hall (517) 263-2161.

Eight or nine growers regularly attend this market in downtown Adrian, selling fresh fruits and vegetables, eggs, honey, and baked goods. Once a month craftspeople are allowed. One grower is strictly organic; his produce includes celery, broccoli, cabbages, cauliflower, beans, and corn.

Albion

Stoffer Plaza, just east of the main street of downtown Albion (Superior), between Cass & Erie streets. Open Saturdays only May and October: Wednesdays & Saturdays June through September. 8:30 a.m.-1 p.m. both days.

This pretty market on the Kalamazoo River has about 10 growers at the height of the season later in the summer. Market master Joyce Holtz, a grower herself for 49 years now, is proud that only growers, no dealers importing fruit and produce, are allowed at the Albion market. Holtz herself grows four kinds of popcorn (white, yellow, strawberries, and calico), and the kernels are hand shelled, which makes for better popping.

Ann Arbor

Just north of downtown at Detroit Street between North Fifth Avenue and North Fourth Avenue. From Huron go north on Fourth. From North Main, go east on Catherine. For easy parking, use the parking

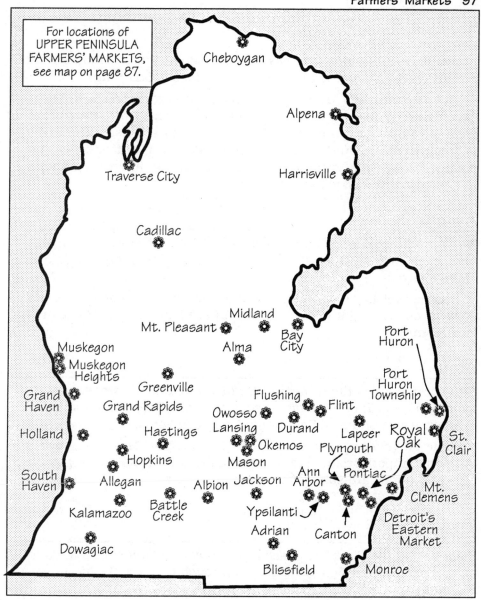

For locations of
UPPER PENINSULA
FARMERS' MARKETS,
see map on page 87.

Cheboygan

Alpena

Traverse City

Harrisville

Cadillac

Midland

Mt. Pleasant

Bay City

Port Huron

Alma

Muskegon

Muskegon Heights

Greenville

Port Huron Township

Grand Haven

Grand Rapids

Flushing

Flint

Holland

Hastings

Owosso

Lansing

Durand

Lapeer

Royal Oak

St. Clair

Hopkins

Okemos

Plymouth

Mason

South Haven

Allegan

Albion

Jackson

Ann Arbor

Pontiac

Mt. Clemens

Kalamazoo

Battle Creek

Ypsilanti

Detroit's Eastern Market

Dowagiac

Adrian

Canton

Blissfield

Monroe

Michigan's Municipal
FARMERS' MARKETS

structure on Ann Street, one block west of Main. **Open**: *January-April, Saturdays 8-2. May to Christmas, Wednesdays & Saturdays 7-3.*

This is one of the largest and liveliest farmers' markets in Michigan. Saturday mornings in the summer are packed with customers coming to buy from the over 100 growers who sell here. The variety is great: from unusual herbs to choice vegetables. A diverse, cosmopolitan crowd adds to the atmosphere, as do the interesting shops in the adjacent Kerrytown complex.

Allegan

Hubbard Street parking lot in downtown Allegan, between Chestnut and Locust streets. **Open** *first or second week of May through October. Thursdays 8-5.*

This market kicks off in May with asparagus and reaches 10 or 12 growers at the height of the season. All the fruits and produce are locally grown.

Alma

City parking lot on the corner of Woodworth & Downie streets, downtown Alma. North of the main street (Superior). **Open** *June through October. Wednesdays & Saturdays. No official hours.*

Some 20 vendors show up at the Alma market. Most are growers but some import produce to sell. In addition to fruits and vegetables, eggs and honey are sold. One farmer grows a number of varieties of squash.

Alpena

Right behind the City Hall, which is at Water and First streets in downtown Alpena. **Open** *2nd week of July through October. Wednesdays & Saturdays 8-2.*

At the Alpena market you have to grow it to sell it. Twenty-three growers sell at this northern Michigan city. One man brings the maple syrup he produces; another sells the honey he gathers. Not a lot of fruit but plenty of vegetables.

Battle Creek

On Jackson Street downtown, in front of McCamly Place (a festival marketplace) and a block from the Stouffer Hotel. Take I-94 Capital

Ave. exit, head north to downtown Battle Creek. **Open** *June through October, Monday, Wednesday & Friday 8-1.*

About 20 growers congregate here at the height of the season. One regular, a native of the Far East, specializes in Chinese vegetables.

Bay City

Columbus at Adams Street, in the Columbus Avenue business district south of downtown Bay City. From I-75, follow I-75 Business Route into downtown and then south. Watch for intersection with Columbus at City Hall. One block east of Washington, the main street of Bay City. Open from first week of June to mid-November. Tuesdays & Thursdays, 2:30-8. (517) 893-5531.

The Hampton Township honeyrock melons found at this large 86-stall covered market are famous for their sweetness. Many of the same farmers can be found at the Midland and Saginaw farmers markets. Some farm families have been selling their produce and foods here for half a century. Strong on broccoli and cauliflower. Lots of sweet corn. Some farmers bring in dressed chickens and ducks.

June is strawberry month. At the first of the month, Benton Harbor-area strawberries are brought in. By the middle of the month, Bay County berries are ripe, and towards the end of the month you can get Alpena-area strawberries here.

Blissfield

Behind the Frosty Boy on corner of Highway 223 and Blissfield Highway, west of downtown Blissfield. **Open** *first Tuesday of June to first week of November. Tuesdays 8-1.*

By the second week of July when the corn and tomatoes and other staple vegetables start coming in, some 12 growers join the five regulars at this small market in the parking lot behind the local soft ice cream emporium. One vendor brings her blueberries, another has raspberries. Two growers are known for their excellent melons.

This part of Lenawee County is the bottom of what was once an early part of Lake Erie. Its soil is especially rich, accounting for the local canneries which originally employed Adrian's large Mexican-American population.

Cadillac

Off Lake Street on Lake Cadillac, downtown Cadillac. One block west of Cadillac's main street, Mitchell. **Open** *2nd week of July through October. Tuesdays & Fridays 8:30-5.*

The beautiful location on Lake Cadillac helps make this a popular market, attracting 500 to 1000 customers a day. You can feed the ducks, take a stroll, or swim nearby. The 20 or so growers come from all over Northwestern Michigan to sell here, providing a full range of vegetables, small fruits, and tree fruits. It does so well there's a waiting list for growers wanting to sell here. The Cadillac market, like many of the best, focuses on homegrown produce and fruits. There are no baked goods or processed foods.

Calumet Farmers' Market

In the parking lot of Coppertown USA in Calumet, in the northern Keweenau Peninsula. **Open** *from some time in July into October. Fridays 9-2.*

Fruits and vegetables. Usually only two growers. When health officials demanded that jams and baked goods only be made in licensed kitchens, participation fell off.

Canton

On Ford at Sheldon Roads in K-Mart parking lot, 3 miles west of I-275. Take Ford Road (M-153) exit. **Open** *last week of July to October 31. Wednesdays 4-8, Saturdays 8-3.*

Canton is the sweet corn capital of Michigan. Farms of 200 to 300 acres provide corn from July through September for many of the state's supermarkets. Eight or so of the growers sell their corn and other vegetables here.

Cheboygan

On State Street downtown in the City Hall parking lot. **Open** *from July to mid-October. Saturdays 8-2.*

The five to ten growers who come to this small market limit themselves to locally grown vegetables and fruits. After someone came up with a load of produce bought wholesale in Bay City, it was decided to prohibit such dealers because it was unfair to the farmers in this northern climate. You can find most all of the usual summer vegetables here, and dried flowers as well.

Detroit's Eastern Market

Just north of Gratiot 1 mile east of downtown. From Gratiot, take Russell north over the Chrysler Freeway. Freeway directions: go onto I-75. Just east of downtown, where I-75 goes north, get off at the Gratiot exit. **Parking:** *free parking in front of the market goes quickly on Saturday, but there's lots of inexpensive space Riopelle and Alfred, a block east of Russell and three blocks north of the main market area.* **Open** *year-round, Monday-Friday 5 a.m.-noon, Saturday 5 a.m.-6 p.m.*

Since the 1890s, this colorful, bustling market has been where Detroiters come to buy produce from local farmers and to find meats, fish, coffee, nuts, produce, fruit, spices, wine, and cheese at the stores around the market. Surrounding the large open-air stall area called "the sheds," where up to 800 farmers or produce dealers can sell their produce, are wholesale-retail specialty shops. The entire area has an earthy atmosphere. Saturday mornings the market is a madhouse, especially from 7 to 10 a.m.

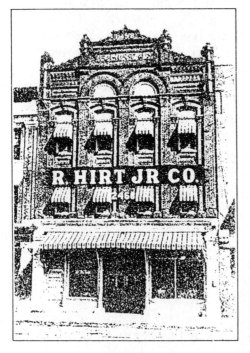

Half the fun of Detroit's Eastern Market is shopping at the old-time wholesalers like Rafal Spice, Cost Plus Wine, Rocky Peanut Company, and R. Hirt (left). Hirt's has been selling cheese and groceries at the market for a hundred years.

By Saturday afternoon, bargains are to be had, because dealers can't afford to be stuck with unsold produce for the weekend. During the week, there are only a few farmers at the market, mostly between 5 a.m. and 7 a.m. They sell wholesale to stores or retail to individual shoppers.

The wholesalers' weekday work is mostly done before sun-up. Around 1 a.m. trucks from the South and Southwest arrive to be unloaded. Farmers in market stalls compete with these out-of-state producers (increasingly growers are coming from Canada) for retail buyers, and a lot of bargaining take place.

Eastern Market is a vestige of old Detroit. There are a great medley of smells and sounds and colorful sights, and a vast variety of food appealing to the city's diverse populations and cultures.

These days the premium small producers are more likely to be found at the royal Oak or Pontiac or Ann Arbor farmers' markets, but if you want atmosphere, value, and a concentration of dealers or specialty foods and wines at very reasonable prices, the Eastern Market can't be beat.

In front of Ciaramitaro's, the third-generation Italian produce business on Market and Winder, you'll see dozens of crates of onions being unloaded, followed by piles of burlap bags of potatoes, as customers buy grapefruit and celery from the stand that's in front of the store, winter and summer. In the Gratiot Central Market, southeast of the Eastern Market sheds across the recessed Fisher Freeway, the aroma of nuts pervades the air of Germack's, the oldest pistachio importer in the U.S. Pungent spices greet you in several Middle Eastern shops; an Islamic slaughterhouse is a few blocks away. Nearby at Capital Poultry, live ducks (a favorite with Detroit's many Poles) and chickens cackle away. Feathers are mixed in the dirt in the gutter outside.

Wholesalers at the market today are likely to be descended from Belgian, German, and Polish farmers who sold at the market generations ago, or from Italian and Lebanese produce peddlers who first catered to Detroit's booming population of industrial workers beginning around 1910.

Dowagiac

Downtown on Front Street at the railroad depot, across from Hooks Drugstore. **Open** *June 1-first week in November, Saturdays 9-5.*

A new farmers' market complements the transformation of downtown Dowagiac, now that the state highway has been rerouted away from the retail district and historic façades have been uncovered. The market is focused on agricultural producers, without having crafts to dilute the image. The market master is committed to seeking out a variety of good growers, not necessarily the same ones every Saturday, and making sure that all niches, including fresh greens and such, are covered. Two highlights: organic produce from Roseland Farms, and a sweet onion akin to the Vidalia onion only a little later in the season, newly introduced to Michigan and grown near Decatur.

Dowagiac abounds in interesting historic buildings, including some eccentric stone mansions, a handsome train station, and an operating old-fashioned sweet shoppe and soda fountain, Caruso's, that still has much the same menu as it did in 1926, when it was last remodeled. Stop at Olympia Books and Prints, downtown across Front Street from the farmers' market, for a printed walking tour. Caruso's is a block north at 130 South Front.

Durand

In front of the railroad depot. From downtown Durand take Main Street east to Russell (just across the railroad tracks), turn right (south) and go a block to Ann Arbor St. Turn right on Ann Arbor. Depot is at the end of the street. **Open** *from the first Wednesday after fourth of July to last Wednesdays through September. Wednesday mornings 8:15-12:15.*

In the background of this lively market is the big, handsome Grand Trunk depot, one of the niftiest depots in the state. In addition to being an Amtrak station on the Chicago-Toronto line, it is a new state railroad museum.

About 25 to 30 growers sell here in the height of the season. Each market day at noon, they have a drawing and give away to two winners big baskets of fruit and vegetables.

One grower is known for his big Howell melons. Margaret O'Brien brings in beautiful cut gladiolus through much of the summer.

Escanaba

Downtown near the city garage. **Open** *June 1-October 15. Wednesdays & Saturdays 6:30-11.*

All of the 10 or 12 growers who sell here are from Delta County. Besides apples there's not much in the way of fruits, but a substantial line of vegetables is usually on hand. Because the Garden Peninsula is warmed by the surrounding lake, vegetables come in at the same time as in mid-Michigan. One family brings up freshly caught whitefish from their Garden, Michigan home.

Flint

Fifth Avenue at Boulevard Drive, across from the post office and just east of the Flint River on the east side of downtown Flint. Water Street downtown becomes Boulevard Drive as it goes east along the river. **Open** *year-round Tuesday, Thursday, & Saturday, 7-5:30. Fish market Fridays 10-6.*

Flint's farmers' market is interesting and lively even in winter, what with two meat vendors, a fish shop, two poultry dealers, several flower stalls, several egg producers, and dealer who imports bulk produce such as 50-pound bags of potatoes and 10-pound bags of white onions. Don't miss Ed Janego's sausage stand. He's been making and selling sausages for over 25 years. Janego promises hot pork sausage that will "curl your tongue."

Flushing

End of Cherry Street. From Main Street in downtown Flushing, take Cherry (at the stoplight) south to the end. **Open** *usually from the first or second week in July through September. Saturdays 7-1.*

All the fruits and vegetables here are homegrown, from the strawberries in June to the pumpkins in September. The location is especially nice: in an old city park, complete with municipal swimming pool, on the Flint River. There are walkways along the tree-lined river banks. Some birdhouses and flowers, both fresh and fried, are also for sale.

Grand Haven

Chinook Pier, on Harbor Drive, on the Grand River, just upriver from downtown. **Open** *first week of June to last week of October. Wednesdays & Saturdays 8 a.m. to around 3 p.m.*

This little market, with its 20 or so growers, has one of the most interesting locations in the state. It's right next to the one of the liveliest recreational boating centers in Michigan. The colorful scene includes expensive sailboats and yachts, big charter fishing boats, a complex of shops, and neat view of the dunes across the river.

Grand Rapids

1147 East Fulton at Fuller, about 1 1/2 miles east of the center of downtown Grand Rapids. **Open** *May 1-Christmas. Tuesdays, Wednesdays, Fridays & Saturdays 7:30-4:30.*

There are about 40 vendors at this municipal market. All but about five grow their own fruit and produce, with a few crafts and flowers, too. Saturdays during the peak of the season are packed at the block-long market. One grower features organic produce.

Greenville

Downtown in an alley near Ann's Pet Shop. From the corner of Lafayette (Greenville's main street) and 57, go one block north. **Open** *at end of first week of July until October 1. Tuesdays and Fridays 8-12.*

This small market swells to about 20 growers at the peak of the season. A grower from Clarksville brings superb cantaloupes. The usual array, from tomatoes and berries, is available.

A transaction at the Midland Farmers' Market. The home of Dow Chemical, Midland has what many consider one of the most pleasant markets in the state. In addition to attracting a number of growers, it has a splendid location in a park right on the Tittabawassee River.

Harrisville

*Just south of the U.S.-23/ M-72 intersection, two blocks west of Lake Huron. **Open** generally from Memorial Day to Labor Day, Wednesdays & Saturdays from 8 or so to about noon.*

This remote county seat has an informal, unregulated farmers' market on county land that attracts five or six growers in season. It's right next to the information center, where you can find out about the Harrisville State Park and the Huron National Forest.

Hastings

*On the Thornapple River north of downtown Hastings. From the main street of Hastings (State), take Broadway north 2 blocks. **Open** May into October. Wednesdays & Saturdays 8 until they run out.*

This pretty spot on the Thornapple is a park. Over 15 growers are there at the peak of the season.

Holland

*Parking lot Holland Civic Center, 150 West 8th St. at Pine, west of downtown Holland. **Open** Wednesdays & Saturdays 8-5. Also Mondays during fruit season, usually late June to early August.*

This is one of the bigger municipal markets, with 79 stalls. Being in West Michigan's fruit belt, it offers a great selection of fresh fruit from late June on.

Hopkins

*In the block-long park on Main Street, between Franklin & Clark streets, across from the fire barn. Hopkins is between Allegan and Grand Rapids. **Open** Wednesdays from 8 until p.m.*

This little town of 600 attracts five or six growers to its farmers' market in the city park.

Houghton Farmers' Market

*Location uncertain. May be across from the Copper Country Mall in the parking lot next to Festival Foods. May be inside the mall. Mall is on M-26 at the west edge of town, up the hill. **Open** from July into October. Wednesday and Saturday 9 to 3 or until sellout.*

Three or four area farmers sell their fruits and vegetables in this northern outpost of Michigan agriculture.

Iron County Farmers' Market (Ironwood)

In Hurley, Wisconsin, just across the state line and Montreal River from Ironwood, Michigan. On U.S. 51 Business Route, across from the Holiday Inn overlooking the river. **Open** *from mid-July into early October. Wednesday from 2 p.m. and Saturday from 10 a.m. to sellout, usually before noon.*

Sweet corn, tomatoes, and cole crops (cabbage, broccoli, cauliflower, rutabagas) are the big crops at this popular farmers' market, one of the very few in the region. There's not much fruit. Some crafts are also on hand. Come early for best selection.

Jackson

119 W. Louis Glick Highway at Mechanic Street in downtown Jackson. Take Cooper Street exit from I-94, head south a mile or so to Louis Glick, turn right (west) two blocks. Open June through October, Tuesdays, Fridays, and Saturdays 7-3:30.

Located in the heart of this old industrial town, the Jackson farmers' market is owned and operated by John Kuhl. His meat market and deli are in the building next to the 30 open-air covered stalls. Some 20 growers are here at the peak of the season, with melons and sweet corn the big draws. The Gibbs family supplies lots of tasty strawberries in June. The Smiths are so famous for their sweet corn that crowds will wait while their truck goes to get another load.

Kalamazoo (Bank Street Market)

Bank Street between Lake & Stockbridge streets in Washington Square, southeast of downtown and south of Upjohn Park. From downtown, take Westnedge south to Vine. East on Vine to east side of the park, south on Water Street, which becomes Bank Street. **Open** *Tuesday, Thursdays & Saturdays 6-6, June through October. In May & November, Saturdays only.*

This big U-shaped market has over 175 growers at the peak of the season. To keep the fruit and vegetables truly homegrown, selling space is limited to farmers in a surrounding 13-county territory. Because the land between Kalamazoo and Lake Michigan is one of the most richly cultivated in the Midwest, there is a great deal of quality produce available here. Asparagus is one specialty of nearby Van Buren and Berrien counties. Strawberries are also here in abun-

Sweet corn sold at farmers' markets is sometimes picked before dawn so it's as sweet as possible. Jackson, Canton, and Royal Oak are a few farmers' markets well known for their excellent sweet corn.

dance during June. In late fall, grapes are brought to market in quantity from the many big vineyards to the west. One farmer with a big following sells fresh dressed poultry—not the skimpy 2 1/2 lb. fryers you find in the supermarket, but plump 4-pound chickens.

Lansing

Just east of downtown on Cedar (one-way southbound) at Shiawassee. From Michigan Avenue, go north on Larch, west on Shiawassee, then south on Cedar. **Open** *year-round, Tuesday through Saturday 8-5:30.*

This big city market occupies two enclosed market halls built in 1938. A smaller, enclosed version of Detroit's fabled Eastern Market, it continues the tradition of big-city markets as places where a broad spectrum of customers come together to shop. Even in winter there is fresh produce brought in from the South, along with locally produced maple syrup, eggs, apples, root vegetables, baked goods, and such. A cheese shop, meat market, and florist are more like stores than stalls. A good bakery features cookies, breads, and meat, vegetable, and cheese pies for $2, and there's a snack bar with coffee. You can sit down and eat at indoor picnic tables or the picnic/playground area by the river across the parking lot. The adjacent Riverfront Park goes from Lansing's north side all the way to East Lansing. It's the pleasantest bike and pedestrian path n Michigan. Two blocks south of the market are several museums, including Impressions 5, Michigan's top children's museum. For more information on related sights, see *Hunts' Highlights of Michigan*.

Lapeer

Nepessing at Court streets in downtown Lapeer. **Open** *Wednesdays & Saturdays 9-2, from second Saturday of May to end of October.*

This pleasant market is situated in the tree-filled courtyard square of the state's oldest (1837) courthouse. About 20 growers show up during the peak of the season. A big draw is "Granny," whose pies, breads, cookies, and rolls attract customers every Saturday from as much as 50 miles away. A lady from Oak Park also comes Saturdays to sell her popular bagels (12 varieties). People also line up for the region's well-regarded strawberries, usually ripe by the second week of June. A couple of weeks later a fine crop of raspberries is usually on hand. Across the street, front-window seats at Dagwood's Deli give a good view of the streetscape.

Marquette & Alger Counties' Farmers' Market

On. U.S. 41, 2 miles south of Marquette. In the parking lot of the ABC True Value Hardware Store, in a commercial strip on the inland side of U.S. 41). **Open** *from the last week in July through mid-September, Saturday 10-3.*

Fifteen growers are committed to selling at this newly organized market, with six or eight expected to show up each Saturday. Products include sweet corn, vegetables, herbs, maple syrup, baked goods, and crafts.

Mason

On Ash Street, 2 blocks west of Jefferson & Ash in the center of Mason. **Open** *mid-July to mid-October. Wednesdays 4-7, Saturdays 8-1.*

Some 6 to 10 vendors sell their vegetables and fruits at this small market. It's on a park which has a playground on one side and a pavilion for the market on the other.

Okemos/ Meridian Township

Behind Meridian Mall in Central Park. On Central Park Road. From Grand River Avenue (M-43), go north on Marsh Road at the Okemos Mall, then go left to Central Park Road. Market pavilion is on right. **Open** *2nd week in July to mid-October. Wednesdays & Saturdays 8-2.*

Located in the middle of 240-acre Central Park, the market pavilion has 15 to 20 growers. The park houses everything from municipal buildings to several miles of trails. A delightful authentic farm house/museum near the market is sometimes open.

Midland

At the foot of Ashman Street on the Tittabawasee River, downtown Midland. **Open** *from the second week of May through October 31. Wednesdays & Saturdays 7-noon.*

This is widely regarded as one of the state's most successful farmers' markets. It's in a park next to the junction of the Tittabawassee and Chippewa rivers, a delightful spot which includes a round pavilion for some of the over 40 growers who sell here. In addition to a wide variety of fruits and vegetables, there is one person selling homemade egg rolls. There are herbs and honey, baskets and bread for sale here.

Monroe

20 East Willow, 1 block north of Monroe & Elm on the south side of the River Raisin. **Open** *year-round Saturday 6-noon. From June through October also open Tuesdays.*

One of the oldest farmers' markets is the state, Monroe's market goes back 60 years. Area farmers formed a cooperative which owns its own enclosed building, permitting year-round operation. In winter, of course, not nearly as much is available: honey, colored corn, potatoes, apples, and such. In the summer the 20 or so growers bring a full array of fruits and vegetables. There are also a good number of fresh and dried flowers.

Mt. Clemens

On Old Gratiot between Clinton & Market streets. Right across from the new County Courthouse in downtown Mt. Clemens. **Open** *from the second week of May to the second Saturday in November. Fridays and Saturdays 8-2.*

This is one of the bigger markets in Michigan, with over 35 growers. Two growers, George Van Houttle and Ron Weig, pick their sweet corn after midnight just before market days, giving you some of the freshest you'll find anywhere. The corn season usually lasts from the last week of July to the first frost.

Mt. Pleasant

Island Park, Lincoln at Main Street, two blocks north of downtown. **Open** *from the third or fourth week of June to the Thursday before Halloween. Thursdays 8:30-5.*

An island in the Chippewa River is the delightful setting for this farmers' market. Some 40 growers come here. A few wholesalers are permitted, but no baked goods or crafts.

Muskegon

Business U.S. 31 at Eastern Avenue, half a mile north of downtown Muskegon. Open year 'round on Saturdays. Also open Tuesdays & Thursdays from May through November.

This popular and venerable institution got its start in 1881, and now is using its sixth site, a seven-acre blacktop surrounded by a park. It's the only outdoor year-'round market in the Midwest, made possible by tarp windbreaks and powerful kerosene-fueled salamander heaters. In the winter you can get apples, pears, winter squash, potatoes, as well as wholesale produce shipped from warmer climates. In the summer some 50 growers sell their fruits and vegetables. One family has supplied fruits from its orchard near Hart, north of here, for the past 80 years. A well-known gladiolus grower from Zeeland also sells here.

Muskegon Heights

Corner of Baker & Center streets on the eastern edge of downtown Muskegon Heights, across the street from city hall. **Open** *May 1 to December 31, Tuesdays, Wednesdays, Fridays, and Saturdays, 7-6.*

Ann Arbor Farmers' Market: one Michigan's liveliest and most colorful. It is packed summer Saturday mornings. The covered, open-air stalls are right next to the interesting Kerrytown complex of shops and just a block away from the amazing sandwiches and foods of Zingerman's delicatessen.

Five or six veteran growers form the nucleus of the up to 15 vendors at this popular little market. The stalls and walkways are covered.

Owosso

In the Armory parking lot on Water Street, 1 block north of City Hall. **Open** *May through October 31. Saturdays 8-12.*

This market includes both farm products and hand-made crafts. About 20 growers attend by the peak of the season. There's lots of sweet corn here, 3 strawberry growers, one person who specializes in herbs, and another who grows certified organic vegetables.

Across the Shiawassee River, you can catch a glimpse of Curwood's Castle, a miniature chateau built by James Oliver Curwood, the popular adventure novelist of the 1920s. Today it's a museum.

Plymouth

On Penniman, right off Main Street in downtown Plymouth. Next to the Penn Theater. **Open** *mid-May to mid-October. Saturdays 7:30-12:30.*

Unlike most farmers' markets in the state, the Plymouth market allows a fair number of dealers who have bought their cheeses or other foods wholesale and resell it here. There are about 15 vendors using the 21 stalls in the roofed structure called "The Gathering." The Penniman Street area has become one of Michigan's most interesting downtown for shopping and restaurants.

Pontiac

2350 Pontiac Lake Road, 1/4 mile west of Telegraph Road in Waterford, Michigan. **Open** *Saturdays year-round 6:30-1. Also open Thursdays From May through December. and Tuesdays from May though October.*

This big market has over 100 growers at its peak and can attract 10,000 on a good Saturday. One growers comes all the way from Ohio to reach this affluent clientele from Birmingham, Bloomfield Hills, and vicinity; another comes from Western Michigan. There are 38 indoor stalls, 32 canopied stalls, and 30 open stalls. Twenty or so craftspeople also sell here. There's a good selection here of everything from herbs to ice cream. Saturdays can be packed, however.

Port Huron

Across from McMorran Place between the downtown commercial district and St. Clair Community College. **Open** *July 18 through October. Saturday mornings until produce is sold out.*

The 15 or so growers here also sell at the Port Huron Township and the St. Clair farmers' markets. They are all small growers, concentrating on the trade they have at these three markets. Some grow miniature vegetables. There are varieties of popcorn, herbs, and flowers.

Port Huron Township

St. Stevens Catholic Church on 32nd Street, 5 miles west of Port Huron. Open mid-July through October. Thursdays 8 until sold out.

Usually the same growers as at the Port Huron market.

Royal Oak

1 mile east of Woodward, 2 miles west of I-75 on 11 Mile Road at Market Street. Take the Woodward exit from I-696, go north on Main Street to 11 Mile Road, then right (east) 3 blocks. **Open** *Saturdays year round 7-1. In summer (June through September), also open Tuesdays, Thursdays, & Fridays. In October also open Tuesdays & Fridays 7-1. In November & December, also open Fridays 7-1.*

House in a huge barn built back in 1927, Royal Oak hosts one of the very biggest and best farmers' markets in the state. Thousands fill the parking lots that surround the market, where up to 150 growers display their fruits, vegetables, and cheeses. There are dozens of varieties of tomatoes alone, and as many kinds of sweet corn. Sweet cherries, bigger and darker than those grown in southern Michigan, come down from the Cadillac area toward the end of July. One grower specializes in organically grown dried beans from Michigan's bean basket, the Thumb. You can find everything from goat cheese to organic eggs here.

St. Clair

At the North end of St. Clair Mall on Riverside Street. **Open** *from the third Wednesday of June to last Wednesday of October. Wednesdays 8 a.m. until sold out.*

Usually the same growers as the Port Huron market.

Sault Ste. Marie
Chippewa County Farmers' Market

In Sault Ste. Marie, Michigan, in the parking lot by the firehouse in the center of downtown. From Ashmun, the main street into downtown Sault Ste. Marie, turn left onto Arlington 1-2 blocks before the river. **Open** *when garden produce is ready (late August or early September into October), Saturdays from 8 a.m. to sellout (past noon).*

Garden vegetables from local farmers are augmented with produce from as far away as Bay City. Some fruit, too. The firefighters next door make good use of the market for boiled dinners (cabbage, carrots, and potatoes with meat).

South Haven

Downtown on Huron Street just off Phoenix Street, in the city parking lot behind the post office. **Open** *July through October, Saturdays 8-1. Also open Wednesdays in July & August.*

This little market is right on the edge of a rich fruit farming area. The eight growers who come here sell all kinds of fruit, form organic raspberries to peaches and blueberries. And they also raise a wide variety of vegetables. Sweet corn is a specialty.

Traverse City

Corner of Parkway and Cass between downtown and the bay, across from the zoo. **Open** *Saturdays 8-1 from Mothers' Day weekend through October. Also open Wednesdays from second half of July through September.*

The large blue canopies covering this big, bustling market area are hard to miss as you enter Traverse City's central area. Up to 8,000 customers are lured by the exceptionally fresh, high quality fruits and vegetables. As many as 60 growers sell here, coming all the way from Newberry in the U.P. and the Bay City area to the south. The sweet corn up here begins to come in by the beginning of August. Corn from longtime local grower Bill Brown draws crowds for its extra sweetness. You can find very good homemade bread here, and apples grown this far north are legendary for their flavor and crispness.

Ypsilanti

Cross & River streets in Depot Town. Open year 'round, Wednesdays and Saturdays 7-3.

Depot Town, a historic railroad district separate from Ypsilanti's central business district, is a splendid setting for this market. The market is housed in a 1875 brick Italianate railroad freight warehouse, near the bars and shops that make this district a popular destination. The old structure holds 25 stalls. At the peak of the growing season, there are about 10 farmers on hand. To remain open all year round, the market allows many more than farmers to sell their fruits and vegetables. There are crafts, a coffee house, cheeses, wholesale produce, and baked goods from the Depot Town Sourdough Bakery across the way (see p. 237). Every Saturday morning, there's live music, sometimes folk, sometimes country, sometimes rock.

The year-round, open-air Muskegon Farmers' Market began as a hay scale auction in 1881; this old photo shows it at a temporary shelter on Spring Street. Today it has its own market shed. It's the state's only open-air market which stays open all year round. With 50 growers selling their fruits and vegetables at the peak of the season, it offers one of the best selections in western Michigan.

Herb Farms

For zesty, imaginative cooking with ordinary ingredients, a small garden of fresh herbs is a wonderful addition to any kitchen. Herbs are easy to grow and require only a small space. Even a window box will do. Sandy soil and lots of sun are the major requirements.

The wide-ranging field of herbs covers a lot of territory: culinary, medicinal, aromatic, and decorative. The decorative side has burgeoned in recent years, thanks to the likes of *Country Living* and *Victoria* magazine, to the point that in some herb shops the dried wreaths and arrangements of herbs and flowers overwhelms the simpler and less profitable living plants. This selective list is focused on recommended shops that sell plants through much of the growing season.

Visiting herb farms is an ideal way to learn about herbs. They're personal places, where the owner-gardener, and possibly a small staff, are knowledgeable, hands-on gardeners who almost invariably enjoy sharing their interest and knowledge with others. So you can get good advice about starting or improving your own herb garden, particularized to your own situation and requirements.

Display gardens at herb farms give a much better idea of landscaping with herbs than any photograph or drawing. In addition, most herb shops carry some recommended books on the cultivation and use of herbs; some have extensive book sections.

Of course, it's good to plan a herb-buying expedition so any live plants you purchase can be taken promptly home, or to your lodging, to avoid having to lock them in a hot, closed car.

For location, see map on page 117.

1 Bellwether Herbs

On northwest corner of Shady Lane and Elm Valley Rd. Take M-22 north 8 miles from Traverse City. Turn left (west) on Shady Lane and head 1/3 mile west. Northwest of Traverse City south of Suttons Bay. **Open** *from May to Christmas. May 1 to Labor Day: Tuesday, Wednesday and Thursday 9-5, Friday 9-7:30, Saturday 9-5, Sunday 10-3. After Labor Day to Christmas: Friday-Sunday, same hours. (616) 271-3004.*

Gail Ingraham was an investment banker in Traverse City until eight years ago, when she decided what she really wanted to do was grow

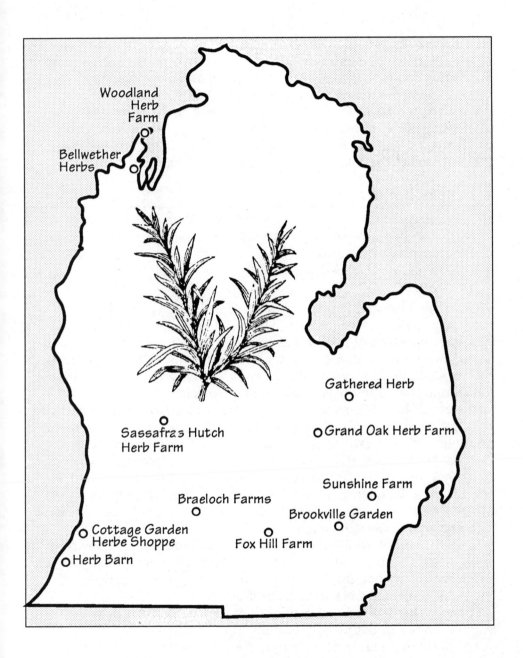

Woodland
Herb
Farm

Bellwether
Herbs

Gathered Herb

Sassafras Hutch
Herb Farm

Grand Oak Herb Farm

Sunshine Farm

Braeloch Farms

Brookville Garden

Cottage Garden
Herbe Shoppe

Fox Hill Farm

Herb Barn

Selected Michigan HERB FARMS

things. Now she has quite an extensive set-up — one and a half acres of herb gardens. You can buy 20 varieties of herb plants ($1.79 to $4 depending on size and type) from the end of May through September. Dried and fresh culinary herbs are sold for 50¢ a baggie.

Just north up Elm Valley Road, Larry Mawby's winery is another interesting place to visit, both for its excellent wines and for the creative graphic panache with which Larry and his printmaker wife, Peggy, promote the wine and embellish the tasting room.

2 Braeloch Farms

*9124 North 35th, near the west side of Gull Lake, northeast of Kalama-zoo. From M-43 a mile north of Richland, turn east onto County Road C at the Stagecoach Stop Inn. When C ends, turn left. Farm is first drive on left. **Open** mid-April-Christmas. Tuesday-Saturday 10-5, Sunday 1-5. (616) 629-9888.*

Growing herbs and perennials is the focus of this most attractive country place at a large farmstead west of Gull Lake. The farm build-ings have been added to and remodeled for different purposes over the years, all within the framework of genteel good taste, in that attractive, historically layered way that makes some places seem richer and more interesting than other places with more clear-cut origins.

The large shop, filled with unfussy dried arrangements and mostly floral gift items, is in the cool ground floor of a big, weathered barn. It's pretty in a relaxed way, sophisticated but not over-decorated or themed. Many small and large gardens and garden plots give visitors ideas for landscaping with herbs and perennials. They also produce cut flowers sold in summer, loose or arranged. The place is perfumed with the chocolatey smell of cocoa shell mulch, bought by the truck-load and sold for $4.75 a bag.

In 1989 owner Cynthia Palmer and her husband fell in love with Allen Beebe's herb and perennial farm while visiting their daughter in Kalamazoo. They bought it on an impulse and moved from Connect-icut, where she had worked as a floral designer.

Prices for herbs are $1.25 a pack (2 or 4 plants), $3 for 3" pots. Supplies may run out by midsummer. Several kinds of borage, calen-dulas, and other plants sold here yield edible flowers, used for crys-tallized cake decorations, floating on drinks, and garnishing salads.

Gull Lake long has been a favorite retreat for wealthy people from Battle Creek and Kalamazoo. Suburbanized in recent decades, it still retains a relaxed country feel. Some very pretty spots are in the vicinity of Braeloch Farms, along West Gull Lake Drive north of the farm.

Around on the lake's east side, **Ross Township Park** has big trees and a pleasant if stony beach; cereal magnate **W. K. Kellogg's estate**, now a Michigan State University biological research station, has a most pleasant public garden walkway behind the Manor House down to the lake. Other worthwhile destinations include the beautiful **Kellogg Bird Sanctuary**, the outstanding **Gilmore Classic Car Museum** (the barns alone are worth a visit), the **Kellogg Dairy**, and **antique shops** in the centers of Galesburg and quaint Hickory Corners and Richland.

3 Brookville Garden

7885 Brookville Rd. 8 miles west of Plymouth in the northwestern corner of Wayne County. Take North Territorial Rd. west from Sheldon Rd. and the M-14 exit there. In about 4 1/2 miles, Territorial swings south, and Brookville Rd. intersects at the north. Garden is at the northwest corner of Brookville and Curtis Roads. **Open** *from April to the weekend before*

Two minutes off I-94 outside Benton Harbor, Nancy John's Herb Barn is one of the most complete herb farm and shops in Michigan.

Christmas. April- June: Wednesday- Sunday 10-5. July-Christmas: Wednesday-Saturday 10-5. (313) 455-8602.

Cynthia Brautigan comes well recommended as a grower of culinary herbs. She grows some 250 varieties, with lots of rosemarys. There's an edible herb garden around the house, and a greenhouse that provides fresh herbs to restaurants year-round. Potted herb plants are sold for $2.50 a 3 1/2-inch pot. Dried herbs and vinegars are also for sale.

4 Fox Hill Farm

440 W. Michigan Avenue, just west of Parma. **Open** *April 15 to October 15. Wednesday-Saturday 9-5, Sunday 12-5. (517) 531-3179.*

One of the largest collections of herbs in the country is in the big greenhouse and garden area by a stately, somewhat decrepit old farmhouse. Since the years of its big Boy, Oh, Boy, Oh Basil Festivals with cook-offs and celebrity judges, Fox Hill has shifted to being a mail-order supplier of plants and fresh cut herbs, and site maintenance has become somewhat lax.

Some 400 kinds of herbs include rarities like asafetida, a culinary herb from the West Indies, and $400 rosemary topiaries. There are 18 varieties of basil, 12 of rosemary, and 30 of thyme. Prices are high in comparison with most herb farms, but if you're looking for something really unusual, this is the place to come. Four public gardens are available to see how the plants look. Fresh-cut herbs must be ordered in advance.

5 The Gathered Herb & Greenhouse

12114 North State Road, 1 mile north of Otisville, 20 miles northeast of Flint, 35 miles southeast of Frankenmuth. Take I-75 to Clio exit, East on Vienna Road (M-57) 12 miles until it dead ends. Then north on State 300 feet. On east side. **Open** *year-round, Tuesday-Saturday 10-6. (313) 631-6572.*

Shelley Carlson wanted to grow things even back when she was a kid of 8. She persuaded her dad to let her dig up their Detroit-area backyard, where she successfully grew vegetables and flowers. She went on to major in botany at Alma College, and when she and her husband moved to the Otisville area, took the opportunity 5 years ago to start her herb growing business.

You can buy some 50 varieties of herb plants here, costing about $2 to $3 a plant. They're all available from May 10 through the summer. A limited variety is available throughout the year. One unusual variety she sells is a $6.50 bay tree in a 4-inch container. Although it will grow to 30 feet, it makes a good house plant. The culinarily adventurous can buy 24 varieties of scented geraniums, whose leaves can be used in jellies, cakes, puddings, and other desserts. There are four varieties of rosemary. Bulk dried and fresh cut herbs are also available.

6 Grand Oak Herb Farm

2877 Miller Road at Lansing Road, half way between Flint and Lansing. From I-69, take Bancroft exit. Right 1/2 mile on Lansing Road to Miller Road. **Open** *Tuesday-Saturday 8-5, Sunday 1-5. (517) 634-5331.*

The name of this herb farm comes from the huge white oak in the front yard. The 350-year-old behemoth is the largest in the state. The 152-acre farm has seven acres in herbs. There are 18 gardens giving visitors a great diversity of ideas about how to plant herbs. There is a salad garden, a Victorian garden, a heritage rose garden, a cottage garden, a lemon pie garden, a tussie-mussie garden, a silver garden, a scented geranium garden, an allium (onion) garden.

You cut your own herbs here, and owner Beulah Hargrove eyeballs your bunch to come up with a price. In basil alone you can find 12 varieties, including spicy Italian, lemon basil, cinnamon basil, and the common sweet basil. Edible flowers are a specialty. There are 54 kinds of scented geraniums, violas, lemon gem marigolds, day lilies, and even old-fashioned heritage roses.

7 The Herb Barn

1955 Greenley Ave. about 2 minutes off I-94 east of Benton Harbor. From I-94 Exit 30 (Napier Rd.), go east on Napier, almost immediately turn south onto Greenley. The garden and shop are behind a farmhouse on the east side of the road in about 1/4 mile. **Open** *year-round except for a month around and after Christmas. May-just before Christmas: Monday through Friday 10-5, Saturday 10-4, Sunday noon-4. Last week in January-April: Tuesday through Saturday 10-5. (616) 927-2044.*

Owner-grower Nancy Johns and her shop manager, Mary Jo Parker, have been able to satisfyingly cover all the wide-ranging aspects of herbs in this attractive small mini-farm and shop: culinary, medicinal and useful, decorative, and landscaping. The shop sells about a hundred kinds of bulk dried herbs and many, many books and Garden Way pamphlets on cultivation, garden design, herb botany and history, recipes and uses. In addition, there are the more usual dried herbs and flowers, loose or in wreaths and decorative arrangements. Some 50

For an idyllic setting, the Woodland Herb Farm near Northport at the tip of the Leelanau Peninsula is hard to match. The cottage shop is charming, and the hidden fragrance garden and pool is delightfully serene.

varieties of seeds are stocked for spring, beginning in March.

Over a hundred varieties of herb plants are typically for sale from May into July and August. Some three dozen common culinary herb plants are generally for sale year-round.

The display gardens are simple, attractive designs well suited to many kinds of houses, new and old, country and suburban. The 16-acre property includes a good-size greenhouse, three acres of garden plots, and a few small outbuildings. It shows what can be done without a big investment; much of it is suited to the smaller spaces of more urban gardeners. It's fun to watch the rabbits and pygmy goats that are housed back away from the shop. A popular summer attraction is small samples of herbal lemonade or teas.

The Herb Barn's location is most unusual: a lazy country road within two minutes of a major I-94 exit. It's quite a convenient stop for anyone heading home to or from Chicago.

8 Mac's Memorables
Cottage Garden Herbe Shoppe

6095 Harrison Street at McCray 10 miles north of Benton Harbor. From I-94 take exit 34 (I-196) north to exit 7 (Hager Shore Road). Head east. Harrison is the first street to the right. Head south to Harrison & McCray. **Open** *year-round, Monday-Saturday noon-6. (616) 849-2211.*

This unusual herb farm has all sorts of specialties. It' s a little one-acre place out in the country, just half a mile away from Lake Michigan. There are some 300 varieties of dried culinary and medicinal herbs. Scented geraniums come in 18 varieties. Teas include herbal and medicinal, black and green. Dried herbs sell anywhere from 25¢ an ounce for rosemary to $8.50 an ounce for ginseng.

Another specialty are supplies for Native American Indian ceremonies, something the local Potawattami population like to buy. There are rattles ($35 and up) and drums ($70 and up), smudge wands, ceremonial tobacco, shaman baskets, and dream catches (hoops hung by your bed to trap bad dreams).

Kevin and Jody McKeown started the shop four years ago, following years of growing and giving herbs away. Kevin is a fine woodcarver and a commercial diver. His carvings are also for sale in the shop.

9 Sassafras Hutch Herb Farm Shop

11880 Sandy Bottom N.E., 7 miles north of Greenville. Take M-57 to Heintzelman Road. Turn right (north) one block. Left onto Sandy Bottom and go over 600 feet. **Open** *from Wednesday before Mother's Day to Christmas. Wednesday-Saturday 10-5. (616) 754-9759.*

You can buy over 250 3 1/2-inch pots of herb plans here, plus dozens of dried herbs. Grower Joyce Kebless has over 40 varieties of scented geraniums (good for making vinegars and for other flavorings). The 10-acre farm has two acres planted in herbs. It's an old Christmas tree farm, and the surrounding pines give the place a quiet, secluded aura.

There are demonstration gardens you can tour and two greenhouses.

10 Sunshine Farm and Garden

2460 North Wixom Road, 4 miles southeast Milford. Take Wixom Road exit from I-96. Go 5 miles north. **Open** *April-December, Wednesday-Sunday 10-5. (313) 685-2204.*

This exceptional herb farm has all kinds of demonstration gardens, complete with labeled plants. There's the classic "Kitchen Cutting Garden," filled with rows of annuals like basil, savory, and fennel which the cook can go just outside to cut fresh. A Shakespearean garden features plants mentioned by the bard. There's a Bible garden and a fragrance garden, a dye garden and a culinary garden, to mention just some of what's here.

There are some 300 varieties of potted herb plants you can buy here. Popular today are the cilantro plants, used in salsas and other Mexican dishes. A 3 1/2-inch pot with 3 or 4 plants is just $2.50. Dill plants are particularly popular these days, used with fish dishes. Dozens of dried herbs are also available.

11 Woodland Herb Farm

7741 North Manitou Trail, M-22. Just west of Northport. **Open** *May-November, Monday and Saturday, 11-5. (616) 386-5081.*

A delightful enclosed garden and a first-rate herb shop are the attractions of Jon and Pat Bourdo's simple farm, the oldest of a number of herb farms in northern Michigan. The small fragrance garden, enclosed in high shrubbery, includes a tiny pool and a fountain surrounded by plants. Visitors are welcome to sit on a bench and take in this serene scene. On one side is a wonderfully weather-worn shed. Inside the crowded shop are products with over 200 varieties of herbs grown on the premises — potpourris and sachets, pesto mixes, and unusual vinegars, dressings, relishes, chilis, and chutneys. Advice and recipes based on Pat's long involvement in herb cookery are available in *Herbs and Spices*, for people interested in flavorings as a way to cut back on salt, and *The Woodland Herb Farm and Condiment Cookbook.*

At Braeloch Farms near Gull Lake and Kalamazoo, Cynthia Palmer has a large old farmstead with lots of space for displaying herbs and perennials and propagating plants, too. Like most herb people, she is a woman who's happy to dig in herself and work in the garden; she can't walk by a bed without stopping to pull any errant weeds.

Organic Farms

To be a certified organic farm requires more than avoiding the use of artificial fertilizers, herbicides, and pesticides. The grower must also take steps to build up the organic content of the soil, by using things like green manure crops, compost, composted manures, and natural minerals such as lime sulfur and rock phosphate. Pest control is done by companion planting and crop rotation, and by using predatory insects, botanical insecticides like rotenone, and dormant oil sprays. In Michigan, a grower must conform to these practices for at least three years to be fully certified as organic.

Not many of the certified organic farms in Michigan sell directly to retail customers. Those on this list do, but even they should be called first to confirm availability. In general, organic fruits and vegetables sell for about 20% above non-organic prices.

SOUTHEAST MICHIGAN

Bailey's Vineyard

Farm is in Troy, on Adams Road, 1/4 mile north of Long Lake in Oakland County. **Call first** *to make arrangements. (313) 545-5786.*

This vineyard was established back in the 1960s in what is now an enclave of suburban Troy. Jim Lemire has four acres in **grapes**, some 13 varieties in all, from Suffolk Reds (a seedless table grape) to various French hybrids such as Vignoles (a premium white wine grape). Prices are as low as 30¢ a pound if you pick them yourself. Another specialty is **Roma** (paste) **tomatoes**.

Black Feet Farm

Near Hudson between Adrian and Hillsdale, at 14155 W. Beecher Road. **Call first.** *(517) 445-2491.*
Rick and Elizabeth Schoolmaster sell both retail and wholesale. They grow **lettuces, celery, carrots**, and **sweet corn**.

Green Acres Farm

6010 Marshall Road near Dexter, west of Ann Arbor. From I-94, take exit 169 (Zeeb Rd.) North on Zeeb 3/4 mile to Marshall Road, turn left. Farm is 1/2 mile down Marshall Road on the right hand side. (Marshall Road is 1/8 mile before Dexter-Ann Arbor Road. (313) 663-4968.

Dan and Norma Green grow four acres of shiitake mushrooms and two acres of vegetables, including lettuce and rhubarb. They are in the transitional phase before qualifying for organic certification.

Hooter Hill Farm

5240 Dexter Townhall Road northwest of Dexter and Ann Arbor. Take I-94 to Baker Road, Go north on Baker to Dexter, west on Main Street. Go under railroad bridge and keep straight on Island Lake Road 3 1/2 miles to Dexter Townhall Road. Turn right and go 1 1/2 miles. (313) 426-3066.

Two acres of organic vegetables — **tomatoes, sweet corn, beans, beets, leeks, carrots**, and **pumpkins** — are grown on Paul and Gwen Guenther's farm, along with a quarter-acre of **strawberries**.

Some organic growers only sell retail at farmers' markets. Renaissance Herb Farm is a regular vendor at the Ann Arbor Farmers' Market, for instance. It's worth checking the farmers' market listings to learn of other organic growers.

Little Organic Farm

6716 Allen Road, near Tecumseh. **Call ahead.** *(517) 423-6859.*

Neal Enke and Nerida Bridgeford have a half-acre of tomatoes, peppers, sweet corn, berries, asparagus, plus specialty and Oriental vegetables. They also sell at the Adrian Farmers' Market.

MID-MICHIGAN

Appleschram

130 West Mt. Hope Highway, about 13 miles west of Lansing and 15 miles northwest of Charlotte. Take M-43 (Grand Ledge Hwy.) or M-50 from Charlotte to Cochran Road, turn west onto Mt. Hope Road. Farm is in 1 1/4 miles. **Open** *seasonally, August thorugh November. (517) 649-8957.*

Thirty-seven varieties of apples, including antique apples, grow in Jane Bush's 17-acre orchard. She also has peaches, pears, and plums. Bush began farming organically six years ago, and the orchard is her sole source of income — a rarity among organic farmers.

Deer Creek Acres

12161 Sharon Road between Chesaning and Saginaw. From west of Chesaning, go north on M-52, 4 miles past intersection with M-57 to Marion Road. Turn right to Sharon Road, then right. Fourth house on left. (517) 845-2766. **Call ahead.**

Larry and Linda Byrne have farmed organically for three years on four of their ten acres. Linda specializes in colored peppers, tomatoes, cucumbers, beans, sweet corn, and strawberries. Also sell at the Owosso Farmers' Market.

Robert & Eleanor Glick Farm

8335 W. Beard Road, 5 miles west of Perry (between Lansing and Flint), just off old I-69. **Call first:** *(517) 675-7316.*

The Glicks have gardened organically for 35 years. They now farm ten of their 40 acres commercially. They sell organic eggs, plus tomatoes and rhubarb. Most is sold to a co-op.

Whetham Organic Farm

*11230 West Mt. Morris Road, four miles north of downtown Flushing northwest of Flint. 7 miles west of I-75. **Call first:** (313) 659- 8414. Also sell at the Flushing Farm Market.*

For over 12 years Clarke and Pat Whetham have been farming their 36 acres without chemicals. They grow assorted vegetables and red raspberries.

SOUTHWEST & WEST MICHIGAN

Gardens Naturally

*3081 100th Street, southwest of Byron Center, about 10 miles south of Grand Rapids. From U.S. 131, take the 100th St.exit 3 1/2 miles to farm and store. The store is **open in May & June** for plants, organic fertilizers and insect controls. **By appointment** the rest of the year. (616) 878-9459.*

Grocery stores are Scott and Lynne Vinkemulder's main customers, but they also take orders for produce, picked or U-pick.

N'Harmony Farm

*6677 12 Mile Road, near Rockford north of Grand Rapids. 2 1/2 miles east of Northwind Drive. **Call first.** (616) 866-1678.*

After quitting a corporate job, Fred Reusch started farming organically 15 years ago. Four of his 18 acres are in vegetables, with another acre of fruit.

Organic Gardens

*32120 Topash Road south of Dewey Lake in the Sister Lakes area of northwest Cass County. From Dowagiac, drive northwest on Middle Crossing Road 7 or 8 miles to Garret Road, turn right 2 miles to the first stop. Farm is on the southwest corner of Garret and Topash. **In season** they maintain a **self-serve table** in front of the house. Otherwise, **call first.** (616) 782-2505.*

A wide variety of vegetables are grown on 1 1/2 acres of Jack and Diane Bower's 5-acre farm, including beets, onions, squash, and potatoes. They will pick to order for customers who call ahead. The Bowers started organic growing six years ago and started selling their produce three years ago.

Red Arrow Organic Gardens

47264 Red Arrow Highway, two miles east of Lawrence, between Paw Paw and Hartford. Red Arrow Highway parallels I-94 and joins the downtowns of Fruit Belt towns. **Call first.** *(616) 674-3488.*

Three acres of organic asparagus, garlic, and onions are grown by Dave and Peggy Marcalletti.

Roseland Farms Market

M-60 near corner of Dailey Road, 5 miles west of Cassopolis, 6 miles east of Niles. **Open** *daily 9-5. (616) 445-8987.*

This serious organic farming venture features some **fruits** and **vegetables, wild apple juice,** and organic **grains** and **meats**. You can buy organically grown beef and pork, sold by halves, quarters, and individual cuts, as well as chicken and turkey.

Some organic farmers are quite familiar with traditional large-scale farming. Gwen Guenther farms over two acres organically on the big farm between Chelsea and Dexter she and her husband Paul own and work.

Sunshower

48548 60th Avenue, 2 1/4 miles east of Lawrence to 48th, 1 mile south to 60th, 1/4 mile. **Open** *year-round. (616) 674-3103.*

Organic pears and **apples,** and many organic **vegetables. Apple cider,** fresh and frozen cider, pear cider, tart cherry **juice** and many variations of **blended juices, apple and pear butter,** also maple syrup and occasionally chestnuts.

Waltz Three-Acre Farm

51782 Correll Road in the northwest corner of St. Joseph County. Take M-60 1 mile east of Leonidas to Correll Road, go north on Correll 1/2 mile. It's the fourth house off M-60). **By appointment or chance.** *(616) 496-7578.*

John Waltz has farmed for 30 years, and for the past four years he and his wife, Linda, have been raising organic vegetables on six acres. Also sells at the Battle Creek Farm Market.

NORTHERN LOWER PENINSULA

Eugene Andrews Farm

8410 N. Wise Road, 7 miles east of Clare, 1 1/2 miles south of U.S. 10. **Open** *during harvest season open all day and evenings as well. Otherwise call first. (517) 465-6554.*

Because he uses commercial fertilizer, lifelong farmer Eugene Andrews is not certified as fully organic, but he does not use herbicides or pesticides on 20 of his 120 acres. His not-quite-organic crops include melons, squash, tomatoes, peppers, cucumbers, string beans, and sweet corn. Some customers drive over 50 miles to buy his hard (winter) squash for making baby food. Sells at Clare and Mt. Pleasant farm markets.

Morning Star Farms

4640 Loeb Road south of Charlevoix. From Charlevoix take U.S. 31 south to the outskirts of town. Take M-66 southeast 1 1/2 miles to Loeb Road, then south 1.2 miles. **Call first.** *(616) 547-6930.*

A wide variety of **dried beans** and **heritage vegetables,** plus **grains** for baking, are the highlights of Paul and Deborah Gelderblom's 20-acre farm.

UPPER PENINSULA

Randy Grego Farm

Between Houghton and Freda on Cove Creek Road. Go west of Houghton along Houghton Canal Road to Smelts Road, less than 2 miles out of town. Smelts becomes Covered Drive. It's 3 1/2 miles to Cove Creek Road. **Open** *3 p.m.-9 p.m. in season. (906) 482-6926.*

About five acres of Randy and Linda Grego's 160-acre farm are used to grow organic vegetables. Randy uses cold frames and greenhouses to grow warm-weather vegetables in the far-north Houghton-Hancock area. He specializes in tomatoes, peppers, cucumbers, eggplant, and okra. The farm is on the way to Freda, where there's a popular restaurant. Randy farms full-time, while Linda runs a children's nursery school in their home.

Hughes Organic Farm

On Calumet Golf Course Road between Calumet and Hubbell. 2 1/2 miles off U.S. 41. **Open** *from the end of July into October, 11 a.m. to 6 p.m., closed Friday and Sunday. (906) 337-5185.*

Over 20 kinds of vegetables are grown on Gary and Patricia Hughes's 12 acres. They've been farming organically for ten years. They grow over 20 varieties of vegetables, including nice tomatoes. (Up here, it can be tricky getting tomatoes to ripen.) They also grow berries. (Strawberries ripen around the first of July up here. Call for U-pick information.) Patricia is a schoolteacher and Gary works in stained glass in the winter.

Rulison Farm

On Donken Road near Pelkie at the base of the Keweenaw Peninsula. **Open** *evenings and weekends.* **Call first.** *(906) 334-2553.*

Dave and Linda Rulison have a 160-acre farm. Ten acres are in trefoil hay, and a quarter-acre is used to grow small vegetables: potatoes, beets, tomatoes, etc. They also sell eggs and organic fertilizer.

Wine Grapes

Beginning home winemakers usually start out making wine with juice or concentrate. However, by advancing to starting with whole grapes and pressing them themselves or having them pressed, winemakers gain more control over how the wine turns out. A key part of that control comes from the amount of contact the pressed juice has with the skins. This affects the wine's flavor and color.

Most commercial wines are made from grapes picked by low-wage hired help paid by the bushel. They can't be depended on to select the best and ripest grapes — a selection process recognized by the German winemaking term "auslese," which means "select." So it's a significant advantage to be able to select the grapes that make up the juice used in winemaking.

Buying direct from a grower means more is known about how the grapes were grown, and on what kind of soil. If the grower also makes wine, it's also possible to taste wine made from those very vines in a different year.

For some groups of friends or relatives, getting together to press grapes and make wine is an annual rite of fall, followed by the suspense and satisfaction of sampling the results over the years, as the wine ages. A good number of home winemakers are Italians or other Europeans who have kept the tradition of winemaking alive in this country for generations.

One bushel of grapes makes three to four gallons of wine, depending on how completely they are squeezed. Prices range from $3.50 to $4 per half-bushel for Concords to $10 and up for vinifera grapes like Riesling.

A few wineries with their own vineyards produce enough grapes that they sell some to home winemakers on a U-pick or picked basis. Availability may vary from year to year, depending on the crop and how much wine they plan to make. Other growers sell only retail. Most of the grapes in southwest Michigan's fruit belt are grown on contract with big producers like Welch's grape juice in Lawton or St. Julian Winery in Paw Paw.

In southern Michigan, grapes usually are picked from the first or second week in September through the month of October. Some years, like 1991, are so hot that harvest begins in August and is over by October. Other years, such as 1992, frost wipes out a good portion of many growers' crops, limiting availability of grapes. A number of winegrowers sell grapes by pre-order on a first-come, first-served basis. So it's best to call ahead, usually by the first of August or so.

SOUTHWEST AND WEST MICHIGAN

Bill Cronenwelt, Sr.

(616) 624-6038. In Lawton, southeast of Paw Paw.

In a beautiful, hilly area just east of the village of Lawton, Bill Cronenwelt grows two varieties of French hybrid wine grapes, Vidal and Foch, and the four main native grapes, purple Concord, amber Catawba, sweet red Delaware, and white Niagara.

In a bad year, like the late May freeze of 1992 that wiped out a third to a half his crop, prices won't go up much. That's because Welch's, which buys two-thirds of the grapes in his area, is so big in New York and Washington, that it's unaffected by local conditions. (Welch's is a co-op, by the way.) Talking to farmers is a living exercise in the meaning of stoicism and taking the long view. Cronenwelt's farm has come down from an ancestor who is said to have brought some of the first grapes to Michigan. Parts of his farmhouse are 130 years old. "We're here for the duration," he says, dismissing the vicissitudes of weather and the world economy.

Fenn Valley Vineyards & Wine Cellar

(616) 561-2396. Between Fennville and Saugatuck. From I-196 or the Blue Star Hwy., take M-89 (exit 34) some 3 1/2 miles east to 62nd St., turn south (right) and in 1 mile east (left) onto 122nd Ave. Sales & tasting room open year-round Monday-Saturday 10-5, Sunday 1-5.

Depending on the size of each year's crop, all of the wine grapes grown here and used in Fenn Valley's own wines may be for sale to home winemakers: the French hybrid grapes Foch, Seyval, Vignoles, Vidal, and Chancellor, and the vinifera grape Riesling. Orders are filled on a first-come, first-served basis; put them in by the second week of August. Fenn Valley will press your grapes into juice if you request it.

Lemon Creek Fruit Farms, Vineyards & Winery

(616) 471-1321. 5 miles east of Bridgman and 7 miles west of Berrien Springs at 533 Lemon Creek Road. From I-94, take the Bridgman exit (16), go north on Red Arrow Highway 2 miles to Lemon Creek Road, then 5 miles. From U.S. 31 2 miles northwest of Berrien Springs, take Lemon Creek Road west 5 miles. Open regularly May-December: Monday-Saturday 9-6, Sunday 12-6. Call for ripeness report.

The Lemon family has grown fruit in this beautiful, rolling area since the 1850s. They were among the earliest farms in southwest Michigan to grow French hybrid wine grapes on a commercial scale, first supplying Tabor Hill, St. Julian, and Good Harbor. In 1984, to market their own produce and add value to it in the production process, they also opened their own winery. For newcomers to the tricky business of winemaking, they've been extraordinarily successful, as proven by many awards in state and regional competitions.

Winemakers can purchase grapes already picked (call ahead to place orders) or pick them themselves. The same grapes are available to customers as the Lemons use themselves: pickers are directed to whatever happens to be ripe. You can taste their results by sampling their wine on the spot. Varieties include Concord, several French hybrids (Chambourcin, Baco Noir, Vignoles, and Vidal Blanc), and Johannisberger Riesling, the viniferous variety that does best in Michigan. Thick-skinned and hardy, Vidal is their leading planting stock. Production is expanded each year; some Seyval vines start bearing in 1992, and Chardonnay and Cabernet Sauvignon in 1993.

Brothers Tim (left) and Jeff Lemon and Jeff's wife Cathy, in the vineyard in late May.

Prices are roughly from 25¢ to 35¢ a pound. Incidentally, grapes for Lemon Creek's own wine is pressed by St. Julian. Many other fruits can be picked here, too. See page 13.

Morrison's Sunnyfield Farms

(616) 657-4934. On the Red Arrow Highway, 2 1/2 miles east of Paw Paw. Or 3 miles west of the I-94 Mattawan. (Go north, not into Mattawan.) Open May 1 until first week in November, daily 9-6.

Concord and French hybrid grapes (Seyval Blanc and Foch) are among the many fruits and vegetables raised and sold already picked on this big, 200-acre farm that's been in the Morrison family since 1835. Call ahead to find out about availability. See page 14 for more.

SOUTHEAST MICHIGAN

HoneyFlow Farm

(313) 796-2344. In the southwest corner of Lapeer County, midway between Flint and Port Huron and 25-30 miles from each. 4 miles west of Almont and 2 1/2 miles due south of Dryden at 4939 Mill Rd. Open from September through mid-October, Thursday through Sunday.

Pick 20 varieties of grapes, including red and white seedless grapes and red and white wine grapes. Grape juice is also for sale. Honey is sold in the comb, liquid, or creamed.

Seven Lakes Vineyard

(313) 629-5686. Northeast of Fenton and northwest of Holly in the northwest corner of Oakland County at 1111 Tinsman Road. From U.S. 23, take exit 79 at Fenton, go east on North and Grange Hall roads to North Leroy Road, north on Leroy to Petts, right on Petts, which becomes Tinsman. From I-75, take exit 101 at Holly, go west on Grande Hall Road to Fish Lake Road on Holly's north side, then north on Fish Lake to Tinsman, west on Tinsman. Open 10-5 daily, 12-5 Sunday, in winter by appointment.

An unusual combination of winery, vineyard, apple orchard, picnic ground, natural area with trails, and ascension point for champagne balloon flights from the Michigan Balloon Corporation. All the varieties of grapes raised here are for sale to home winemakers; most buy juice by the jug or barrel. Wine grapes include Vignoles, Seyval, Vidal Blanc, Aurore, Chancellor, Cascade De Chaunac. Table grapes are Concords, Buffalo, and Suffolk Seedless Red. Call for brochure.

Foraging for Edible Wild Plants

By ELLEN WEATHERBEE

One of the most pleasant aspects of driving through the country-side is seeing the many different plants and habitats you pass. Many of the best wild edible plants are found along these roadside areas. Sometimes the plants themselves will be obvious; other times a special collecting technique is needed to find something tasty.

Roads pass through all kinds of plant habitats, giving even some-one with casual interest in foraging a chance to find many kinds of plants. But finding some low-lying habitats requires specialized knowledge. Some wild plants are hidden in specific localities. Wild rice is found in shallow lakes. Cranberries grow in bogs. Blueberries are in both bogs and other acid areas. Often local parks officials will know of any good collecting places for the common plants. Michigan state parks and many other parks have a "browse rule" allowing a visitor to collect a small amount of fruit, nuts, and mushrooms for personal use.

CAUTIONS! In the midst of this bounty, be aware of three cautions: permission, poisonous look-alikes, and pollution.

1. Always stop and get permission from the property owner.

2. Take care that the plant is the correct one you meant to get; check plant descriptions and photos. Better yet, take a class in identification. Always pay attention to plants which have poisonous look-alikes. Several are mentioned above, such as the cattail, grape, and onion imitations. In addition, wild carrot can be confused with hemlock, which can kill the unsuspecting eater. Wild carrot is woody and not worth the bother, but is frequently collected, as novices think it is easy to identify. Avoid the daylilies which grow alongside the road in profusion. Many books recommend their use, but do not eat them as they have caused many stomach problems in the Midwest, especially in Michigan.

3. Roadside pollution from cars and sprays is a constant problem. Try to collect in a little-used area which does not have evidence of spray. Call the county road commission to see what is used on the road weeds.

Here are some of your best bets for Michigan wild edible plants:

Asparagus

Easy to find if you know where to look. Asparagus can be spotted in the fall when it is feathery, yellow in color and waist high. Look along open, sunny fencerows, and under fruit trees. Birds like to eat the red seeds of the asparagus and drop them, complete with fertilizer. In spring, the young shoots begin to push their way up through the soil near where last year's tall, feathery seed stalks have tipped over and caught, perhaps in a nearby fence or among wads of old grass. Cut the young shoots off at ground level and return several times at intervals of four to six days. Rinse well and snap off the stalks to keep the remaining tender parts. Boil or steam in a small amount of water until just tender. Add salt and butter.

Taste: Wild asparagus tastes as good as cultivated asparagus and can be prepared using the same recipes. Snap off the stems where they break easily and peel the stems of the outer skin if they are tough.

Difficulty of finding: Chance of finding wild asparagus is 80% if the site is along an old farm road which had asparagus planted occasionally in a nearby farm garden. An old fence makes it easier to spot the old stalks.

When to harvest: The first shoots appear toward the end of April (early May in northern areas), and the plants continue to produce spears through the end of June.

Berry Bushes

Strawberries, raspberries, and blackberries like to grow in the sun between a wooded area and the road or in old fields. Blueberries prefer acid woods or open acid bogs. They all have edible fruit when thoroughly ripe; their leaves also make a nice tea.

For a berry pie, mix four cups of fruit with two tablespoons flour and 1/4 cup honey, 1/2 teaspoon cinnamon and juice from a lemon. Cover with oatmeal or crumb topping and place in a pie shell.

Wild tea is easily made: simply pour boiling water over dried or fresh leaves and add honey, if desired.

Taste: Wild fruit is delicious. Wild strawberries are outstanding. Make a jam if you just find a small amount. Blueberries are another favorite. The other fruits taste similar to the domestic varieties.

Difficulty of finding: Chances of finding wild berries are 80% for at least a good tasting. Chances are greater than 60% that there will be a patch large enough to preserve. Try the areas which are changing from old fields to filling in with a few young trees. Collect a few leaves for tea while collecting the fruit to eat raw or cooked.

When to harvest: Strawberries are found from the end of May through mid-June. Blueberries ripen from July through the first half of September. Blackberries and raspberries are found in July and August.

Cattails

Many wet areas have cattails as the most common plant. In the early spring, cut the young shoots (under 12 inches) just where the plants root in the muck. Cut away the outer plant fibers until reaching the tender inner core. It can be eaten raw, boiled, or stir-fried.

When the plant is older and reaches about two feet tall, the flowering stalk appears. The brown, fuzzy top is the female part from the previous year. Take the top portion on a new stalk before it opens up completely. It will be about six inches long and 1/2 inch wide. Remove the outer tissue and boil until tender, about eight to ten minutes. Serve with butter. The inner stalk-like core remains — hence the name: wild corn-on-the-cob. It is a favorite of many children. Do not confuse cattails with iris. The poisonous iris leaves fit together in a tight V shape rather than rounded as in cattails.

Taste: Young cattail stalks are average in taste. The cooked cattail spikes are quite tasty served hot with butter.

Difficulty of finding: If the timing is right (and it may take a few tries to spot the young shoots or the young still-tight flower heads) and there are cattail marches available, chances of finding good edible portions are 90%. Two pieces of equipment are helpful: rubber boots to prevent wet feet and a hat to ward off red-winged blackbirds who are usually protecting their nests in the marshes.

When to harvest: Young shoots are found in mid to late spring.

Elderberries

This shrub huddles in many a wet roadside ditch. In late May or early June, elderberries have masses of flowers all over their opposite-stemmed branches. Blossoms can be collected for tea. Later in the summer, the ripe fruit makes good cooked fruit; it is a bit too astringent to eat raw for most tastes.

Taste: Cooked in pies or made into wine, elderberries are considered by many a delicacy.

Difficulty of finding: If the timing is right, the white flowers and the subsequent dark fruit are quite obvious. Ditches should be overgrown with shrubs and have at least temporary moisture in them. If these conditions are met, elderberry flowers and fruit should be found 70% of the time.

When to harvest: The berries ripen in late August.

Found in ditches and along swamp borders, elderberries ripen in late August and make great jams and jellies as well as fillings for pies.
1) Flowering elderberry bush. 2) Mature fruit. 3) Flower and leaf arrangement. 4) Bark of the elderberry bush.

Garden Weeds

Weeds of good taste and nutrition tend to grow in sunny waste places at the edge of farm fields and any disturbed area which is in the open. Tasty weeds include **lamb's quarters** and **amaranth**. **Sheep sorrel** likes older meadows as well as the disturbed ground. These plants are all available throughout the spring and summer when soil remains disturbed (as in garden sites). All of these vegetables should be collected while still young (under four inches tall). Wash well and steam or boil a few minutes until just barely tender.

Taste: These weeds are high in vitamins and very good to eat, especially the young lamb's quarters. Served with either buttered and plain or wrapped in fancy Greek filo dough. The taste is something like fresh spinach.

Difficulty of finding: 90% chance of finding in a disturbed area, such as garden soil.

When to harvest: They grow from mid-April through September, but must be harvested young, before they get tough.

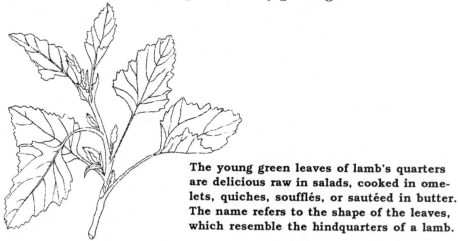

The young green leaves of lamb's quarters are delicious raw in salads, cooked in omelets, quiches, soufflés, or sautéed in butter. The name refers to the shape of the leaves, which resemble the hindquarters of a lamb.

Grapes

Found in both sunny and shaded places, grapes have several uses. The young leaves make a wrapping for rice and other foods. Steam grape leaves for one minute, place rice inside them, and steam for an hour. Ripe grapes can be used for jellies, jam, and pies. There are several species of wild Michigan grape: some are native and others are remnants of cultivated vineyards. Be aware of moonseed, which looks like grape and which is poisonous. Moonseed often grows intertwined with grape. Moonseed has only one seed and no tendrils on the plant; grapes have more than one seed and have tendrils.

Taste: Steamed grape leaves are very good and add a European feel and taste to even a bland mixture steamed inside. Grape jams and jellies are excellent and so flavorful that some people dilute the juice a bit before using.

Difficulty of finding: Grapes are easy to find along the edges of woodlots or draped over small trees. Best are the old domestic vines that were abandoned on the public lands. In these habitats, chances that grapes will be found are 90%.

When to harvest: Ready to use in late August and September.

Japanese knotweed

This plant of Asiatic origin has been used for an ornamental because it grows rapidly and has masses of tiny white flowers. The plants are clonal and grow tightly together in large clumps along the roadside, both in town and country. They resemble a cross between bamboo and cattails. Cut the young shoots (under ten inches) and boil.

Taste: Belongs to the same family as rhubarb and has a similar flavor. A little dish of stewed young knotweed is tasty.

Difficulty of finding: Since the plants grow prolifically once they are established, there is a 70% chance they will be found.

When to harvest: Early spring just as spring wildflowers peak.

Spring shoots of Japanese knotweed taste like its rhubarb relative when boiled. They grow in clumps along roadsides. Note where you see them in summer, and come back at spring wildflower time for a tasty sauce for custards or vanilla pudding.

Jerusalem artichokes

Roadsides are one of the easiest places to spot Jerusalem artichokes. The tall stalks of summer persist throughout the winter and help to locate them. As with most tubers, the underground parts become mushy in the spring because the plant's energy goes into making the new growth. In summer, the tubers are just beginning to form. Dig into the ground under the old stalks. Rinse the tubers well; they will range in size from the size and shape of a pencil to that of a fat cigar shapes. Eat raw or boil.

Taste: The tubers taste best when cooked a few minutes, either boiled or sautéed. They are relatively bland and could use a touch of wild onion to perk them up.

Difficulty of finding: These sunflowers are difficult to spot unless in flower at the end of summer. Then they are commonly seen. If the localities are found then, the forager has a 90% chance of returning after frost to dig them.

When to harvest: Collect in fall or winter, or in early spring before growth occurs.

Milkweed pods

These plants are easy to recognize but are too old to be used for food by their mature stage. Young shoots (up to six inches tall) and the young pods (up to one inch long) are what you want to eat. Use a knife to cut the edible part, wash well, and boil in two waters to get rid of the bitter taste. Bring a pot of water to boil, add the cleaned milkweed and boil hard one minute, throw off the water and repeat in a second pot of boiling water. The milkweed will take another few minutes to become tender. Serve with a bit of salt and butter.

Taste: If collected when under one inch long, these pods are delicious. Young shoots and older pods are only medium good.

Difficulty of finding: Chances of finding milkweeds growing in old fields or along roadsides are 60%. Everyone remembers where they are in the fall, but for some reason people have trouble finding them when they are ready.

When to harvest: Collect the young shoots in spring.

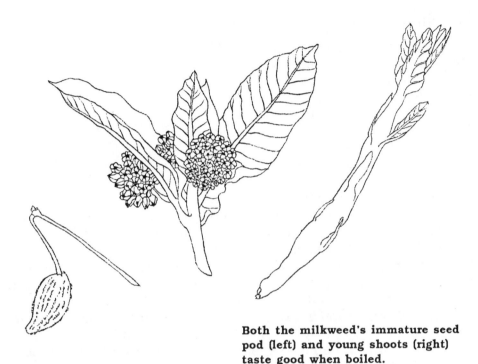

Both the milkweed's immature seed pod (left) and young shoots (right) taste good when boiled.

Mints

Mints grow in a variety of places from very wet to very dry. All mints have opposite leaves and square stems. The smell and flavor vary, but most taste good and are said in the old herbals to "clear the mind." Bee balm and catnip grow in dry areas. Bee balm is the wild oregano the people of European backgrounds like to collect. Catnip is more pleasant for cats than for people. Most mints of wet places make delicious tea. Pour boiling water over the leaves and steep until light brown.

Taste: Some of the wild mints are absolutely delicious. Others are almost moldy in flavor. Still others are almost hot or peppery. Experiment to find which ones are tasty in the area.

Difficulty of finding: The nicely flavored mints are most secretive, found in cold streams. The dry-area bee balm is more readily found. Chances are 30% for the wet-area mints, 80% for dry-area varieties.

When to harvest: Collect mint any time the leaves are fresh-looking and green.

Michigan's Delicious Morels

There are over 2,000 kinds of wild mushrooms. but the most prized is the easily identifiable morel. It tastes so delicious that literally hundreds of thousands search for it every spring. It can be a challenging hunt, but once you find one, more are likely nearby.

Morels have the virtue of having a distinctive appearance. You're not likely to confuse them with poisonous varieties. Take along a sharp knife and a basket when you head for woods. Use the knife to cut the mushrooms just above the ground (plucking them may get them dirty).

All Michigan morels have caps pitted with little hollows. May is the big month for finding morels in Michigan. They can be found in both northern and southern parts of the state. When springs are warm and wet, morel crops are biggest. When the spring has been cold and dry, there may be almost no morels to find.

Old orchards are a favorite place to hunt morels, but beech-maple forests, oak woods, and burned-over meadows are also choice spots. Although morels have an unmistakable appearance, it's surprisingly difficult for novice hunters to spot them because they blend into the background of last fall's dead leaves and grass. Spotting them becomes easier with practice.

Don't expect morels to taste like supermarket mushrooms. They have a distinct flavor unlike any other. The flavor is delicate and easily diminished by overcooking or an overdose of seasonings. The best method of preparation is also the simplest. Clean the morels carefully. If you wash them, blot them dry with paper towels. Cut off the stems and slice the caps lengthwise. Melt a generous amount of butter or margarine in a frying pan, cover the bottom of the pan with morels and salt lightly. Sauté about five minutes on each side and serve immediately. Morel stems are tough, but them may be chopped fine and used to flavor soups and gravies.

(Based on an informative pamphlet prepared by the Michigan Travel Bureau and the Department of Natural Resources.)

Onions

All of the wild onions are edible. Most are quite intense in flavor. The wild leeks are the "ramps" of Appalachian Mountain fame. Wild chives grow in lawns and fields. Wild leeks grow in rich woods and river flood plains throughout the state. And wild garlic prefers old fields. Cut up small amounts of young plants to add a nice zest to salads and soups. Do not confuse with death camus, which grows along the sand dunes and in fens; it does not smell like onions.

Taste: The taste and strength of wild onions varies from the delicious (and intense) flavor of the wild ramps to the garlic-like flavor of some of the thin varieties. Try them until finding a comfortable level of intensity. If they are very strong, they can be boiled once, drained, and then used for a more palatable sautéing.

Difficulty of finding: Your chances of finding wild chives in lawns, garlic in old fields, and wild leeks in mature woods varies from 60% to over 90%.

When to harvest: Wild leeks are at their peak in the spring, about two weeks after the tree leaves appear.

Ostrich fern

The best of the edibles is the ostrich fern found along banks of rivers and streams. It has long been collected commercially in Maine and Nova Scotia. The only other fern that looks like it is sensitive fern, which has a rounded stem, where there is an indentation in the stalks of the ostrich fern. A brown, fertile fron overwinters; young shoots which stick through the low mucky soil in early spring. Cut a few green fiddleheads (and young shoots) from each clump of ferns; return in several days for another batch. cover with boiling water and simmer until tender, about eight minutes. This fern transplants well and is frequently found in gardens.

Taste: Absolutely one of the very tastiest plants well worth any time and effort to find them. Don't over-collect. Pick no more than twice on the same plants several days apart.

Difficulty of finding: Depending on the available flood plains, chances range from 20% to 40% of finding these delicious shoots.

When ripe: From the end of April through the third week of May.

One of the choicest of the wild plants is the ostrich fern. 1) a mature clump of ostrich fern. 2) 10-inch fronds. 3) the groove in a frond. 4) fiddleheads 4-inches high. 5) collection of fiddleheads, ready to cook.

Shrubs

A variety of shrubs and bushes have edible fruit. Highbush cranberry, hackberry, nannyberry, and serviceberry provide an uncommonly tasty treat. Highbush cranberry has opposite branches and thick bunches of red fruit which hang down. The smell is not pleasant, but when cooked with a touch of lemon and sweetened, they make a nice dessert. Collect after a hard frost in the fall. Nannyberry is also known as wild raisin and is collected after a frost. Don't be surprised to chase out a flock of partridges; they often spend time in clones of nannyberries. Serviceberries, found throughout the state, are one of the nicest early shrubs to flower. The fruit which follows in late May and early June can taste as good as blueberries.

Taste: Serviceberries are especially tasty, somewhat resembling flavorful blueberries. Highbush cranberry smells bad when raw (and when cooking), but actually tastes like cranberries when cooked, sweetened, and cooled. Use only wild plants, as the domestic species doesn't lose the bad flavor. Nannyberries and hackberries are OK edibles that are ready to eat after the first frost.

Difficulty of finding: These shrubs are more difficult to recognize, as most people think they all look alike. Start watching for different twig and flower patterns. Chances of success are 40%.

When to harvest: Serviceberries ripen in late May and early June. Collect cranberries and nannyberries after a hard frost.

Sumac

There are a number of sumacs. Most are edible. Stay away from the poison sumac found in wet areas; it has dangling greenish-white berries. The redheaded sumacs are the ones to use for tea and lemonades. Do not boil, as the plant becomes very bitter. Simmer the completely ripe, red heads in water or make sun tea by covering with water and setting in the sun for several hours. Strain through cheesecloth or a clean pillowcase and add honey to sweeten.

Taste: Sumac makes a very tasty beverage as long as it does not boil and as long as the heads are completely ripe.

Difficulty of finding: This familiar shrub is easy to find in poor dry soils of the state, especially in the Lower Peninsula. All of the edible types have red fruits. Chances of spotting this plant are 80%.

Violets

All shapes and sizes of violets are found in wooded and grassy areas along roadsides. Blue violets have the most flavor and can be eaten raw or put into salads. When the flower is picked, more take their place. Much of the seed setting is done without the true flowers so the future of the plant is not usually harmed if a few flowers are taken. A pretty jam, jelly, and syrup can also be made from the flowers.

Taste: Flavor is good enough, but the color makes it especially attractive, whether in jams, salads, or syrups.

Difficulty of finding: Since the violets are so frequent in woods, lawns, and scrubby areas, they should be found in 90% of the areas early in the spring.

Watercress

Look in any slow-moving stream or in protected coves of rivers. Watercress has a terminal lobe and small pairs of leaves down the stem. The rootlets are usually bright white. Watercress takes up pollutants, so if it is to be used raw, soak in a few drops of Clorox per quart of water for 20 minutes. Rinse thoroughly and use raw in salads or cooked in soup. (See nettle soup recipe.)

Taste: Wild watercress tastes just like fresh domestic watercress — pleasant and nippy, like mustard leaves. Use it for a perk-up flavor in soups and salads.

Difficulty of finding: Watercress is sometimes found in creeks and river banks but much of it is polluted. Be sure to follow instructions above. Found in about 30% of such sites.

Wintercress

This plant grows in sterile, sandy woods and is more common in the northern part of the state. The leaves are shiny and evergreen; the fruit is a bright red berry. All parts of the plant are nice for tea. Steep cut up pieces in simmering water. Add honey to taste.

Taste: Wintergreen makes a nice tea either by itself or mixed with berry leaves.

Difficulty of finding: In southern Michigan, chances are 20% it will be found. If looking around bogs or other acid woods. In northern Michigan, chances are 70% it will be found.

For more information and recipes for wild edibles, see Ellen Weatherbee's book, Edible Wild Plants, A Guide to Collecting and Cooking *($14.95). Contact Ellen Elliott Weatherbee, 11405 Patterson Lake Drive, Pinckney, Michigan 48169. Phone: (313) 878-9178.*

Cider Mills & Apple Orchards

Don't look for quality apple cider at a supermarket. It won't be as fresh and probably has preservatives, which add an aftertaste. Michigan ranks second to third nationally in apple production and has a great supply of cider mills, some of which are over a century old. While hard cider is waning in popularity, the healthy, tasty benefits of sweet cider are making it increasingly in demand. Don't look for bargains at cider mills. (A gallon costs anywhere from $2.50 to $4.) Quality is what you're after. And while you're there, get some fresh-picked apples. The taste of fresh apples eaten within a day of being picked are far superior to the ones you find in a store which are typically weeks off the tree.

No batch the same. Cider is a blend of several varieties of apples. When the cider-maker creates a blend, it's hardly a scientific process, so no two batches of apple cider taste the same. And from week to week, different varieties of apples ripen, changing the blend and the resulting taste. As the fall season progresses and more varieties ripen, the taste tends to get richer and sweeter. Cider at the beginning of September isn't likely to be nearly as good. Wait until at least mid-September for the beginning of the real cider season. Flavor peaks in October in the south and November in the north of the state.

Each cider mill has its own unique taste. This is a result of individual presses, the philosophy of blending the apples, and where the apples are grown. One important advantage of buying cider at a mill is the total absence of any preservatives, in nearly every case. Though preservatives extend shelf life, they can leave an aftertaste. All the cider mills listed in this guide produce cider purely from pressed apples, with nothing else added unless noted. Until about half a century ago, apple cider was the number-one juice drink in America. In the 1940s, apple juice was perfected by filtering and pasteurizing the juice so that it could have a long shelf life. Cider isn't pasteurized.

Philosophies of cider making vary considerably. Many like to use predominantly Jonathan, Red and Golden Delicious apples, with Northern Spy another popular cider variety. Others believe the best cider has the greatest varieties of apples, the more kinds the better. Another variable is the amount of particles the cider-maker allows to filter through. Some cider connoisseurs believe the superior flavor is in the cloudy-looking, thicker drink that comes from allowing more of the pulp to filter through.

Michigan's superior-tasting apples. Michigan is roughly even with the state of New York in apples production. Both trail the state of Washington, where orchards have been planted in the state's eastern desert and irrigated. Because of Michigan's cooler climate, it apples are sweeter and more flavorful than apples from Washington. But because our weather is more variable, Michigan apples don't have the cosmetic appeal of Washington apples. Michigan also offers a much greater variety of apples than Washington. The big fruit farms in that state pretty much stick to Red Delicious, Golden Delicious, and Granny Smith, while here some 20 major varieties are grown and another 40 are not uncommon. At most Michigan orchards of any size you will find the legendary Northern Spy along with the much more recently introduced Gala and Mutsu varieties.

There is one commercial growing region in the state that surpasses all the others. This is "Peach Ridge," an eight-by-twenty-mile

Apples growing in an orchard near Leslie, south of Lansing. Although Michigan's billion-pound-a-year apple crop is dwarfed by the production of Washington State, the Wolverine State's apples are tastier because of Michigan's cooler, more variable climate. That also makes Michigan apples less uniform in appearance. Far more varieties of apples are grown commercially in Michigan than Washington.

ridge just northwest of Grand Rapids, where 16,000 acres of orchards are planted. The 200-foot elevation drains the cold spring air, preventing dangerous frost which would damage the delicate fruit buds.

The rise of Empires and Galas. As for trends in apple-growing, there is an increase in Gala and Empire apples. Empires, similar to but a little smaller than a McIntosh, have grown in popularity with growers because they bear early and store better, remaining crisp and flavorful on into April. Gala is an American newcomer that has quickly won acceptance because it is an early apple with exceptional sweetness and flavor. On the decline are Paula Reds, an early apple which doesn't store well, and Winesaps, which color poorly.

One half to three fourths of the roughly 20 million bushels of apples grown a year in Michigan are used for applesauce, pie fillings, and other processing. Ten percent of the rest is sold directly to customers at farm stands. Competition in the apple market is now worldwide, with countries like Argentina, Chile, New Zealand, and South Africa exporting huge quantities and lowering prices. Wholesale prices have become so low (8¢ a pound in recent years) that many Michigan apple farmers could not make it without a retail fruit stand to sell apples and cider directly to customers. Hence the recent upsurge in cider mill operations.

Antique apples, after a renaissance about a decade ago, are unfortunately waning in popularity. We talked to more than one farmer who was bulldozing his decades-old Snows to make room for more productive dwarf and semi-dwarf trees that are the mainstays of modern orchards. If you see any Gravensteins or Snows for sale, by all means give them a try.

Tips on finding great cider. For those in search of the very finest-tasting cider, here are a few pointers. Many believe that the old fashioned rack and cloth press, in which the pulp is squeezed through a cheesecloth-like filter, makes the best cider. It's more time-consuming to make cider this way, the cleanup is more difficult, and less juice is extracted, but aficionados claim it makes a better cider than the modern continuous presses which work faster and use rice hulls as a pressing agent.

In early September the cider is still going to be tart. Many say the later in the fall you wait, the better the flavor. The cider-maker has more fully ripened varieties to use in the blend. Another factor is the quality of the apples used. A good cider-maker will never use "drops" for cider, but rather the same quality sold for eating whole.

In making cider, three critical differences affect taste. Some cider-makers filter the cider a good deal more than others, creating a much clearer liquid with the virtue of lasting longer before it turns. Some equate this with a higher-quality product. However, as many others feel that a good cider needs body and deliberately permit a considerably greater amount of pulp particles to filter through. "If you can read a newspaper through a gallon of cider," says one old-timer, "it's no damn good!"

Another variance in cider-making philosophy concerns the apple varieties used in the blend. Some make tasty cider with only three kinds of apples. But many feel that the more varieties, the better the cider. One of the key aspects in the art of cider-making is choosing the proportion of tart and sweet apples. Northern Spies, for example, are a tart apple common used in making cider, while Yellow Delicious are a popular sweet variety. One person who makes renowned cider keeps the proportion of tart apples to a minimum. Others use more tart apples to create a cider with more zing.

POPULAR MICHIGAN APPLES

The state of Washington grows more apples than Michigan, but far more varieties are grown here. That makes for a much more interesting selection for the buyer. Washington grows just three kinds of apples, while Michigan apple farmers grow some 60 varieties. Also, the cool climate makes Michigan apples far superior in flavor. Here are some of the most popular, listed in order of ripening:

Jonagold. A 1940s cross between Golden Delicious and Jonathan, this fine eating apple likes Michigan's cool climate. The original strain is yellow with a red blush. It ripens in early September.

McIntosh. One of Michigan's most popular apples, the McIntosh ripens in mid-September. It originated as a chance seedling on John McIntosh's Ontario farm around 1800 and is a premiere cool-climate apple. Although easily bruised, it is a crisp apple with a snappy flavor. Added with restraint to a cider blend, it adds wonderful aroma and an interesting tang.

Cortland. These dark red apples, developed in 1915, ripen about a week later than McIntosh. Their flesh is very white and resists browning when sliced. Not as tart as a McIntosh.

Jonathan. Michigan grows more of these semi-tart, all-purpose apples than any other state. Discovered in New York in 1800, this brilliant red apple turned out to grow even better in Michigan. By the Civil War it was planted widely in the state. It's a juicy, fragrant apple, good for cider and for eating fresh. It's ready in late September.

Empire. Ripening in early October, Empire is the most popular new variety planted in Michigan. A Cornell University horticulturist crossed Delicious and Empire apples in 1966 to create a variety that has the more interesting flavor of McIntosh but stays crisp longer and won't bruise so easily because it is firmer. Smaller than a McIntosh, it also has thinner skin. The Empire has spread like wildfire in Michigan as apple farmers choose what to plant next.

Gala. Bred in New Zealand in the late 1930s, it came to the U.S. in the 1970s. Part Golden Delicious, it is one of the best eating apples you can find. It ripens in early October.

Red Delicious. More for its appearance than its flavor, Red Delicious is America's most popular eating apple. It originated as a chance seedling in Iowa in the late 1880s. Twenty-seven strains have evolved. Some of the old strains, less cosmetically attractive than the most popular contemporary commercial varieties, have more flavor. This apple has been bred to be sweet, crisp, durable, and pretty, but it lacks interesting flavor. Ripens in early October.

Golden Delicious. Yellow in color, Golden Delicious has a richer, tangier flavor than the Red Delicious. A chance West Virginia seedling in the early 1900s led this choice apple to become second only to Red Delicious in worldwide production. A favorite of cider-makers, it is also a choice eating apple. It's one of the three main varieties grown in Washington, but Michigan's cooler nights produce a more flavorful fruit. They mature toward mid-October, about a week after Red Delicious.

Ida Red. This cross between a Jonathan and Wagener was first developed at an Idaho experimental station in the early 1940s. Now Michigan is the biggest producer of this sweet yet tart all-purpose apple. It ripens in October and keeps exceptionally well.

Northern Spy. Descendants of a seedling discovered at the end of the 18th century in New York is still grown widely by Michigan apple farmers because it is a classic favorite for pies, cobblers, and other commercial processing uses. It ripens in mid-October. The spicy flavor makes it a favorite eating apple for some. Often included in a cider blend to add tart tang to the cider.

Mutsu. A cross between the Golden Delicious and the Japanese Indo, the light-green Mutsu is large, sweet, and flavorful. The flesh is firm and juicy, with a slightly spicy flavor. Quite popular outside the U.S., it is fast becoming a Michigan favorite. They mature toward mid-October.

Rome Beauty. Ripening in late October, the Rome keeps well until mid-summer. The Rome makes one of the best baked apples you can get. Pop it in the microwave for 10 minutes and you'll find its flavor really comes out. The Rome was discovered in southern Ohio along the Ohio River in 1816. Ranks sixth in the number of apple trees in Michigan.

Granny Smith. This distinctive green apple came out of Australia in the mid-19th-century. A Sydney man named Smith named it for his wife, widely known as Granny Smith. Somewhat tart but still a great eating apple, it has become the world's third most widely grown apple.

SOUTHWEST MICHIGAN

1 Calderwood Farms

2993 Lemon Creek Road, 2 1/2 miles west of Berrien Springs in Berrien County. From I-94 exit 16 at Bridgman, go north on the Red Arrow Highway 3 miles to Lemon Creek Road, east 8 3/4 miles. Open for peaches, pears, and apples: August 5-October 31 (10-6, Monday-Saturday). (616) 471-2102.

At this big 300-acre fruit farm, U-pick is available for both summer and fall apples. Ready-picked apples are $7 to $10 a bushel, U-pick apples are 20¢ to 25¢ a pound. Cider ($2.50/gallon) is pressed from the many varieties of fall apples grown here. Farm managers Nancy and Jim Calderwood are the fourth generation of Calderwoods to farm this land.

In late August and early September, there are also peaches, pears, and plums — picked or U-pick, except for peaches that are all picked. Stanley plums are good for canning as well as eating; sweet Santa Rosa plums make for good eating out of hand.

2 Culby's U-Pick

*A few miles east of Benton Harbor. From I-94 exit 30 (Napier Rd.), go east on Napier 2 miles, then north on Blue Creek Rd. 1/2 mile. **Open** approximately August 1-October 31, 9 am.-6 p.m. Closed Mondays. (616) 944-5996 or (616) 927-2315.*

Apple varieties are Earligold, Jersey Mack, Empire, Akane, Ida Red, Connell Red, Red and Golden Delicious, Jonathan, and Winesap. Late varieties of peaches are here to pick, usually through the first half of September, along with sweet potatoes.

3 Diversity Farms

A few miles west of Paw Paw on 45th St. and County Road 374 in the heart of the Fruit Belt in central Van Buren County. County Road 374 and 45th Street. From Paw Paw, take the Red Arrow Highway to Lake Cora golf course, then north 1 mile, west 1/2 mile to northwest corner of 374 and 45th. (616) 657-6283.

Early to late apples, Bartlett and Bosc pears, Concord grapes.

4 Fruit Acres Farm Market

Northeast of Benton Harbor, off I-94 at Coloma exit, on south side of exit. Open late May through October. (616) 468-3668.

The apple season at this varied farm market begins here with summer strawberry apples. Cider is available daily. Grapes are also available in late summer and fall, along with most every kind of Michigan fruit and vegetable in season. Sweet corn is a specialty.

5 Gatchell's Farm Market

*Just east of Benton Harbor. From I-94, take exit 29 (Pipestone), go east on Meadowbrook 4 miles to 5040 Meadow brook. Or take Meadowbrook west from M-140 4 miles. **Open** daily 9-8. Asparagus: late April to early June. Fruit: July through October. (616) 944-5779.*

A simple, old-fashioned farm market in an area of rolling hills and tidy fruit farms. Fall fruit includes pears, plums, peaches, and apples.

6 Hillside Orchards

*2 1/2 miles southeast of Baroda in central Berrien County. On Fleisher Lane. Take U.S. 31 to Hinchman Road, west 2 1/2 miles to Fleisher Lane, south to end of Fleisher Lane. **Open** Monday, Wednesday, and*

Friday, 7:30 a.m.-6 p.m. (616) 471-7558.

You can enter the packing house of this mostly wholesale, 116-acre fruit farm to get good prices on plums, peaches, and a large variety of apples, including Paula Reds, Empire, Ida Reds, and Jonathans. Summer fruits are also grown here.

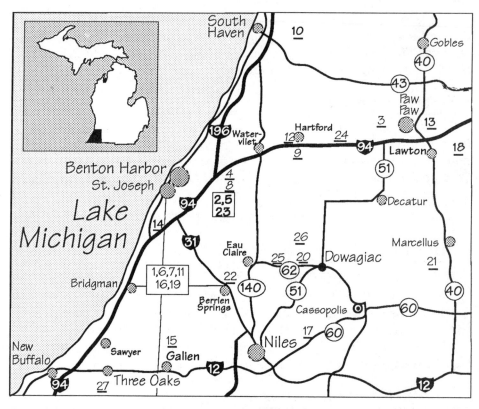

Cider Mills & Apple Orchards

SOUTHWEST
MICHIGAN

Key

7   Farm Stand/ U Picks: pp. 154-165

🛡   Federal Highway

(140)   State Highway

⊛   Cities & towns

7 Johanson's Apple World

*8700 Keehn Road, 2 1/2 miles east of Bridgman just west of Baroda. Keehn is just off Lemon Creek Road, between Holden and Cleveland roads. From I-94 exit 16 at Bridgman, take the Red Arrow Highway north to Lemon Creek Rd., and go east 2 miles to Keehn. **Open** August 15 to end of October. Daily 10-dusk. (616) 422-2426.*

Former mechanical engineer Roy Johanson has planted 700 to 800 apple trees since 1975, some 16 varieties in all. He's best known for the tasty Mutsu, which you can pick for $6 a half bushel. Other varieties are $5 a bushel. Homemade jams and jellies are also available, as is honey.

8 Jollay Orchards

*2 miles south of the I-94 Coloma exit at 1850 Friday Rd. (Friday is the main north-south road at the exit.) **Open** weekends only. (616) 468-3075.*

Entertainment agriculture. Hayrides take weekend visitors to pick apples and pumpkins.

9 Klug Orchards

*A mile southwest of Hartford at 65980 66th Ave. From I-94 exit 46, take County Rd. 687 (it's the main north-south road) south 1/2 mile, then west a mile on 66th Ave. to 66th St., northeast corner. **Open** mid-July through October 9-7 daily. (616) 621-4037.*

Free samples of the fruits and vegetables grown on this 80-acre family farm are always available. Most produce is available picked or U-pick, except for some older apple varieties on trees too big to be picked without ladders. There are tomatoes and other vegetables, peaches, and apples starting with the Williams Red in summer. Other varieties are Macintosh, Jonathan, Paula Red, Delicious, and Winesap (both Turley and Stayman). Apple cider, pressed in nearby Hartford, comes either with or without preservatives. There are also pumpkins, gourds, squash.

10 Lacota Depot

*6 miles east of South Haven on Phoenix Rd. From I-196, take Phoenix east. **Open** July through October. (616) 253-4586.*

This Fruit Belt train station is conveniently surrounded by fields and orchards. Fresh cider is for sale, and produce is available at the farm market or U-pick. Fruits available in fall include raspberries, peaches, some nectarines, plums, pears, melons, and 20 varieties of apples. The sweet corn season extends into September, and melons and vegetables into October.

The Kal-Haven Trail from South Haven to Kalamazoo goes right by here. A bike trail on a converted railroad bed, it offers bicyclists and hikers a delightful combination of villages and hamlets to explore and fruit farms of all kinds. For a free map and brochure, call (616) 637-2788, daytime, 7 days a week in summer.

11 Lemon Creek Fruit Farms & Winery

5 miles east of Bridgman and 7 miles west of Berrien Springs. At 533 Lemon Creek Rd. A mile east of Baroda. From I-94, take the Bridgman exit (16), go north on Red Arrow Hwy. 2 miles to Lemon Creek Rd., then east 5 miles. **Open** *regularly May-December: Monday-Sat 9-6, Sun 12-6. Other times by appointment. (616) 471-1321.*

The Lemon family has grown grapes and other fruit here, in the beautiful, rolling fruit-growing area between Baroda and Berrien Springs, since the 1850s. In recent years, to make up for dwindling profits in wholesaling fruit, Bob, Tim, and Jeff Lemon have taken up winemaking with considerable success. But Lemon Creek remains a diversified fruit farm with many kinds of fresh fruit for sale, packaged or U-pick. In September and October, these include raspberries, peaches, plums, pears, and eight kinds of apples. The Lemons also sell all the varieties of grapes they use in making their award-winning wines. (See the chapter on wine grapes, page 132.)

Between the farmhouse and orchards is a metal building housing the winery, fruit sales room, and wine-tasting counter. Visitors can picnic at tables outside the sales room.

12 McFarland Fruit Farm

Just north of I-94 exit 46 at Hartford. Located at Shell gas station just off I-94. **Open** *July 1-October 31, 9-7. (616) 621-4036.*

A gas-station freeway outlet of an adjacent family fruit farm. Perfect for people who are always on the road and don't have time for a leisurely drive in the country. Fall produce includes apples and grapes, and, through September, peaches, prunes, plums, raspberries, melons, and tomatoes.

13 Morrison's Sunnyfields Farm

*On the Red Arrow Highway, 2 1/2 miles east of Paw Paw. Or 3 miles
west of the I-94 Mattawan. (Go north, not into Mattawan.)* **Open** *May 1
until first week in November, daily 9-6. (616) 657-4934.*

This rambling but quaint farm stand under a huge tree dates from
the 1930s; the 200-acre farm has been in the Morrison family since
1835.

Apples are sold picked only. Varieties include Jonathan, McIntosh,
Empire, Mutsu, Red Rome, and Red and Golden Delicious. Cider is
made from these apples in fall; honey, jams and jellies, and popcorn
are sold here, too.

In fall there are also other fruits for sale — cantaloupe and some
peaches into September, and still later, grapes — both Concord and
French hybrid used in making wine. Fall produce includes, into
September, Peaches 'n' Cream sweet corn, beans, peppers (many varieties are grown). There are also Asian vegetables, including eggplant
and various greens, broccoli, tomatoes (also available U-pick), and
squash.

Next door the owner's Taiwanese wife runs Annly's Chow, a good
Chinese restaurant that serves fresh fruit pies for dessert. (It's open
year-round except January until 8 p.m.; closed Sundays and Mondays.) For a quick overview of the village of Paw Paw, see the entry on
Morrison's in the farm market chapter.

14 Nye's Apple Barn

*Just southeast of St. Joseph and immediately north of I-94 exit 27 at
Niles Ave./M-63 (the old road to Berrien Springs).* **Open** *daily May
through October, 9-6. (616) 429-0596.*

The retail sales "barn" just north of the freeway exit looks completely suburban, but the produce sold here are actually raised quite
near here, in the Nye Brothers' Orchards on Hollywood Road. Catering
to St. Joseph's old-money resorters seems to be a big part of the business here; peaches and pears are shipped UPS. Nye's grows hardy
mums for sale for fall planting starting in mid-September. Cold cider
made on the premises is available in year-round.

Late summer and fall fruits sold here include apples, blueberries,
cantaloupes, grapes, peaches, pears, plums, and raspberries. As for
fresh-picked vegetables, there's eggplant, greens, peppers, pumpkins
and squash, sweet corn, and tomatoes. There's U-pick for raspberries,
peaches, apples, and other fruits and vegetables.

15 Phillippi Fruit Farm

In the southwest corner of Michigan, 6 miles north of Galien on Cleveland Ave. Turn onto Cleveland Ave. from U.S. 12 in Galien. Open 9-6 daily. Cider mid-September to first week of November. (616) 422-1009.

Five families now grow fruits and vegetables for this third-generation farm market. Summering Chicagoans are its major customers.

The hydraulic cider press has been going since 1972. The cider is pure and good here. They don't use apples picked off the ground. The dozen types of apples grown include Gala and Golden Blush. Peaches and plums are also available in the first half of September.

All kinds of vegetables are sold in season at the 40' x 60' market shed. Lake Michigan, just seven miles away, makes Berrien County, in Michigan's southwest corner, a prime fruit-growing area. "It's like a big furnace," says Steve Fox, the farmer here. "It keeps our temperatures 5° to 10° warmer in the fall." Even more important is the lake's delaying of premature warming in the spring, reducing the chance that newly formed buds will experience a sudden cool spell and die.

16 Quint's Fruit Farm

5 1/2 miles east of Bridgman, 5 1/2 miles west of Berrien Springs. 497 E. Shawnee Rd. From I-94 take Exit 16 (Bridgman). Go north on Red Arrow Highway to first stoplight (Lake Street), turn right. Lake Street becomes Shawnee Road. **Open** *July through September. (616) 422-1375.*

At Quint's you can get picked or U-pick peaches, grapes, and apples in season. Cider is also on hand.

17 Roseland Farms Market

On M-60 5 miles west of Cassopolis and 6 miles east of Niles. Store is a red cottage on the north side of M-60 about 1/4 west of Dailey Rd. **Open** *daily 9-5. (616) 445-8987.*

"Wild apple juice" — cider pressed from the many kinds of old apple trees on this organic farm— is what's sold here, fresh in fall and frozen other times. Roseland Farms was started by Merrill and John Clark after he got his PhD. in biochemistry from nearby Notre Dame and was working in that field. Its main product is organically raised grains and meats. But the Clarks enjoy getting involved in all aspects of sustainable, chemical-free agriculture, from research and education to growing and marketing vegetables and fruits grown on the farm.

A fall trip to the country to buy apples, cider, and pumpkins is, for many urbanites, their strongest connection with the rural world around them. Direct sales to consumers have become increasingly important to farmers, since few can rely on wholesaling fruit to support themselves.

The **apples** in the old orchard include some Snow apples, Winesaps, and others they haven't really identified. Some years they turn out prettier than others, depending on the pests and diseases around, but the apples for sale *are* organic, and they *do* taste good. You can also buy organically grown beef and pork, sold by halves, quarters, and individual cuts, as well as chicken and turkey.

18 Schultz's Fruitridge Farms

1 1/2 miles south of Mattawan on County Road 652. (Mattawan is between Paw Paw and Kalamazoo a mile south of I-94. Take Mattawan exit 66 south to Mattawan; main street becomes 652 and leads to farm. **Open** *August 1- October 31. (616) 668-3724.*

Peaches, apples, plums.

19 Shafer Orchards

About 6 miles southeast of Bridgman and I-94 in west central Berrien County. Take I-94 Exit 16 (Bridgman). Turn north onto Red Arrow Hwy., east at light onto Lake St. which becomes Shawnee Rd. Go 5 miles to Hills Road, south 3/4 mile to Shafer Road. **Open** *August through first half of October. Monday through Saturday, 9 a.m.-dark. (616) 422-1972.*

Shafer sells vegetables as well as U-pick apples, grapes, peaches, and plums. Cut flowers are also available.

20 Sprague's Old Orchard

Between Eau Claire and Dowagiac 1 1/2 miles northwest of Indian Lake. On 33085 Middle Crossing Rd. at Indian Lake Rd. From M-62 between Eau Claire and Dowagiac, go north on Indian Lake Rd. to farm. **Open** *daily except Sunday July-December, 8 a.m.-6 p.m. (616) 782-2058 or (616) 782-8578.*

The same family has farmed this exceptionally beautiful old farm and orchard since 1868. It has a Civil War-era house and big trees. Antique farm implements are displayed by the sales barn.

Ten to twelve varieties of apples are grown here, and all are used in making cider with a rack and cloth press. The farm and orchard have been tended by the same family since 1868. Peaches are also sold, along with squash, sweet corn, some tart cherries, dried flowers, Indian corn, and gourds.

Most fruit is sold picked only: cherries, raspberries, blueberries, plums, apples. U-pick: apples, sometimes peaches and plums. Also for sale: sweet corn, fall squash and pumpkins, Indian corn, gourds, and dried flowers (both loose and in arrangements).

21 Spirit Spring Farm

In northeastern Cass County. Take M-40 4 miles south of Marcellus and go west 1/4 mile on Hoffman Rd. Or, from M-60 at Jones, go 5 miles north on M-40, then 1/4 mile west on Hoffmann. **Open** *September through October, Thursday-Sunday 11-7. (616) 646-9379.*

This 30-acre farm features an astounding 200 kinds of apples, including all sorts of antique varieties. It was planted just a dozen years ago, but many of the trees are now bearing. The cider may be the most unique-tasting in Michigan because it is a blend of some 20 to 30 varieties. (The kinds vary with the season.) For eating you kind buy here the highly prized Spitzenburgs, which ripen in mid- to late-October. Or try the eccentric and ugly Hubbard Nonesuch; "every bite is a new experience."

22 Stover's U-Pick & Farm Market

On U.S. 31, 3 1/2 miles north of Berrien Springs. Take I-94 to exit 28, go south on U.S. 31 8 miles. From South Bend, go north on U.S. 31 24 miles. **Open** *June-November, 8-8, closed Sunday. (616) 471-1401.*

This diversified operation in the heart of Berrien County's fruit region offers many kinds of vegetables and fruits, including apples in fall, along with cider and caramel apples.

Late summer and fall fruits, available picked or U-pick, include red and black raspberries, peaches, plums, grapes, apples, and pumpkins. Fresh vegetables grown here include squash, tomatoes, peppers, broccoli, cauliflower, and brussel sprouts.

23 Sunrise Farms

*On Hillandale Road just east of Benton Harbor. From I-94 take Exit 30, east on Napier. 2.6 miles. **Open** June 5-October 15, 9-6. (616) 944-1457.*

This big (200-acre), attractive family farm, run by Jim Culby and his sons Larry and Mike, makes a wonderful picking destination for people who like authentic farm atmosphere without entertainment. A good deal of its business is wholesale, so there are lots of big crates around. The drive is dirt, wet to keep the dust down, and the buildings predate World War II. (The picturesque farmhouse was built by talented designer-builders from the House of David in Benton Harbor.) An 1835 log cabin has been moved to the site and furnished by Jim's late wife to look pretty much like it did in pioneer days. It's open to visitors. They are welcome to use shady picnic tables and a barbecue grill.

You can buy picked or U-pick blueberries, red raspberries, nectarines, sweet and tart cherries, and 11 varieties of peaches. (Early peaches make the best eating.) Peppers are another specialty here; they come sweet and hot, in green and red. Other vegetables for sale are sweet potatoes, cucumbers, and tomatoes, including Roma tomatoes for sauces and canning.

24 Sunshower

*2 1/4 miles east of Lawrence at 48548 60th Ave. Go east of Lawrence on the Red Arrow Hwy. to 48th, 1 mile south to 60th, 1/4 mile west. **Open** year-round. (616) 674-3103.*

Organic pears and apples, and many organic vegetables. Apple cider, fresh and frozen cider, pear cider, tart cherry juice and many variations of blended juices, apple and pear butter, also maple syrup and occasionally chestnuts. U-pick by arrangement only.

25 Tree-Mendus Fruit Farm

*2 miles due east of Eau Claire; 5 miles northwest of Berrien Springs. On East Eureka Road, off M-62. From I-94, take M-140 (Watervliet exit 41) south about 14 miles to M-62, go east 1/4 mile, look for signs. **Open** from late June through mid-October. Hours from the last week in June-*

Labor Day: daily except Tuesday 10-6. After Labor Day through 3rd week in October: Friday-Monday 10-6. Summer ripe & ready report: (616) 782-7101. Winter phone: (616) 461-4187. **Fall weekend admission fee** *($2/child, $4/adult) includes orchard tour and entertainment. Fee credited to purchase of fruit.*

During the 1960s, fruit farmers began to find it hard to make a profit simply selling their fruit wholesale. Trucking strikes, farm labor boycotts, and erratic prices led farsighted growers to think about diversifying. The most successful grape- and apple-growers have succeeded by combining direct-to-consumer sales with recreation.

No one has done this better than Herb Teichman of Tree-Mendus Fruit. He has transformed his father's Skyline Orchards, tucked away on a scenic, hilly road west of Indian Lake, into a well-organized, attractive visitor destination, aggressively promoted while still personal and low-key.

Tree-Mendus Fruit artfully provides a pleasant day in the country for a generation of Americans who no longer have relatives down on the farm. In addition to 560 acres of U-pick orchards, there's a big **picnic area** and 120-acre **nature park** with **hiking trails** through wooded wildlife areas with ponds. Visitors can fill **water jugs** at a deep well.

Teichman manages to focus on fruit and teach visitors a lot about it. He doesn't run a carnival, as some well-known cider mills and orchards do. He loves to talk to customers when time permits. His outstanding **orchard tours** cover the evolution of fruit varieties,

Some growers really go in for pumpkins and other squash in a big way — with elaborate pumpkin displays or by growing an unusual variety of squash. For more on this favorite fall crop, scan the farm market and U-pick chapter,

techniques from grafting and pruning to harvesting, depending on the season. One-hour tours (from $3 to $5/person, depending on options, with a $40 minimum) are given by appointment, on short notice when possible. On the weekend of the Cherry Pit Spitting Championship, and on Saturdays and Sundays after Labor Day, musicians and comic characters circulate in the orchard, and an orchard admission fee ($4/adult, $2/child) is charged, which includes a narrated orchard tour by wagon. The fee is credited toward purchase of fruit.

Teichman's "old-time apple museum" has grown from a few dozen antique apple trees to a remarkable collection of over 300 varieties from around the world. Here you can taste the Spitzbergen (Thomas Jefferson's favorite), the Westfield Seek-No-Further, and the tasty, tart, crisp Calville Blanc, which goes back to 1627. Modern marketing demands apples that look uniformly attractive, ship well, and can be picked at once. Such requirements have eliminated many old favorites. About 50 antique varieties are for sale here.

Apples you pick yourself cost 38¢ a pound, while antique and unusual varieties are more like a dollar. Jams, apple butter, frozen peaches and cherries, homemade cherry topping, and the farm's distinctive varieties of cider and cherry cider are for sale in the Tree House Country Store. Waffle boat desserts, cooked while you wait, have peaches, cherries, or apples in season and lots of whipped cream. On crisp fall days, pickers and hikers can warm themselves by the big fireplace.

Fall fruits also include peaches, plums, pears, and pumpkins. All are grown on the farm and sold U-pick or picked. Recently the Teichmans have gotten into experimental vegetables, traditional and exotic, for sale when available.

26 Wicks Apple House

*North of Indian Lake between Eau Claire and Dowagiac. 52281 Indian Lake Rd. From I-94 Watervliet exit, go south 10 miles on M-140, turn left onto Columbia Rd. Where it ends, turn left onto Indian Lake Rd. **Open Mem. Day through October, 8-6. Closed Mon. except holiday weekends.** (616) 782-7306.*

This farm market has grown into a cider mill, bakery, gift shop, and a very pleasant, informal restaurant for breakfast and lunch — all without losing too much of the flavor of the family farm it remains. Three generations of Wickses help grow asparagus, tart cherries, Stanley plums, apples, and Concord grapes that are sold here, along with other Michigan produce whenever possible. No U-pick, but customers can select their own apples from big orchard-run crates. You can see cider being made on weekends from the end of September through October; explanatory signs tell you what's happening. The free Cider Fest on the second weekend of October features live country music, square dancing, and horse-drawn wagon tours of the farm.

27 Williams Orchard

4 miles south of Three Oaks, almost in Indiana. At 107 Paw Paw St. At the light in Three Oaks, go south 4 miles. **Open** *late July to mid-November. Cider available mid-September to mid-November. Daily 8-6. (616) 756-9417.*

Ken Williams, age 73, runs this fruit farm established by his grand-parents shortly after the Civil War. They bought fruit trees from a traveling salesman and started the orchard which continues to this day. Today Williams grows 50 acres each of peaches and apples. Back in 1910, his dad would load a wagon with fruit and sell it in areas of Indiana where fruit was less plentiful. Some of the neighbors would lease a boxcar, fill it with fruit, and take it to North Dakota, where they would sell it right off the car.

Williams is not one to have his apples pressed too early. "Summer apples," he points out, "don't make much more than colored water." He likes to wait until his apples are "firm ripe" to pick them, then takes some to a neighbor to be pressed into cider. For eating apples, he's best known for his Golden Delicious. He also sells honey. Five pounds are $6.50. U-pick apples cost $8 to $10/ bushel.

WEST MICHIGAN

1 Bin-An-Oan Orchards

12 miles south of Grand Rapids at the corner 84th and South Division. From US-131 take exit 74 at 84th Street. East on 84th. First farm on left. **Open** *July through December, Monday-Saturday 9-6. (616) 455-4278.*

The 14 acres provide a full-time occupation for former biology teacher Abe Moerland. Here he grows apples, pears, peaches, plums, pumpkins, and some vegetables. Northern Spies are a favorite of the 20 to 25 apple varieties grown. A rack and press cider press makes cider in the fall, with fresh baked doughnuts.

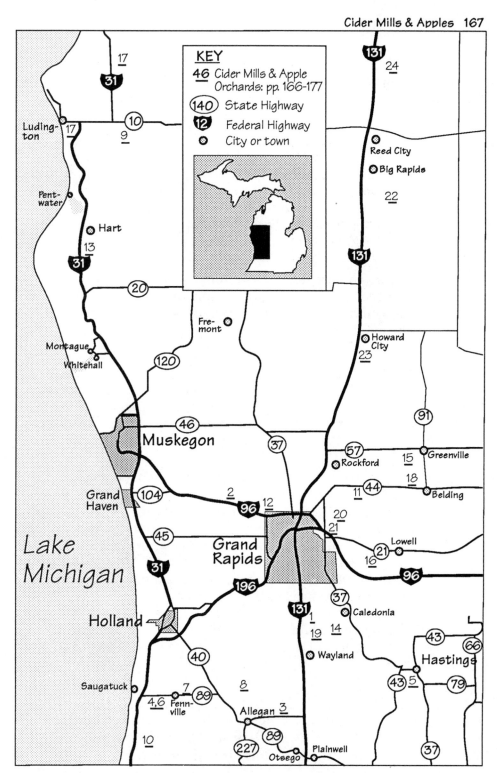

KEY

<u>46</u> Cider Mills & Apple Orchards: pp. 166-177

(140) State Highway

12 Federal Highway

◎ City or town

Cider Mills & Apple Orchards WEST MID-MICHIGAN

"Bin-An-Oan" means "garden of peace" in Chinese. It's a legacy of Mrs. Moerland's parents, who were missionaries in China.

2 Vince Brown Farms

Near Nunica, east of Grand Haven and south of Muskegon, on 8th Ave. From Grand Rapids or Muskegon, take I-96 to exit 25 (near Marne), then north 4 1/2 miles on 8th Ave. From Grand Haven, take 104 east to Nunica. At Nunica, take Cleveland east to 8th Ave., go north 1 1/2 miles on 8th Ave. to farm. **Open** *June-November. June-October: Monday, Wednesday, and Friday 7 a.m.-8 p.m., Saturday 7-5. In November, Monday and Saturday 9-6. (616) 899-2333.*

U-pick apples and picked peaches, plums, apples, and grapes, along with cabbage, broccoli, tomatoes, and sweet corn. Most of other fall favorites are on hand, too: squash, pumpkins, Indian corn, corn stalks, gourds, and cider.

3 Brown's Ridge View Fruit Farm

About 25 miles south of Grand Rapids and about 2 miles due west of Martin on 116th Ave. (M-222). From U.S. 131, go less than a mile west on M-222 at Martin exit. **Open** *June-October. Summer hours: Monday through Saturday, 8-8. After Labor Day: Monday through Saturday 9-6. (616) 672-5245.*

An unusual combination of topography — hilly uplands, wooded in part, and bits of muckland — makes for a more varied and interesting landscape and variety of fruit than at many fruit farms. Bosc and Bartlett pears are grown here; fall apples include Red and Golden Delicious, McIntosh, Ida Red, Empire, and Gala. Everything is available picked or U-pick, and the savings can be substantial. Most trees were planted in 1955 by Jeff Brown's grandfather, as suburbanization was encroaching on his old orchard in Byron Center.

In fall, cider is pressed with a rack and cloth press. An increasing number of special weekend attractions include horse-drawn wagon rides and a haunted house. But this farm still feels like a farm and not an overgrown retail store and amusement park.

4 Conifer Lane Farm Market

On M-89 about 6 miles southeast of Saugatuck and 3 miles west of Fennville. Turn east onto M-89 from I-196 exit 34 or the far more scenic Blue Star Highway south of Saugatuck. **Open** *from mid-July through*

October, 9-6. (616) 561-2524.

Both Conifer Lane and the Dutch Farm Market are run by the Ed Raak clan, who have 100 acres of orchards on two farms in Allegan County. Their cider is a secret blend which creates a drink on the sweet compared to tart side of the spectrum. In the peak of the fall season they sell some 15 varieties of apples, including the increasing rare (but delicious) Snows, Wolf River (a good cooking apple), Transparent (good for apple sauce), and Winter Banana.

Get a free cup of hot cider when you visit, and if you bring a gallon jug, you can fill it up for just $1.75. Fresh doughnuts are available, as are various vegetables, jellies & jams, and taffy apples. U-Pick apples are about $10 a bushel.

From August into September, great quantities of peaches are available. Also on hand: specialty cheeses, and free recipes.

5 Cotant's Farm Market

Just south of Hastings about 25 miles southeast of Grand Rapids. On M-37 1 1/2 miles south of Hastings, and half a mile north of the M-79 intersection. **Open** *mid-April-Halloween, Monday-Saturday, 9-6. Closed Sunday. (616) 945-4180.*

Apples, baked goods and fresh pressed cider are for sale.

6 Crane Orchards and Cider Mill

Southeast of Saugatuck and 1 1/2 miles west of Fennville on the north side of M-89. From I-196 exit 34, go east on M-89. **Open:** *Hours of* **Crane's Pie Pantry** *and restaurant: open year-round. May-October: open daily 10-5 except Sunday 11-5. Nov.-March: Tuesday-Saturday 10-5, Sunday 11-5, closed Monday. April: open weekends only.* **U-pick** *open beginning in late July daily 9 a.m.-6 p.m. (616) 561-5126.*

U-pick apples and peaches are the big draw at the Gary Crane Farm on the north side of M-89. Glo Haven, Loring, and Red Skin peaches are available through the first week of September. Fall apples start with Gala in early September, followed by Empire, McIntosh, Cortland, Jonathan, Red Delicious, Golden Delicious, Ida Red, and Rome. Most trees are dwarf for easy picking.

The Crane family, which has been growing fruit here for six generations, has also developed one of Michigan's pleasantest and most successful agri-tourism projects on the old family homestead. Next door, surrounded by orchards, is the Crane House bed and breakfast. Across the road on the south side of M-89 is Crane's Pie Pantry and

Restaurant in the lower level of an old barn. It's a cheerful, homey hodgepodge of interesting farm artifacts, where visitors can eat plump apple pies (also available frozen), soups, and sandwiches — all very tasty and satisfyingly prepared. Cider is available by the glass or jug, fresh in season and frozen the year 'round. More kinds of picked apples are for sale here, along with some raspberries in season. Cold storage facilities at big producers like Crane's insure that apples stay crisp through winter.

7 Dalton Farm

Just east of Fennville. On 55th at M-89. From I-196 exit 34, go east on M-89. No hours; someone's always on hand in season. (616) 561-2210.

You can buy or pick your own peaches, raspberries, nectarines, or apricots here, but the biggest crop is apples. There are 18 varieties, beginning with Early Blaze in the last half of August. Granny Smiths are a major variety grow at Dalton's. Antique apples include the legendary Tolman Sweet, once the country's leading sweet apple, and still favored by the local Dutch population. It ripens in October. Also on hand are the now-rare Opalescent apples, one of the most beautiful-looking apples. It ripens in late fall to a dark red, almost purplish shade and has the reputation as a fine baking apple. Opalescents were first discovered in Barry County, Michigan.

Fennville is famous for its fall Goose Festival, held on the third weekend of October. It's also the home of an excellent Mexican restaurant, run primarily for the many Mexican-Americans who came to the area first to work as pickers and then to take full-time jobs in canneries in Fennville and Holland. Su Casa, open daily for breakfast, lunch, and dinner, occupies the rear room of a Mexican grocery store at 306 Main, just west of the Shell station.

8 Dendel Orchard

On 127th Ave., Six miles north of Allegan and some 23 miles southwest of Grand Rapids. Take A-37 (a major north-south road between Allegan and Hudsonville) to 127th Ave., then 3/4 mile east. **Open** *June 20-October 31. (616) 793-7255.*

Peaches are on sale from July 25 through October. Plums, pears, and apples are all available in fall, picked or U-pick. Apple varieties include Red Free (like a Jonathan but ripens early and keeps better than most early apples), Transparents, Grimes Golden, King, Paula Red, Ida Red, Spy, McIntosh, Jonathan, and Red and Golden

Delicious. A continuous-belt cider press produces cider in quantity that's treated with preservatives and sold at Meijer and Harding stores.

9 Dolson's Sugar Ridge Orchards

About 7 miles east of Ludington. From Ludington or U.S. 31, take U.S. 10/31 east to Scottville, then take Scottville Rd. south from the town center 1 1/2 miles. Go east on Conrad Rd. 1 mile, then south on Darr Rd. less than a mile to 1688 Darr. **Open** *summer and fall, daily 10-7. (616) 757-3552.*

Apples grown here near Lake Michigan include standards like Macintosh, Jonathan, Red and Yellow Delicious, newly popular favorites like Mutsu, Empire, and Ida Red, old standards like Rome Beauty and Winesap, and some "gourmet" apples like Ozark Gold, Blushing Golden, and Molly's Delicious, a big, very early apple that's sweet like sugar. Several kinds of freestone and cling peaches are grown, as well.

Bob Dolson isn't into agritourism, so if you want his cider, which is made from a good variety of apples, you have to order it ahead.

10 Dutch Farm Market

7 miles north of South Haven on 109th Ave., just east off I-196, exit 26. **Open** *daily May 15-November 1, 8-7. (616) 637-8334.*

Peaches, grown in almost every variety suited to Michigan, are the mainstay of the fruit farm here, along apples, but the highway produce stand also carries home-grown plums, plus other produce purchased elsewhere: vegetables, cider, specialty cheeses, sausages, doughnuts. No U-pick here, but most of these fruits are available U-pick at Conifer Lane on M-89 west of nearby Fennville, owned by the same family.

11 Grass Lake Orchards & Farm Market

About 8 miles northeast of Grand Rapids and 4 miles southeast of Rockford on M-44 (also known as Belding Rd.), just across from Lake Bella Vista. 1 1/2 miles east of Beltline/Wolverine Dr. **Open** *May to mid-December, Tuesday-Saturday 9-6. Also open Sundays noon-5 in October only. (616) 874-7194.*

Stanley plums, pumpkins, and apples. Apple varieties include: Ida Red, Early McIntosh, Empire, Fuji, McIntosh, Red and Yellow Delicious, Northern Spies, Rome, and Jonathan. Apple gift boxes are a big deal here at the holidays. (Controlled-atmosphere storage keeps apples fresh.)

To eat on the spot or take home: fresh cider (pressed elsewhere) and apple doughnuts and caramel apples made on the premises. Homemade pies ($6 and $7) can be baked to order.

Other farm products are for sale: maple syrup; comb honey; pickles; and decorative corn stalks. Country crafts are made by the owner's daughter. Extra fall attractions include straw for kids to play in, a cornstalk archway, and special events like a rabbit show.

12 Happy Apple

On the northwest outskirts of Grand Rapids at 2390 Four Mile Road N. W. From I-196, take the Walker exit, go north on Walker, then right (east) on Four Mile Road. **Open** *July-November, Monday-Saturday, 9-6. (616) 784-0864.*

This 200 acre-farm includes a big 30-acre blueberry patch. Of the four kinds of blueberries grown, the Blue Crop, ripening in mid-July, taste best. Also grown are apples, peaches, pears, sweet corn, and other vegetables. Cider is made and sold, too.

13 Hill Crest Fruit Farm

Between Muskegon and Ludington, 2 miles north of Shelby and 3 miles south of Hart. Turn west at the Oceana Golf Course; orchard is first farm past it. **Open** *year-round. (616) 861-2955.*

Cherries, peaches, pears, plums, and apples. No U-pick, and no cider, either. "We don't want to mess with lower-quality apples for cider," says the owner. "We try to raise sharp-looking apples." Many varieties of each fruit are grown, some old and some new. Apple varieties, for instance, include McIntosh, Cortland, Spies, Winter Bananas, Baldwins, Hubbardston, Mutsu, Ida Red, Wealthy, Grimes Golden — "most everything but Empires."

The Hart-Montague Trail, once a railroad line, now a bike/hiking/cross-country ski trail, runs right near here through the pretty, rolling orchard country between Montague and Hart. For more information, call the chamber of commerce at Silver Lake (616-873-5048) or White Lake (616-893-4585).

14 Hilton's Apple Acres

About 12 miles south of Grand Rapids and 4 miles southwest of Caledonia, on 108th St. 4 1/2 miles west of M-37. (108th St. is the southern county line of Kent County.) From U.S. 131, take the Caledonia exit, go east 2 miles on 100th St., then south on Kalamazoo Ave. 1 mile to 108th St. and east 3/4 mile to farm. **Open** *July 1-Dec. 24. Monday-Sat 9-6 Open Sundays 1-5 in October only. Opens Memorial Day to July 1, Friday and Saturday 9-6 for winter apples and country crafts. (616) 891-8019.*

This multifaceted country destination offers a picnic area, farm animals to pet, and hayrides and orchard tours by appointment. There's U-pick for Red Haven peaches and pumpkins. Other home-grown produce for sale includes apples, pears, sweet corn, and many other vegetables. Summer apples are followed by Red and Yellow

What most visitors to cider mills in the fall don't see is the amount of work it takes to prune the thousands of trees found in most commercial orchards. A full-size apple tree can take an hour to trim. Without trimming, there will be more apples, but they'll be smaller.

Delicious, Empire, Ida Reds, and Jonathans. Cider is made from apples grown here but pressed elsewhere. It's sold in fall, along with caramel apples and fresh doughnuts in seasonal variations. Also for sale: honey, jams, and maple syrup, plus country crafts and gifts. Apples are kept in cold storage and sold year-round, even when the retail store is closed. Just call.

15 Klackle Orchards

2 miles west of Greenville and about 25 miles northeast of Grand Rapids on 11466 West Carson City Rd. (M-57). From U.S. 131, take the Greenville/M-57 exit, go about 15 miles east. **Open** *July-October, daily 10-6. (616) 754-8632.*

Apples, peaches, pumpkins, squash, honey. U-pick apples, summer and fall red raspberries. Fresh-pressed cider and doughnuts.

16 Orchard Hill Apple and Angus Farm

About 15 miles southeast of Grand Rapids on Cascade Rd., 5 1/2 miles east of the village of Cascade, between I-96 and the Grand River. From I-96 take Lowell exit, 1/2 mile north to blinker, turn west on Cascade Road. 2 1/2 miles from blinker. **Open** *August 1 January 1, daily 9-6. (616) 868-7229.*

For sale picked: apples, plums, pears, pumpkins, and vegetables. Many extras to make this a rural destination: a bakery, farm animal exhibit, demonstration beehive, and maple syrup display. For a nearby scenic drive that's especially nice in fall, take M-21 from Lowell to Ada. Two covered bridges are in beautiful sites near here: the Fallasburg Bridge on the Flat River north of Lowell and another one across the Thornapple River in the center of Ada. Small parks are by both.

17 Orchard Market

2 locations in Mason County. **Ludington:** *1 block south of the light at the U.S.10/U.S. 31 intersection.* **Freesoil:** *corner of U.S. 31 and Freesoil Road.* **Open** *May to mid-November. May-August: 8-7 daily. September to mid-November: 8-6. (616) 464-5534.*

West Michigan's diverse fruit-growing region extends north up through Mason and Oceana counties; north of that, it's mostly cherries. Fruits grown and sold at these popular, well-regarded markets include strawberries, cherries, peaches, plums, and apples. Homegrown vegetables include asparagus, sweet corn, potatoes, cabbage, broccoli, cauliflower, and more. Also jams, honey, maple syrup, baked goods from nearby Amish farms.

18 Paulson's Pumpkin Patch

20 miles northeast of Grand Rapids, 3 miles west of Belding on M-44. **Open** *August-October, daily 9 a.m.-dark. (616) 451-6595.*

Apples, winter squash, pumpkins, Indian corn. See page 33 for notes on scenery around Belding.

19 Ritz Orchard

10-15 miles south of Grand Rapids and a mile east of the village of Moline and A-45. At the corner of 9th and 144th. From U.S. 131, take Dorr exit (or Caledonia exit), go east to A-45, then north (or south) to Moline, and a mile east on 144th. **Open** *July through February. Market open July-February. Cider available second week of September usually through January. (616) 877-4732.*

Wayne and Carol Ritz now run this 93-acre fruit farm, which goes back in the family over a century. It's in hilly, picturesque Dutch country, 30 miles east of Lake Michigan. Among the 14 varieties of apples grown here is the unusually sweet Tallmann Sweet, favored by the local Dutch for frying. In July the very early Transparent apple is ripe. It is used for applesauce. In addition to apples, the Ritzes' market sells locally collected honey and locally grown dried flowers and corn, and grapes, peaches, pears, plums. Also, cider, doughnuts, honey, and popcorn.

20 Robinette's Apple Haus

4 miles east and 4 miles north of Grand Rapids. on 4 Mile Road. **Open** *Fresh cider begins day after Labor Day. Monday-Saturday 9-6, Sunday 1-6. After Christmas Monday-Saturday 9-5. (616) 361-5567.*

This heavily wooded 125-acre farm has 40 acres of apple trees, as well as sweet cherry and peach trees. All of the eight to ten varieties produced are used in making cider. Wait until October or November to get a fuller, more complex flavor. The Apple Haus also has a bakery, where doughnuts, breads, and pies are made. Sandwiches and soups are served at lunch. After March they freeze gallons of cider to sell until the next fall crop.

21 Sietsema Orchards and Cider Mill

*On the northeast side of Grand Rapids, north of where I-196 turns west from I-96. From I-96, take the East Beltline exit, go 2 miles north on Beltline to Knapp Rd., east on Knapp 300 ft. Market **open** end of July to mid-May, Cider from mid-September to mid-May. Monday-Saturday 8-6. (616) 363-0698.*

This big 300-acre fruit farm concentrates on apples, but they also raise and sell six varieties of peaches as well as pears and grapes. The farm was established in 1934 and is now run by the third generation. Their early apples, Jersey Macs, Apollo Reds, Paula Reds, and Lodis, kick off the season, followed by another 11 varieties, including Spies (the world's best pie apple because it holds its shape), Rome Beauties, and Mutsu, which marketers are starting to rename "Crispin."

Unlike many urban fruit farms that make cider, this still feels like a farm. Jonathans are the major part of their cider blend, made with a rack and cloth press. Doughnuts and caramel apples are made during the fall. Other fall fruits include pears, grapes, and (into September) peaches. Also for sale: caramel apples, popcorn, and honey.

22 D & D Stout Orchards

*About 15 miles southeast of Big Rapids and 35 miles north of Grand Rapids. From U.S. 131, take Stanwood exit, go east into Stanwood. Take Pierce Rd. east to 135th Ave., south for 7/10 mile. **Open** June-October, Monday-Saturday, 9-7. (616) 823-2119.*

Fall fruits at this big fruit farm include not only apples but raspberries, melons, peaches, pears, plums, and grapes, along with tomatoes, squash, and pumpkins. There's cider, too.

23 Watts Orchard

*At the southwest edge of Howard City, about 30 miles north of Grand Rapids and 15 miles south of Big Rapids. Washburn Road, southwest corner of the Howard City village limit. From U.S.131, take Big Rapids exit (18), go east to second road, south to orchard signs. Or take old U.S.131 out of Howard City to Washburn Road, west to sign. **Open** July 2 or 3 until first week of November. (616) 937-4094.*

Tart and sweet cherries, peaches, apples, plums, pears, apricots. Also, vegetables and cider.

24 Will-lane Farm and Orchards

About 10 miles south of Cadillac, 20 miles north of Big Rapids, and a mile north of LeRoy. From U.S. 131, take Mackinaw Trail into LeRoy, continue north on Mackinaw Trail a mile to 17 Mile Rd. Go west on 17 Mile half a mile, look for sign to orchard on corner of 17 Mile Road.
   Call ahead for times. (616) 768-4305.

Apple, peaches, pumpkins, and **cider** are produced on this working farm with animals. Some U-pick. Free horse-drawn hayrides to orchard and pumpkin patch.

NORTHERN MICHIGAN

1 Amon Orchards and U-Pick

*Just east of Traverse City overlooking the East Arm of Grand Traverse Bay. On the east side of U.S. 41, 2 1/2 miles north of where it intersects with M-72 in Acme by the Grand Traverse Resort. **Open** year-round. January-April: Saturday 10-5. May-October: daily 9-6. November & December: Saturday 10-5. (616) 938-9160 or (800) 937-1644.*

Amon's offers more than the cherries that make it and Traverse City famous. In the fall: raspberries, apples, plums, peaches, pumpkins, cider and doughnuts. Try the tasty cherry cider for something different. You can pick fruit and enjoy a splendid view of Grand Traverse Bay. And you can press your own apple cider with a hand crank. Amon's gives a lot of entertainment for your money. And there are free samples of an interesting variety of homemade cherry products, from barbecue sauce to the best-selling cherry fudge sauce. Cherry products can be shipped UPS.

2 Apple Valley Orchards

*About 15 miles north of Manistee and 15 miles south of Frankfurt at 11240 Milarch Rd., between Onekama and Bear Lake. From U.S. 31 3 miles north of Onekama, turn west onto Hwy. 600 at the Blarney Castle gas station. In 1 1/4 miles, take a left at the Y. Follow sign to Apple Valley, look for the two-story red farmhouse. **Open** May-December. No set hours. Leave money in jar if no one's there. (616) 889-4343.*

In the Meister family of German farmers who first settled Onekama and founded the town's first church, the sons went downstate, got ed-

ucated, worked, but eventually all returned, and now a second generation of college-educated sons has come back to the family farm up
north. Peaches, nectarines, and apples are the fall crops of this big
fruit farm, which also sells to Mrs. Smith's Pies.

There's no U-pick here, but plenty of tips and advice from Mrs. I. R.
Meister if you catch her in. For instance, she says the best apple pies
combine different kinds of apples. And Michigan apples taste better
than the ones grown in Pennsylvania. That's why fruit buyers for Mrs.
Smith's Pie comes all the way up here to buy pie apples. Mrs. Meister
was shocked to realize that Mrs. Smith's frozen pies tasted better than
her own, until she asked the corporate apple-buyer for their secret:
mix varieties. They use Golden and Red Delicious, Spies, and
Jonathans. Despite their reputation for blandness, Delicious make
good pie apples, I. R. says, because they're not too acid. Even better for
pies she likes the tangier Spy Golden, her favorite of the 15 apple
varieties grown here.

3 Cripps Fruit Farm

12 miles west of Alpena on Werth Road. Call for directions. **Open** *for
cider in October. Saturday 10:30-5:30, Sunday 12:30-5:30, weekdays
9:30-6:30. (517) 727-2005.*

Elaborate pumpkin displays form the centerpiece of this farm. Take
a $2.50 hay wagon ride through pumpkin patch where over 3,000
pumpkins have been turned into such things as pirate ships and
space shuttles. Dozens of pumpkins hang from a big 75-foot "pumpkin
tree."

Francis Cripps doesn't rush his cider, waiting until the peak month
of October to press. His five-acre apple orchard grows seven or eight
varieties, and he uses Delicious apples as a base in his blend, along
with McIntosh, Cortland, Northern Spies, and others. Along with cider
they make fresh doughnuts, caramel apples, and sell pumpkin-carving
tools ($2 for a single tool, $12 for a set). A big favorite is strawberry
cider: apple cider flavored with strawberry juice.

4 Elzinga's Farm Market

10 miles south of Charlevoix or half a mile north of Atwood on U.S. 31.
Open *mid-June-December 20. Hours through color season: Monday
through Saturday 6-6. (616) 599-2604.*

A homey, general-purpose farm stand, Elzinga's sells apples,
peaches, pears, and a big variety of homegrown seasonal vegetables.

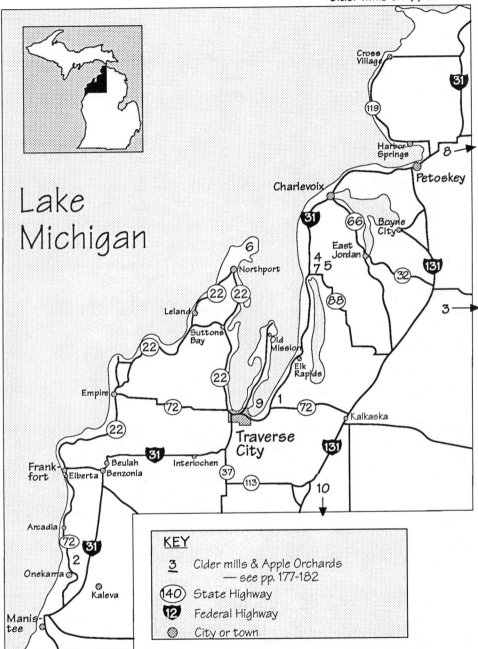

Lake
Michigan

Cross Village

31

119

Harbor
Springs

8 →

Petoskey

Charlevoix

31

66

Boyne
City

131

East
Jordan

4
7 5

32

3 →

88

6

Northport

22 22

Leland

Suttons
Bay

22

Old
Mission

Elk
Rapids

22

Empire

72

9 1

72

Kalkaska

22

31

Beulah
Benzonia

Interlochen

Traverse
City

131

Frank-
fort
Elberta

37

113

10
↓

Arcadia

72

31

KEY

<u>3</u> Cider mills & Apple Orchards
— see pp. 177-182

140 State Highway

12 Federal Highway

City or town

2

Onekama

Kaleva

Manis-
tee

Cider Mills & Apple Orchards
NORTHERN LOWER PENINSULA

It's a favorite stop of American Spoon Food's Justin Rashid on the way to Traverse City, because he can sit in the lunchroom, enjoy a quick sandwich, coffee, and a piece of good fruit pie, and look out and watch the workings of the farm.

5 Friske Orchards

Some 15 miles southeast of Charlevoix on Docter Road. Two miles off U.S. 31 east of Atwood on Ellsworth-Atwood Road. Watch for sign at Docter Road intersections. Farm market **open** *year-round Monday-Saturday 9-6. Cider mid-September through March. (616) 588-6185.*

Brothers Richard and Neil Friske grew up on this 250-acre fruit farm which their German immigrant parents started 30 years ago. It's on the northern fringe of fruit farming, made possible by the moderating effects of Lake Michigan two miles away. The exceptionally cool early fall weather makes for about the best apples you can find anywhere, they say. Even the common Red Delicious grown here makes a Washington State counterpart pale by comparison.

The Friskes grow 20 varieties, including most of the new popular types—Gala, Mutsu, Braeburns, Fujis, and Jonagold. A lot of Northern Spies are grown, which Neil calls "the best pie-making apple in the world."

The brothers take a serious interest in making good cider. They believe the best is made with a proper blend of *all* their varieties, not just the standard few used by most cider makers. They also stand by their rack and cloth press. Though it makes for more work, the press allows just the right amount of body, say the Friskes.

The Friskes also sell the fall peaches, pears, and plums they grow on their big farm. They also collect and sell their own honey, jams and jellies, and apple butter.

6 Kilcherman's Christmas Cove Farm

North of Northport near the tip of the Leelanau Peninsula on Christmas Cove Road. Take M-201 north from Northport. When it veers right, stay straight (you'll be on De Long Rd.), then take next left onto Christmas Cove. **Open** *daily 10-5 in September and October. (616) 386-5637. Call before making a special trip.*

In recent years, third-generation fruit farmer John Kilcherman has become intensely interested in the history of old apple varieties. He grows 170 kinds of **antique apples** on his farm and sells many of them at this attractive farm stand. For special occasions, he makes up sampler boxes of them, complete with his own informative booklet. His wife, Phyllis, sells objects decorated with Scandinavian rosemaling.

Nearby Christmas Cove is said to have been named by grateful passengers on a ship that found safe harbor there during a big storm at Christmas time.

7 King Orchard

*Between Traverse City and Charlevoix, 2 miles east of Eastport and U.S. 31 on M-88. **Open** July through November, Monday through Saturday 10-6, Sunday 12-6. Cider available September 25-November 15. (616) 544-6479.*

John and Betsy King's fruit farm is one of the farthest north in Michigan. Situated on top of a drumlin 35 miles north of Traverse City, their land wouldn't be able to grow fruit commercially if it weren't for Lake Michigan just three miles to the west. The big lake keeps their microclimate temperate and regular enough to escape the killing frosts

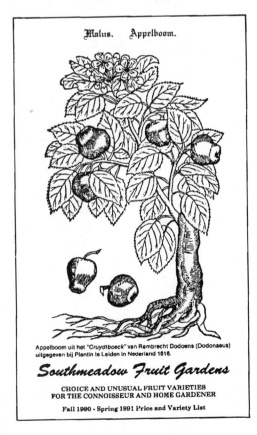

Malus.   Appelboom.

Appelboom uit het *"Cruydtboeck"* van Rembrecht Dodoens (Dodonaeus) uitgegeven bij Plantin te Leiden in Nederland 1616.

Southmeadow Fruit Gardens

CHOICE AND UNUSUAL FRUIT VARIETIES
FOR THE CONNOISSEUR AND HOME GARDENER

Fall 1990 - Spring 1991 Price and Variety List

Antique apple illustrations and assorted tips and apple history enliven the annual price lists of Southmeadow Fruit Gardens, Lakeside, MI 49116. Its specialty is rootstock of "choice and unusual fruit varieties for the connoisseur and home gardener." Many antique apple varieties come from amateur pomologists who scour old orchards for antique apples like the many russets, "fascinating and delicious sorts of apples yet virtually unknown to the general public . . . . They never know what delectable eating hides underneath the rough exterior." Southmeadow's fat 100-page annotated catalog (about $10) makes interesting reading.

experienced just a few miles farther inland and to the north. This extreme northern location makes for unusually high-quality McIntosh apples. The cooler nights produce better coloring and a crisper apple.

John King grew up in Flint, but learned fruit farming working summers on the Old Mission Peninsula while attending Michigan Tech. After managing farms, he bought this 40-acre orchard 12 years ago. Now some 22 varieties of apples are grown. He and Betsy also make cider and grow tart and sweet cherries, peaches (available into September), apricots, and nectarines. Their hilltop orchards and proximity to the lake help prevent potentially devastating freezes of 16 or 17° F. below zero which would kill the buds. They also sell dried flowers, jams and jellies, and produce (sweet corn, tomatoes, melons) in season.

8 Knaebe's Mmmunchie-Crunchie Apple Farm

5 miles southwest of Rogers City on Karsten Road. From the U.S. 23/M-68 intersection outside Rogers City, go 4.1 miles west on M-68, then 1 1/2 miles south on Karsten Road. Also Also reachable from I-75 via M-68 at Indian River (about 28 miles). **Open** *early August-early November. Monday-Thursday noon-7. Saturday and Sunday 10-5. Closed Friday. (517) 734-2567.*

Apples and cider, along with pumpkins, gourds, and Indian corn.

9 Underwood Orchards

Southeast side of the Old Mission Peninsula just north of Traverse City. Go 2 1/2 miles out Center Road (M-37), turn right on McKinley Road. **Open** *mid-June to December 23, daily 9-6. (616) 947-8799.*

The retail outlet of this large apple and cherry orchard has been slicked up and gentrified in suburban style, befitting the suburban character of the southern part of the beautiful Old Mission Peninsula. In the fall: apple cider, cherry-apple cider, pumpkins, and apples, along with garden vegetables. Fresh fruit pies and good cinnamon rolls are specialties of the bakery.

10 Willies Apple Haven

About 4 miles east of Cadillac. From town, go 2 miles est on M-55, then south two miles on the Wexford-Missaukee County Line Road (s 49 Road). **Open** *weekends, Aug. 15 to Nov., 8-6. (616) 775-2714.*

U-pick or picked apples (McIntosh, Ida Reds, Paula Reds, Yellow and Red Delicious, Empires, Cortland, Northern Spy).

MID-MICHIGAN including OAKLAND COUNTY.

▼   *The numbers before each entry are keyed to the map on p. 184.*

1 Al Mar Orchard

5 miles southwest of Flushing on Duffield Road at Beecher Road, 1 mile east, 2 miles north of the M-21/M-13 junction. **Open** *year-round. Monday-Saturday 9-6; Sunday 12-6. Cider made year-round except August. (313) 659-6568.*

There are some 24,000 apple trees on this 160-acre fruit farm, with some 24 varieties including Jonagold and Mutsu. Kids can see the farm's resident reindeer and llamas and go on hayrides. At the market shop, there are cherries, grapes, pears, and plums for sale in addition to apples. The bakery here specializes in fresh pies, apple dumplings, and apple cider doughnuts.

2 Asplin Farms

Five miles east of Durand, four miles west of Swartz Creek on Miller Road. One mile south of I-69, exit M-13, 1/2 mile east of M-13. **Open** *Tuesday-Thursday, noon-6, Friday noon-11 p.m., Saturday & Sunday 10-6. (313) 621-4780.*

Wendell Asplin's philosophy is "the more different kinds of apples, the better the cider." He also eschews a weak, watery blend. The Asplin cider is sweet, mellow, rich, and thick. A bachelor who also raises Christmas trees on his 80-acre farm, Wendell started his mill in 1973 while selling real estate in Birmingham, Michigan. By 1982 his Christmas tree and cider businesses were doing well enough to allow him to move back here to his boyhood home on this farm. He sells "fried cakes," along with the cider. They're like doughnuts, but being made without yeast, they're more dense.

Country music plays a big part in Asplin's life. Two songs he recorded in Nashville a few years ago both reached 52 on the national charts. Every Friday night from mid-April to mid-December he has a country music show featuring a local band. There's a $1 per person admission charge and no alcohol.

3 Baynes Apple Valley Farm

Between Midland and Saginaw on Midland Road. 3 miles south of Freeland on M-47. **Open** *year-round, Monday-Saturday 9-6, Sunday noon-6. Open until 8 September & October. (517) 695-9139.*

This cider operation has been going since 1939. On 25-acres an unusual variety of apples are grown — 40 in all. Antique apples include Dutchess, Deacons, Gravenstein, Red Astricam, and Russets. The tasty Jon-Grimes are so popular that they are pre-sold before they are even picked. The Gravenstein, available in mid-August, are great-tasting and well worth asking for.

Baynes is also famous for its fruit pies, especially the apple pie

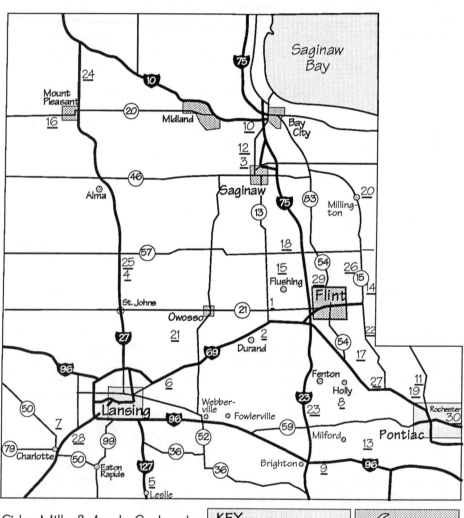

Cider Mills & Apple Orchards
MID-MICHIGAN

KEY

46 Cider Mills & Apple Orchards: pp. 183-194

12 Federal Highway

140 State Highway

⊙ ▢ Cities & towns

(10-inch is $5.99). They also have cider doughnuts, muffins, cookies, and whatever else they feel like baking that day.

4 Beck's Cider Mill

7 miles north of St. Johns on Maple Rapids Road. Take U.S. 27 to Maple Rapids Road, then east 1/4 mile. Open for cider Labor Day to mid-January. Daily 8-8. (517) 224-4309.

This 80-acre orchard produces 10 standard varieties. The blend creates a slightly tart cider. You can also buy doughnuts, home-baked pies, caramel apples.

5 Blossom Orchard

Between Lansing and Jackson on east side of U.S. 127, north of Leslie. Open August-December. Tuesday-Sunday 9-5:30. (517) 589-8251.

U-pick apples. Also peaches, pears, plums, and pumpkins, along with honey and popcorn.

6 Clearview Orchards

Northeast of Lansing at 1051 Barry Road. From Haslett, take Haslett Road to Green Road, to Barry Road. 2 miles east on Barry to farm. Open late August to late October. (517) 655-1454.

U-pick apples.

7 Country Mill

Southwest of Lansing at 4648 Otto Road. Take U.S. 27 to Potterville, west on Vermontville Road, 3 miles to Otto Road, north 1/2 mile. Open August to Christmas, Tuesday-Saturday, 9 a.m.-6 p.m., Sunday 11 a.m.-6 p.m. (517) 543-1019.

There's been an apple orchard here since the Civil War, and some of the ancient trees are still producing. Today there are 26 varieties on the 50 acres of trees. People come all the way from out of state to buy the Mutsu variety, a combination of a Japanese and Golden Delicious apples. The Gala, from Australia, has the taste of pears. The Fuji is also popular.

Owners Bernie and Ann Tennes have been here for 22 years. He's a retired agricultural engineer and she was a social worker. They've added a complete bakery, with apple pies ($5 frozen), apple crisp doughnuts, and apple bread. Also popular is an apple cheese spread. There's a sit-down area for those who want to eat at the mill.

Recently the U-pick operation has been boosted with a rubber-tire train holding 120 passengers. It takes visitors out to the orchards and back. Halloween features a haunted lane, complete with goblins who jumps out. They start making cider in August, but the peak season begins the second week of September.

8 Diehl's Orchard and Cider Mill

6 miles south of Holly, 7 miles north of M-59 (Highland Rd.) at 1479 Ranch Road. Follow Milford Road to East Rose Center Road to Ranch Road. Cider pressed from Labor Day to March or April. **Open** *year-round, Monday-Saturday 9-5, Sunday 1-6. (313) 634-8981.*

Sue Diehl grew up on this 70-year apple farm and came back 40 years ago to run it with her husband. Their 75 acres grow 10 varieties, all of which are used to make a sweet, mellow blend. Also available: freshly baked doughnuts, honey, jams and jellies, popcorn, and candy. Picnic tables encourage picnicking; hayrides in the fall.

9 Erwin Orchards U-Pick

Between Milford and South Lyon at 61019 Silver Lake Road. From I-96, take exit 153 at Kensington Metropark, go south 1 mile, left onto Silver Lake Road. Orchard is in 1/4 mile.
Store opens *in July through January, Monday-Saturday 8-6, Sunday 9-6. Picking daily from late August, 9-6. (313) 437-4701.*

This U-pick operation includes some of Michigan's most desirable apples: McIntosh, Red Delicious, Golden Delicious, Ida Red, Northern Spy, Mutsu Empire. Fall raspberries are also available U-pick. Next door at the Country Store, find ready-picked apples, plus cider, doughnuts, caramel apples, apple butter, jellies, baked goods. honey, and popcorn. Call for wagon ride times. Nearby Kensington Metropark has trails, boat rentals, nature center, and farm.

10 Gehringer's Orchard and Cider Mill

5 miles west of Bay City and east of Midland at 919 Salzburg Road. **Open** *for cider September through February. 9-6 in the fall, 9-5 thereafter. (517) 667-0130.*

On this small old farm seven kinds of apples grow on 10 acres. The cider here his especially sweet, using a foundation of Red and Golden Delicious apples. They make good apple doughnuts and sell well regarded Golden Delicious eating apples.

11 Goodison Cider Mill

4295 Orion Road, Oakland Township north of Rochester. Take Roches-
ter Road north to Orion Road, bear northwest 3 miles. **Open** *Sept*
though December, 9-7 weekends, weekdays 11-6. (313) 643-7333.

CPA Bob Steinheiser recently bought this cider mill and can be
seen in the fall in overalls pressing sweet cider with a rack and
cloth press. He filters the cider after pressing, creating a lighter,
less syrupy product, which many cider-lovers prefer. Doughnuts are
made fresh daily here, along with caramel apples. Also for sale are
maple syrup, honey, crafts, and vinegar aged right here. Steinheiser
has added a picnic and playground area, along with a petting zoo.

12 Green Apple Barn

10 miles north of Saginaw and east of Midland on North River Road,
1/2 mile south of Freeland Road. **Open** *May-December, 10-6 daily,*
from January-April 10-5 Monday-Saturday. (517) 695-2465.

This 80-acre centennial farm now has four generations of Lea-
mans working here, from the 88-year-old grandfather to the eleven-
year-old great-grandchildren. A big part of their business is dried
flowers, raised on 15 acres and air-dried or freeze-dried. Jack
Leaman makes the cider, using nine varieties of apples he grows on
ten acres. People in these parts, he tells us, like the tart cider favored in New England. Rather than using a base of Delicious apples,
which makes for a sweeter, more watery cider, Leaman uses relatively more Jonathan and Winesap apples to make a thicker, tarter
apples. Early in the cider season, before the fall varieties ripen in
early October, he mixes pears into the blend to sweeten the early
apples, normally quite tart.

Green Apple Farm is known for its Northern Spy apples, a legendary tart apple many like to eat out of hand but which is a favorite
for pies. A small bakery turns out batches of doughnuts, breads, fruit
pies, coffee cakes, and cookies, including a popular sour cream
cookie. The farm also offers U-pick raspberries in July and U-pick
blackberries in late August.

13 Long Family Orchard & Farm

4 miles east of Milford and just west of Farmington Hills on Commerce
Rd., 1/3 mile west of Bogie Lake Rd., north of Huron Valley Hospital.
From the north, take M-59 to Bogie Lake Rd. (near Alpine Valley Ski

Resort), south to light and west 1/3 mile. From the south, take Hagger-
ty north to end. **Open** *May-October. Call for hours. (313) 360-3774.*

In September and October, U-pick or picked apples, along with
cider and caramel apples. In October, pumpkins, gourds, squash,
decorative cornstalks.

14 Masters Orchard

*10251 East Richfield Rd. near Davison, just east of Flint. 1/2 mile off
M-15.* **Open** *September 15-January. (313) 653-5677.*

Ready picked or U-pick apples, along with cider, popcorn, and
honey.

15 McCarron's Orchards

*West of Flint and just northeast of Flushing on West Carpenter Road.
Take I-75 to Pierson Road, exit west 4 miles to Elms Road, north 1
1//2 miles to Carpenter, 3/4 mile.* **Open** *year-round. Cider pressed
first week September until middle of May. Monday-Saturday 9-6,
Sunday 11-5. Apples available early August to June. Bakery open
year around. (313) 659-3813.*

Pat McCarren has been growing fruit for the past quarter century.
He takes care to mix two-thirds tart (especially Jonathan) and one-
third sweet (Golden Delicious) to create a cider that is sweet and
flavorful enough but not too syrupy. This proportion gradually
changes beyond fall as the starch in the stored apples breaks down
into sugar. To keep the right taste he cuts down on the sweet apples
and uses more tart.

McCarrons' 35 acres of apple orchards produce 19 varieties of
apples. Not long ago the Mutsu, Gala, and Fuji were the hot new
apples. But the newest hits are Jonagold (a cross between Jonathan
and Golden Delicious giving making a spicy, juicy, rosy red apple)
and King Luscious, an unusually large apple.

The McCarrons also have a full-time bakery, making from scratch
white and whole wheat bread, cinnamon rolls, and a big variety of
fruit pies. In November they make pecan and pumpkin pies.

16 McIntosh Orchards

*5 1/2 miles west of Mt. Pleasant on M-20 (W. Remus Road) on the
south side of the highway.* **Open** *second week of September to
February. Monday-Saturday 8-5:30. (517) 773-7330.*

Dan Hill of Montrose Orchards presses 12,000 to 15,000 gallons of cider a year at his family orchard just north of Flint. Just before this picture was taken in May of 1992, a sudden freeze knocked out the entire apple crop from their 7,000 trees. An M.S.U. grad in horticulture, he is part of a clan that has been raising apples for over half a century.

Ed McIntosh has been running the 50-acre apple orchard his father started in 1932 since he came out of the service in 1946. Unlike a lot of fruit farmers, he doesn't grow a large number of varieties, just six or seven. His early batches of cider are pressed with Red Delicious, McIntosh, and Jonathans, and as the season progresses, the Jonathans give way to Northern Spies. He makes caramel apples in October. The 10,000 gallons of cider he presses a year in his rack and cloth press sell for just $2.50 a gallon.

17 Mitchell Farm

3 miles north of Holly and about 10 miles south of Flint at North Holly Road and Mitchell Road. From I-75, exit 108, go south on Holly Road 3 miles. **Open** *late April-July 1 & late July-Nov. 1. Daily 10-6. (313) 634-4753.*

In September and October, there are **apples**, **cabbage**, **ear corn**, **Indian corn**, **popcorn**, **broom corn**, **pumpkins**, 12 kinds of **squash**, and **gourds**. On October weekends, you can pick your own pumpkins. Well into September, the Mitchell Farm sells their **sweet corn**, **tomatoes**, **peppers**, and **cucumbers**.

18 Montrose Orchards

*1 mile east and north of Montrose, northwest of Flint. On Seymour Road. Market **open** daily. Monday-Saturday 9-6, Sundays 12-6. Cider made year-round. (313) 639-6971.*

Dan Hill has been fruit farming for over half a century and knows as much about apples as anyone in the state. He grows 60 acres of apple trees on his 180-acre farm. He points out that while the state of Washington can grow prettier, more pointed apples, Michigan's flatter, less colorful apples are clearly more flavorful.

When it comes to making cider with his rack and cloth press, he says more important than the number of varieties pressed for a batch is the proportion of sweet to tart apples used. Unlike most cider-makers, Montrose filters his cider after squeezing the apples, producing a clearer cider that has less bacteria and stays fresh longer. The flavor doesn't suffer, he says, and people sensitive to the pectin in cider drink it more comfortably.

Empire is the apple of the future, in Montrose's view. Far superior to the trendy Fuji and Gala varieties, it's like a McIntosh but not as large. It's darker, stays firm longer, with a thinner skin. He also likes his Molly Delicious, a premium early season sweet eating apple which ripen in late August and early September.

In fall the market also sells plums and pears grown here, as well as locally collected honey and popcorn grown on the farm nearby. The Montrose bakery makes fruit pies, breads, and doughnuts, plus pull-apart bread which contains blueberries, cherries, or raspberries, all grown here on the farm. In the fall there are wagon rides and pumpkins along with the cider.

19 Paint Creek Mill

3 miles northwest of Rochester on Orion Road between Adams and Rochester roads. Cider available Labor Day to December 22. (313) 651-8361.

There's no orchard at this historic old grist mill. They buy apples to press. There are also fresh homemade doughnuts, handmade caramel apples, fruit pies, and fudge and candies. An adjoining restaurant is open all year.

20 Parker's Orchard

Some 15 miles east of Frankenmuth and 1 mile east of Millington at 8355 South Oak Road. 1 1/2 mile east of M-15 and 1/4 mile north of Millington Road. **Open** *September through January, Monday-Saturday 9:15-6; Sunday 1-5:15. (517) 871-3031.*

Six varieties of traditional apples are grown in Gordon Parker's 32-acre orchard; some are over half a century old. All are used to make sweet cider. Bring your own gallon jug and get it filled for $2.40; otherwise it's $2.70 a gallon. Also for sale are fresh doughnuts, jams and jellies, and popcorn.

21 Poor Man's Ponderosa

20 miles northeast of Lansing and 1 1/2 miles north of Laingsburg at 6831 Meridian Road. 6 miles south of M-21 at Ovid. Cider available only in October. Restaurant open year-round. (517) 651-6718.

This fourth-generation German farm has turned the old farmhouse into a restaurant featuring hamburgers made with beef raised right here. The house is perched on "Poverty Knob," affording a nice view of the surrounding countryside. The 35-acre apple orchard is half mile away. It yields 10 varieties, including Empires and Paula Reds. Owner Brad Schlicher blends Ida Reds with Red and Golden Delicious apples in his rack and cloth press. He waits until October to get fully mature fruit for pressing, and closes the cider mill by the end of the month because, as he puts it, "We're way out here in the sticks, and nobody much comes any later than October." You can also get fresh doughnuts with your cider. Schlicher also grows 10 acres of strawberries, for sale in June.

22 Porter's Orchard & Cider Mill

12 miles east of Flint. 1 1/2 miles east of M-15 in Goodrich. On Hegel Road. Cider pressed September 15 through April. Year-round market **open** *Monday-Saturday 9-6, Sunday 1:30-6. (313) 687-2476.*

Porter's has some of the best tasting apple cider you'll find any-where in the state. Apple trees were first planted here in 1921 by a former Flint tool-and-die maker. Now there are some 30 varieties over 90 acres, tended by third-generation fruit farmer Ray Porter. Using a rack and cloth press (many say this makes the best cider), he's a proponent of "the more different kinds of apples, the better." As many as ten varieties at a time are pressed. The best cider, he

A landmark on U.S. 27 north of Lansing is Uncle John's Cider Mill up on the hill. The complex is run by the fourth generation of apple-growers. The Beck family first started farming here in 1890.

says, is in November, when the apples have matured to their peak in sweetness yet remain firm and flavorful.

Porter also sells excellent jams and jellies, popcorn, and locally collected honey and maple syrup. Homemade cider doughnuts are also available.

23 Spicer Orchards Farm Market

*About 20 miles south of Flint and 10 miles north of Brighton. 1/4 mile east of U.S. 23. and 3 miles north of M-59 on Clyde Rd. Just east of the Clyde Rd. exit. **Open** year-round 9-6. (313) 632-7692.*

Fall fruits grown on this high ridge include apples, raspberries, peaches, plums, pears. All are available U-pick or ready-picked. Picnic tables enjoy a sweeping long view to the south; the orchard sits atop a long glacial moraine. The pleasant sales room sells cider, doughnuts, honey, preserves, and baked goods from the bakery.

24 Stan's Cider Mill

*A little north of Mt. Pleasant. Go 2 miles north of Rosebush on Old 27 and turn east onto East Vernon Road. **Open** September to end of November, Monday-Saturday 9-9, Sunday 12-6. (517) 433-5849.*

Stan's doesn't have its own orchard, but has pressed the apples it buys for over a decade. In addition it sells homemade doughnuts and caramel apples on weekends.

25 Uncle John's Cider Mill

*7 1/2 miles north of St. Johns on U.S. 27. **Open** August 15-January 5. Daily 9-9 through October, 9-6 from November on. (517) 224-3686.*

This fourth-generation farm has 90 acres of apple trees growing many varieties of apples, including McCallas, Vikings, Spartans, as well as more common varieties. They make a good apple bread here, and the bakery also puts out doughnuts and fruit pies.

Uncle John's barn has become a theater of sorts, where visitors sit around and watch cider being pressed and doughnuts being made in a glass-sided kitchen. Each weekend in September and October, there's a weekend fair — cars, arts and crafts, and more. "Ya'll pay us a visit — just call fer a free calendar of events," you are urged. There are free wagon tours, U-pick pumpkins, and a picnic area by a small stream.

26 Uptegraff's Orchard

*Just northeast of Flint and 4 miles north of Davison at 5350 North Gale Rd. 1 1/2 miles north of Richfield between Irish Road and M-15. **Open** mid-August through the fall. Daily 1-6. (313) 653-4577.*

Five varieties of U-pick apples from semi-dwarf trees, plus cider. There is also a quarter-acre of grapes.

27 Vallee of Pines Fruit Farm

*Between Clarkston and Holly in northwest Oakland County at 9500 Bridgelake Rd. Take Dixie Highway (U.S. 24) 3-4 miles north of I-75 Clarkston interchange to Rattalee Lake Rd., 1 1/2 miles east to Bridgelake Rd., north to farm. **Open** in season. (313) 625-3027.*

Apples and cider, and many other fall fruit as well: grapes, raspberries, peaches, pears, and plums. No U-pick.

28 Witte Orchards

*Some 6 miles southwest of Lansing on M-99, 1 1/2 miles south of Holt Rd. On east side of divided M-99, which begins as Logan St. in Lansing and goes to Eaton Rapids. From I-96, take Logan/M-99 exit south 4-5 miles but remember, it's on the east (left) side of road. **Open** August 15-October 31, Monday-Saturday 8:30-7, Sunday noon-7. (517) 646-6543.*

Many varieties of apples in season, plus cider, apple butter, popcorn, pumpkins, herbs, and ornamental corn.

29 Wolcott Orchards & Cider Mill

On the northern edge of Flint but south of I-475. On West Coldwater Road between Clio and Jennings roads. From I-475 take the Clio Rd. exit, go south to Coldwater and turn west. **Open** *daily, year-round, 9-6. (313) 7879-9561.*

Wolcott's features a wide variety of apples, including less common varieties such as Tallmann Sweet, Maiden Blush, Winter Banana, Greening, and Steel Red. The orchard has been in business almost 100 years. Parts of its cider mill are that old, too. Because it is open all year, it stocks a variety of other items: doughnuts, nuts, flours, juices, and more.

30 Yates Cider Mill

East of Rochester on the east side of Rochester Hills. On East Avon Road near 23 Mile Road at Dequindre. **Open** *September 1 to end of November. Daily 9-7. (313) 651-8300.*

This is one of the few remaining water-driven cider mills left in the country. The original Yates gristmill dates from 1863. It's powered by the Clinton River which was diverted into a canal. It was converted into a cider mill in 1876. There is no commercial orchard here; the apples are brought in from other orchards. They also sell doughnuts, caramel apples, cotton candy, hot dogs, and knackwurst, and there is a fudge shop in the back. Remodeling in a gentrified vein has stripped much of the original character away from the old mill.

Yates can get uncomfortably crowded in the peak of the season. Sundays are the worst. Early mornings and late afternoons are less crowded. The Rochester-Utica State Recreation Area across the road has facilities for picnicking and hiking

MACOMB COUNTY AND THE THUMB

▼ *The numbers before each entry are keyed to the map on p. 196.*

1 Apple Barn Cider Mill

5404 Chapman Road, 9 miles north of Lapeer, 1 mile east of Highway 24. Open with peaches, pears and raspberries at beginning of August. Cider begins in September. Open daily 10-5 weekdays, until 6 or 7 weekends. (313) 793-2853.

Until recently this was the popular Reynolds Berry Farm and Cider Mill. Now it's owned by Carolyn and Jim Skinner. Jim is a chef from Detroit (he once worked at the legendary London Chop House) who describes their move to the country as a "mid-life crisis." (He's 50.) He says he had never tasted better cider than that made on this 20-acre farm. Some 17 varieties are grown here, pressed into cider with a rack and cloth press when they have at least five varieties to blend. The secret, Jim feels, is not to put too many Northern Spies or other tart varieties into the blend. By the last two weeks of October, you get cider with the fullest variety of flavors.

Skinner will be making doughnuts throughout the day on weekends, so customers will have the special treat of eating them while truly fresh. There is homemade candy, honey, maple syrup, and an expanding array of things like wooden toys and furniture.

2 Armada's Apple Orchard

In the northeastern corner of Macomb County, half a mile north of Armada. at 75600 North Ave. From the main four-corners in Armade, take North Ave. straight north. Open September-December, 10-6. (313) 784-8448.

This old-fashioned U-pick apple orchard also sells cider and caramel apples.

3 Blake's Big Apple Orchard

1 mile south of downtown Armada at North Ave. and 33 Mile Rd. in northern Macomb County. From the main four-corners, take North Ave. south one mile. Open May-December. (313) 784-9710.

A big selection of U-pick fruits and vegetables are grown on this 90-acre farm: apples, pears, peaches, pumpkins, tomatoes, usually

Port Austin

Caseville
10

Pigeon
142 Elkton
Bad Axe
Harbor Beach
142

Sebewaing

Lake
Huron

Caro
Cass
City

Vassar

Millington

North
Branch
18
2

Sandusky
Port Sanilac

Marlette

Croswell
13
Lexington

Lapeer
1

Imlay City Capac

Almont
7

Romeo
12

4 2
3

Richmond

New
Haven
5,10,
11,14

8
Lakeport
Port
Huron

9
St. Clair

Marine
City

New Baltimore

Utica

Lake
St. Clair
Mt. Clemens

Algonac

Canada

Key

7   Cider Mills & Apple Or-
        chards: see pp. 195-200

140   State Highway

12   Federal Highway

   City or town

Cider Mills & Apple Orchards
MACOMB COUNTY & THE THUMB

20% below market price. One of the few places with U-pick peaches. Because pickers must be careful to pick only the ripe peaches, most peach farmers don't let the public near their trees.

Animal farm, wagon rides, pony rides.

4 Blake's Orchard and Cider Mill

17985 Armada Center Rd., 3 miles west of Armada in northern Macomb County. **Open** *June 1-December 23. (313) 784-5343.*

Run by the same family as the Big Apple Orchard, this 400-acre farm is more entertainment-oriented. It also features fall pears, apples, and pumpkins. 30 varieties of apples make for good cider.

For visitors there are 20-minute tours of the 150-acre orchard on a tractor-train/trolley ($1), an animal petting farm, and demonstrations of pressing apple cider (a 45-minute operation).

5 Bowerman's Westview Orchards

65075 Van Dyke (M-53) at 30 Mile Rd., 2 miles south of Romeo. From M-53/Van Dyke, take Romeo exit, follow signs to Orchards, Downtown to old part of the road. **Open** *July-April, Monday-Sunday 8-7. (313) 752-3123.*

Fall fruits sold already picked include peaches, pears, plums, and apples. Vegetables include sweet corn, broccoli, squash, onions, and winter cabbage. Also sweet cider and honey. Romeo is an especially old country town, settled in the early 1820s, known for its beautiful historic houses.

6 Coon Creek Orchard and Cider Mill

78777 Coon Creek Rd., 4 miles northwest of Armada in northwestern Macomb County. Call for directions. **Open** *daily July-November. (313) 784-5062.*

Fall fruits include peaches, raspberries, apricots, pears, apples, and pumpkins. Also, petting farm, hayride, and cider.

7 Hill's Orchards

Some 18 miles east of Saginaw and 25 miles northeast of Flint, about 6 miles southwest of Caro. At M-81 and Fenner Rd., a mile east of Watrousville. **Open** *daily year-round 9-6. (517) 673-6894.*

A big produce market at an 80-year-old fruit farm features apples grown here and local produce in season. Cider is made from some half-dozen apple varieties as long as the supply of apples lasts, usually into early summer. There are also 25 flavors of ice cream.

8   McCallum Orchard

About 13 miles northwest of Port Huron and 4 miles northwest of Lakeport. From M-25 about a mile north of Lakeport State Park, go west on Harris Rd. 3 miles. 10 miles north of Port Huron on M-25 and 3 miles west on Harris Road. **Open** *May-December, 8-6 daily. (313) 327-6394.*

U-pick fall produce includes raspberries, plums, peaches, pears, grapes, apples, pumpkins, and squash. (All this is also available picked.) Also for sale: cider and doughnuts, plus jam, apple butter, popcorn, honey, mums, and gifts. This is quite a rural place, not a suburbanized farm destination.

9   Pankiewicz Farm Cider Mill

Near Richmond between Mount Clemens and Port Huron. Take I-94 to 26 Mile exit, go about 2 miles east to County Line Road. Turn north (left), go 3 miles to Lindsey Road. Turn right to farm. **Open** *2nd week of September through October. Weekends only, 10-5.*

The little 12-acre apple orchard here is tended as a hobby by autoworker Stanley Pankiewicz. He blends five or six standard varieties to make his cider, and also makes fresh doughnuts.

10   Rapp Orchards

(63545 Van Dyke Rd. between 29 and 30 Mile roads, less than 4 miles south of Romeo and 10 miles northeast of Rochester. West side of road. From M-53/Van Dyke, take Romeo exit, follow signs to Orchards, Downtown to old part of the road. **Open** *daily year-round. (313) 752-2117.*

Many fall fruits and vegetables are grown and sold here: pears, plums, peaches, and apples — Red and Golden Delicious, McIntosh, Jonathans, Empire, Red Gold, Ida Red, Paula Red, Fuji, and Mutsu. Jams and honey, and fresh cider are available in season. (It's pressed elsewhere, from their own apples, on a rack-and-cloth press.) U-pick pumpkins. Sandwiches and cheese are for sale at a deli counter; a picnic area may be installed soon.

11 Southview Orchards

2 1/2 miles south of Romeo at 63910 Van Dyke Rd. (M-53). From M-53/Van Dyke, take Romeo exit, follow signs to Orchards, Downtown to old part of the road. **Open** *August-February, 8:30-6:30. (313) 752-2512.*

Over 40 acres here produce peaches, pears, plums, and apples. Over 15 varieties of apples include the legendary Golden Russet, the flavorful Mutsu, and the Northern Spy. Bushels of apples start at $8. Cider is made beginning October 1, when the apples are mature enough to make to make a good drink.

12 Stony Creek Orchard and Cider Mill

3 1/2 miles west of Romeo and about 10 miles northeast of Rochester at 2961 West 32 Mile Rd. , due east of downtown Romeo. 2 1/2 miles east of Rochester Rd. **Open** *September-March. (313) 752-2453.*

Apples, pears, cider, and pumpkins. Also, honey, jams and jellies, maple syrup. U-pick on weekends in autumn.

13 Tringali Orchards

4 miles north of Lexington and 24 miles north of Port Huron at the base of the Thumb. 3457 Lakeshore Rd. (M-25). **Open** *year-round 10-6, daily except Wednesday. (313) 359-8158*

Year-round produce and fruit market with cold storage for home-grown apples, potatoes, onions, squash, etc. Peaches in season (no U-pick). U-pick or picked apples and pears. In fall, cider. Also, herbs and spices, eggs, honey, and popcorn.

14 Verellen Orchards & Cider Mill

63260 Van Dyke (M-53), 3 miles south of Romeo. From M-53/Van Dyke, take Romeo exit, follow signs to Orchards, Downtown to old part of the road. Open July-May. (313) 752-2989

Homegrown fruit for sale picked: peaches, apples, plums, pears, and grapes. Fresh doughnuts daily. Cider in season.
Also for sale: honey, eggs, potatoes, jams and jellies.

SOUTHEAST MICHIGAN

▼   *The numbers before each entry are keyed to the map on p. 202.*

1 Alber Orchard and Cider Mill

Bethel Church Rd., Manchester. 2 1/2 miles north of Manchester on M-52, east on Bethel Church Rd., 3 1/2 miles. **Open** *from first in Friday September through Thanksgiving, 9-6 daily. (313) 428-7758.*

Situated in the picturesque hills near the quaint village of Manchester, Albers has been in the same family for a century. Some of the century-old Northern Spy trees are still producing. Albers makes some of the best tasting cider in the state. Its sweet flavor usually peaks around the latter part of October. The traditional rack and cloth press has also been here over a century.

It's a small orchard, only ten acres, but there are 28 varieties of apples. Most rare is the tangy, sweet McCoun, which ripens in the second or third week of October. It's well worth asking for.

There's no U-pick at Albers, but they sell delicious doughnuts from the Washtenaw Dairy in Ann Arbor and German pretzels from Benny's Bakery in Saline. Albers' caramel apples are also excellent.

Grazing sheep are a common sight on hilly back roads in the

Country singer Wendell Asplin makes rich, thick cider on his 80-acre farm east of Durand. The singer of two Nashville hits, he presents live country music at Asplin Farms Friday nights from mid-April to mid-December.

southwestern part of Washtenaw County. It has long had more sheep than any other county east of the Mississippi.

2 Apple Charlie's

38035 South Haven Road, 1 mile south of New Boston, 6 miles south of Detroit Metro Airport. Take I-275 exit B11, then 1 mile west. **Open** *August until end of January. Cider Labor Day until end of January. Daily 9 until dark. (313) 753-9380.*

Apple Charlie Grover has been working here since age 15. He maintains a good cider has a good foundation of Jonathans, Winesaps, Red Delicious, and a few McIntosh for aroma. Too many Macs and you get a watery cider. Too many Red Delicious and you've got too sweet and syrupy a blend.

3 Davies Orchard & Cider Mill

On Willow Road, 9 miles southwest of Detroit Metro Airport. Take I-275 to exit 8 (Will Carleton), west 1/4 mile to Waltz Road, north 2 miles to Willow Road, west on Willow, 1 1/4 miles to orchard. **Open** *mid-September through November, 9-7. (313) 654-8893 or 654-6019.*

U-pick and picked apples (ten varieties), plums, pumpkins, honey and fresh apple cider.

4 Frank's Orchard

Between Ann Arbor and Dexter on Dexter-Ann Arbor Road, 1 mile west of Zeeb Road, north side of road. From I-94, take Zeeb Road exit north, then west on Dexter-Ann Arbor Road. **Open** *September-November. Weekends 9-7, weekdays to dark. (313) 662-5064.*

U-pick and picked apples, plus cider and picked pumpkins.

5 Hideaway Orchard

On M-52, 3 miles south of Adrian. 8 miles north of the Ohio-Michigan border. **Open** *end of June through January, 9-5. Closed Mondays. (517) 263-0060.*

Homegrown fruits for sale include sweet and tart cherries, plums, nectarines, peaches, and apples. These can be made up into fruit baskets. Fresh cider in fall. Vegetables include squash, peppers, tomatoes, and pumpkins. Also: jams, jellies, maple syrup, honey.

6 Kapnick Orchards

4 miles southeast of Tecumseh. From M-50 less than a mile east of Tecumseh, go 4 miles south on Rogers Hwy. **Open** *year-round. Monday-Saturday 8-8, Sunday 10-8. (517) 423-7419.*

This big operation buys its vegetables from other area farmers (and from California in the winter) and grows its own fruits on 140 acres. There are over 20 varieties of apples. Also available are peaches, pears, plums, and nectarines. You can pick your own cherries, strawberries, raspberries, and blueberries. The Kapnicks press their own cider, and have a bakery which makes fresh doughnuts.

A festival is held here the second weekend of each October. The entertainment, food and drink, and activities draw some 10,000 visitors a day.

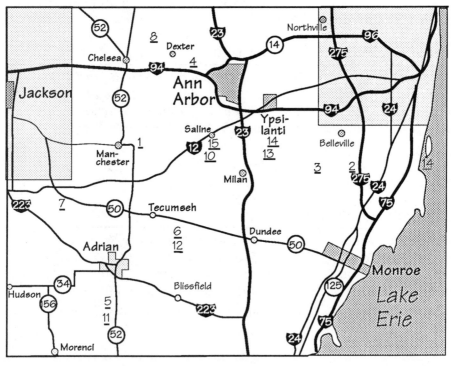

Cider & Apples
SOUTHEASTERN
MICHIGAN

KEY

<u>4 6</u> Cider mills & apple orchards, pp. 200-205

(140) State Highway

12 Federal Highway

⊚ ▨ Towns and cities

7 Keeney Orchards

5300 Monroe Road (M-50) west of Tipton. Tipton is five miles west of Tecumseh. **Open** *September and October. (517) 431-2400.*

The Keeneys raise 60 to 70 acres of **apples**. The standard varieties are available: McIntosh, Jonathan, Red and Yellow Delicious, and Ida Red. The operation is totally U-pick. They charge $5 a bushel. Hidden Lake Garden, a beautiful landscape garden/ conservatory/ natural area owned and run by Michigan State University, is nearby. It's a fine place for fall hiking.

8 Lakeview Farm and Cider Mill

12075 Island Lake Road, 4 miles west of Dexter and about 12 miles northwest of Ann Arbor. From I-94, take the Baker Rd. exit, north on Baker to Dexter, west on Main Street to Y at Huron River. Take right fork under bridge. At the next Y (soon), take left fork onto Island Lake Rd. **Open** *for cider September 15 to Thanksgiving. Tuesday-Saturday, 9-5. U-Pick raspberries in August. (313) 426-2782 (in season a recording gives callers daily update of which apples are ripe and what blend was used in the last cider pressing).*

A dozen years ago, Woody and Marilyn Begres dropped out of academia (he was a tenured professor) and started this fruit farm. They planted 2,000 apples trees on their 15 acres, plus raspberries and strawberries. The 27 varieties include some famous and wonderful antiques: Rhode Island Greenings, and Newton Pippins.

Cider is pressed Tuesdays and Fridays, usually with five to ten varieties. This is the only cider mill we know in which the varieties of apples used are listed for the buyer. This way those who prefer to stock up on a blend of their particular liking will know ahead what's available. Some like cider with a Golden Delicious base, some like the tarter Northern Spies, and others want Paula Reds in a blend.

Also available are doughnuts, Indian corn, gourds, pumpkins (both U-pick and picked), U-pick raspberries into October, homemade raspberry and strawberry syrup, dried flowers and wreaths.

9 Lesser Farms

On Island Lake Road, 5 miles west of Dexter and about 12 miles northwest of Ann Arbor. From I-94, take the Baker Rd. exit, north on Baker to Dexter, west on Main Street to Y at Huron River. Take right fork under bridge. At the next Y (soon), take left fork onto Island Lake

Rd. **Open** *summer and fall: Mon.-Sat. 9-6, Sun. 1-6. (313) 426-8009.*

This 450-acre farm primarily raises hogs and cattle, but it also has an orchard. Red Haven peaches sell for $12 per 3/4 bushel. They're in short supply, so order ahead. There are plenty of prune plums and a seven-acre apple orchard. Varieties include Northern Spy and go for $9 a bushel. Lesser also sells honey from his hundred beehives: for $3.50 for 3 pounds or $6 for 6 pounds.

Island Lake Road is an especially scenic country road (partly dirt) that leads into the band of glacial lakes making up the beautiful Pinckney Recreation Area. There's also a commercial trout farm on the road. On the way to Lesser Farms, about three miles west of the second Y, Dexter Townhall Road leads north to the beautiful Silver Lake and many miles of hiking trails through dense upland forests and wetlands full of wildlife.

10 William Lutz

11030 Macon Road south of Saline. From U.S. 12 just east of the mill pond at the west end of town, take Monroe Street 4 miles south. **Open** *September-October. U-pick after October 16. (313) 429-5145.*

Apples.

11 Marvin's Fairfield Orchard

On M-52 4 1/2 miles south of Adrian and the M-52/ U.S. 223 intersection and 7 miles north of Ohio state line. **Open** *August-December daily 9-6, Sunday 12-6. (517) 436-3378.*

This 70-year-old orchard grows peaches, pears, plums, and apples on 20 acres. Some antique apple varieties are here which you won't easily find elsewhere. The Red Astrachan came originally from Russia in 1835. It's an early summer apple that's good for applesauce and pies. The Black Arkansas, a hard apple that ripens late in the season, is a good keeper. There are also Russets and Transparents. A newer variety worth asking for is the Golden Blushing, an attractive cross between Yellow Delicious and Jonathan.

There's also a cider mill here, and Mrs. Marvin, a schoolteacher, is famous for the doughnuts she makes on fall weekends, several batches a day.

12 Red Apple Orchard

4 1/2 miles southeast of Tecumseh at the corner of Billmyer Hwy. and Sutton Rd. From M-50 about 4 miles east of Tecumseh, go south on Ridge Road about 3 miles to Sutton, go west 1/2 mile to orchard. **Open** *for cider second week of September through first week of December. Monday-Saturday 9-5:30, Sun 11-5-30. (517) 423-4012.*

Fourteen kinds of apples are grown on this 23-acre fruit farm. The cider preferred by customers here is a blend of half tart and half sweet apples. By the last week of September and on through November you get the peak flavor that comes from having the most variety of types to blend with. You can also pick your own apples for just $6 a bushel (approximately 50 pounds).

13 Wasem Fruit Farms

6580 Judd Road, 6 miles northeast of Milan. 3 miles east, 1 mile south of U.S. 23. **Open** *for cider usually from Labor Day until May daily 9-6. After Christmas, cider is pressed Thursday mornings, doughnuts made Friday mornings. (313) 482-2342.*

Leola Wasem and her husband planted the first semi-dwarf apple trees in the region back in the 1940s. Now her daughter and son-in-law run the orchard, raising peaches, pears, plums, and cherries as well as a whopping 26 varieties of apples. Try the tasty Prime Gold which ripens by Labor Day. An antique apple grown here is the Golden Russet.

The rack and cloth press takes a blend of at least three to five varieties to make a cider well liked by locals. Also sold are popcorn grown in Indiana, honey, and apple butter. You can also pick your own apples.

14 Wiard's Orchards

South of Ypsilanti. Take I-94 to Huron St. (exit 183) at Ypsilanti, then go south 4 miles. Follow the signs. **Open** *year-round, 10-6 daily. (313) 482-7744.*

From a farm established in 1853, Wiard's has grown into a verita-ble circus of attractions. The centerpiece remains the apples. Nine varieties are grown on 200 acres. The rack and cloth press blends as many of the nine as are ripe, with the peak number in the first or second week of October. You can pick your own apples, peaches, and pears in the fall, as well as asparagus, strawberries, cherries, pears, and peaches earlier in the season.

This is a fun place to take kids, but if you like your farm stands and U-picks pure and simple, it's not the place for you. The atmosphere in fall is more like a continual country fair. Tour busses lumber down the dirt road to U.S. 23. There's live country music every weekend in September and October from noon to 6. There are fire engine rides, train rides, wagon rides, pony rides, a petting farm, a haunted barn, orchard tours, apple butter-making demonstrations, face-painting, candle-making, and even a straw maze for kids.

Along with fresh produce and tropical fruit purchased elsewhere, there's plenty else to eat coming from a full-line bakery and butcher shop. Hot dogs, caramel apples, candies, and nuts are also for sale.

15 Windy Ridge Orchard and Cider Mill

1 mile south of Saline. From U.S. 12 in the center of town, at the intersection of Saline-Ann Arbor Road, go south on Saline-Milan Road (the continuation of Saline-Ann Arbor Road). Orchard is in 1 mile. **Open** *weekends mid-September through October. (313) 426-2900.*

Apples and pumpkins, fresh cider and doughnuts. Hayrides and petting corral.

SOUTHERN MICHIGAN

▼   *The numbers before each entry are keyed to the map on p. 207.*

1 Canaan Farm Orchard

On 44th Street, 2 miles north of Climax, half way of between Kalamazoo and Battle Creek. From I-94 take Exit 88, go 2 miles east on Michigan Ave. to 44th St., south 1 mile; orchard on right. **Open 9-6** *daily in September and October. Cider pressed mid-September through Halloween. (616) 746-4066.*

This old farm from the 1860s has been run by Brad Roof, a descendant of the original owner, since 1986. Here you can find one of the old, less pretty, but much more flavorful Red Delicious strains. Roof prides himself in waiting for his apples to be fully ripe before pressing them into **cider**, something not all cider mills are careful to do. His 20-acre orchard grows nine varieties of **apples**, all of which he uses when ripe in his blend. Also for sale are **pumpkins** and **squash**.

2 Glei's Orchards

A few miles northeast of Hillsdale and east of Jonesville at 3500 Milnes Rd. From U.S. 12 between Moscow and Jonesville, turn south at the flasher light onto Milnes Rd., go south 4 miles. **Open** *year-round, Monday through Saturday 8-6. (517) 437-4495*

This big facility grew out of a farm started in the 1890s by Karl Gleis. Now it includes a two-acre bedding plant nursery, Christmas tree farm, and fresh produce market. The 80 acres of apple trees (25 kinds in all) produce 30,000 bushels a year. Those 2 1/2 inches and smaller are screened and used for cider. (Many of the rest go into supermarkets.) Controlled-atmosphere storage keeps apples fresh and crisp all year. Varieties include the crunchy, flavorful Gala, the Jonagold (today the #2 apple in Europe), and, coming into

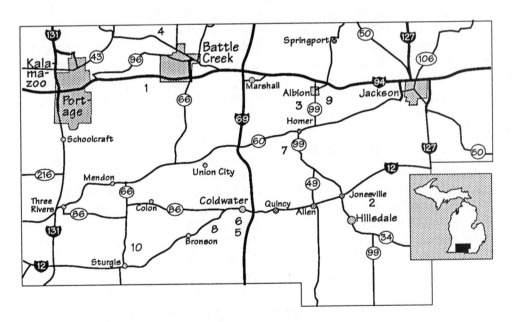

Cider Mills &
Apple Orchards
SOUTHERN
MICHIGAN

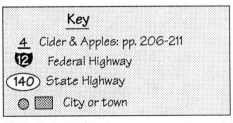

Key

4   Cider & Apples: pp. 206-211

12   Federal Highway

(140)   State Highway

◉ ▦   City or town

production in 1992, the Fuji, which co-owner David Glei says "has an excellent flavor but looks like trash."

Cider is made from September 10 to May. Unlike most cider mills, Gleis puts a small amount of potassium sorbate to extend the shelf life of the cider it sells directly to customers. They use a couple of dozen varieties in their rack and cloth press.

The farm market features homegrown vegetables in season (tomatoes, melons, cukes, peppers, sweet corn, cabbage, broccoli, cauliflower, and squash), supplemented by tropical fruit and produce bought at the big Detroit markets in the off-season.

U.S. 12 from Clinton to Jonesville and Allen is dotted with interesting visitor destinations: the engaging Southern Michigan Railroad that runs between Clinton and Tecumseh (weekends only, summer and fall), and St. Joseph's shrine in the Irish Hills, Stagecoach Stop (an exceptionally entertaining family-run make-believe village, worth an all-day excursion, open weekends through September), and the Grosvenor House in Jonesville, a historic house museum that's the apogee of Gilded Age splendor (open weekends, 2-5, June through September). Finally, in Michigan's self-proclaimed antiques capital of Allen, there's the Green Top Antique Mall (a charmingly quirky collection of buildings just west of town) and many other antique shops. For more on the area, see *Hunts' Highlights of Michigan*.

3 Harrison's Orchard

About a mile south of Albion on Condit Road. (Albion is between Jackson and Marshall on I-94). From M-99/Superior St., Albion's main street, go south over the river and take the first right. Orchard is in a farm on the left. **Open** *from Labor Day until apples run out, sometime between January and March. Monday through Saturday 9-5, also open until Christmas on Sunday 1-5. (517) 629-6647.*

The scale, simplicity, and picture-perfect tidiness of this family operation is like something out of the 1940s. The turn-of-the-century farm's a classic, and neat as a pin. The cheerful sales room and cider-making building are super-clean, painted fresh each year. **Apples** include some uncommon old favorites: Northern Spy, Red Rome, Tolman Sweet, and Winesap. The cider, made with a rack and cloth press, is multifaceted and unusually good.

People in Albion rave about the ladyfinger popcorn, sold dried right on tiny ears. (It's too small to fit into a normal sheller. You shell it by rubbing two ears together.) Popped, it's very small and tasty. Pumpkins are also sold here in fall.

4 Hillcrest Orchards

Between Battle Creek and Kalamazoo on North 46th St. From M-89 between Battle Creek and Gull Lake, go north 1/2 mile on 46th St. **Open** *late August to December. Monday-Saturday 9-6, Sunday 10-6. (616) 731-4312.*

This big 800-acre farm has 600 acres of apple trees growing 19 varieties. Red Delicious is the most common variety on the farm, not because it tastes best, but because of its eye appeal.

The cider-making philosophy here is to use as many kinds in the blend as possible. The press is the newer, faster hydraulic type which uses rice hulls as a pressing aid. The maker lets the freshly pressed cider sit 24 hours to allow the sediment to settle out, create an clearer cider that has a longer shelf life. They make over 30,000 gallons a year here.

5 McCollough Brothers

About 5 miles south of Coldwater on South Angola Road. From U.S. 69 take the Copeland Road exit just inside the Michigan line. Go west briefly on Copeland to Angola Road (Old 27), then north 2 1/2 miles. **Open** *September 1-November 1. 9-5 daily (Sundays if someone is on hand).*

Wendell McCollough's dairy farm has had a farm stand for over half a century. Now apple cider is the main draw. The 39-acre orchard produces most of today's standard varieties. This is near Amish territory, and four to eight Amish pickers take in the annual harvest. The old screw press turns out about 1,500 gallons of cider a year. Also available in season are pumpkins, squash, and honey.

6 Pleasant Acres Farms

1 1/2 miles south of Coldwater on Old U.S. 27. From I-69, take the first exit south of Coldwater, follow Business Route 69 signs toward town. **Open** *from mid-May through Thanksgiving, depending on weather. 10-5:30 Monday through Saturday at least. In season (July into October) open daily 9-6. (517) 278-8689.*

Farm stand sells its own produce in season, supplemented by wholesalers. **Apples, peaches, pears,** and **plums** are grown here, along with asparagus, strawberries, sweet corn, tomatoes, melons, and many other vegetables. Cider is made in fall.

7 Rowbotham's Orchard

*Southwest of Homer and southeast of Marshall on 23 Mile Rd. between T Dr S and County Line Rd. **Open** for apples Sept 1, for cider October 15 to Christmas. 9-5 daily. (517) 542-3958.*

This is a place where you can get some of the best cider anywhere. Some people like it so much they buy a dozen jugs to freeze and enjoy throughout the year. Unlike most cider mills, the owner here won't even begin pressing his apples until mid-October, when the full, ripe flavor of the varieties used has been achieved.

Phil Rowbotham has been running the cider mill for 52 years. The 40-acre farm earlier belonged to his grandmother. It's a small operation, turning out about 8,000 gallons a year. Rowbotham says the best cider comes from November apples, when they've had time to get more body. His half-century old-fashioned rack and cloth press requires no filtering, giving the cider a little bit of sediment to add character. "When you can read a newspaper through a gallon," he states, "you haven't got good-bodied cider."

McIntosh, Jonathan, plus Red and Yellow Delicious are used to make the cider. Eleven varieties of apples are for sale, including Empires and Gala. Fresh doughnuts are also made here, and squash and pumpkins are for sale in season. It's a picturesque, pleasantly old-fashioned farm that makes for a pretty drive from Albion, Marshall, or Hillsdale.

8 Schlubatis Orchard

One mile south of Coldwater on Old U. S. 27, the Old Angold Road. Take I-69 exit 10. Open all year, daily, 8-6. (517) 278-8887.

One of the larger orchards in the region. Willard Schlubatis has 135 acres of apple trees which he has been tending since moving here in 1942. By mid-September the cider, made with Jonathans, Golden Delicious, and other varieties, is getting sweet. Around Labor Day his Bartlett pears are getting ripe, and he also sells a few squash.

9 Sweet Seasons Orchard

Close to M-60, just west of Concord, at 15787 Allman Rd. Concord is about 10-11 miles southwest of Jackson and 7 miles southeast of Albion. Allman is an east-west road where M-60 angles away; if you're coming from the west, make a hard left a little ways before you come to the blinker light. From the east, it's the first road west of the blinker. Look for sign on M-60. Drive west on Allman about 3 miles. **Open** *daily 10-6 from the day after Labor Day to the day before Christmas. (517) 524-8535.*

It's a pretty drive out to this tidy family operation. Plums, pears, raspberries, and tart pie cherries are also grown here; the early fruits are sold at the Jackson Farmers' Market. In addition to common commercial apples, a number of old-time apples are here: Snow Apple, Wolf River, and Steel Reds. Cider is made on the premises. The kitchen makes six kinds of donuts, caramel apples, peanut butter popcorn balls, and apple cookies.

10 Weiderman's Fruit Farm

28749 Hackman Road, 5 miles north of Sturgis. Go north from town on M-66, then 3/4 mile east on Hackman. **Cider mill open** *September through December, 9-6 Monday-Saturday.* **Market open** *May through December. (616) 651-2273.*

This cider man dates from the 1940s. The 30-acre farm includes a **pear** orchard, asparagus and strawberry patches, and a sizable vegetable growing area. The eight-acre **apple** orchard is planted with 10 varieties. Peak time for **cider**, pressed in a rack and cloth press, is Halloween. Owner Allen Weiderman believes the more varieties in the blend, the better. **Doughnuts** are also made here in fall.

Not all Red Delicious apples have an insipid taste. Sometimes you can get an older strain (there are some 27 different types of Red Delicious in all) that doesn't have the now-famous Red Delicious perfect appearance but tastes a lot better.

Most apples shipped long distances to supermarkets from places like Washington State are developed for looks rather than flavor. The newer strains of Red Delicious, America's most popular apple, are especially insipid. Michigan is fortunate to have a century-and-a-half-old heritage of commercial apple-growing and a cool climate producing dozens of kinds of flavorful apples, including less than beautiful antique varieties like this.

Outstanding Bakeries

In choosing bakeries for this chapter, our criteria have been mainly how good they are, and to a lesser degree how unusual, with consideration also given to atmosphere, value, and location. It's especially interesting to visit bakeries that take you into the everyday life of very different worlds close to home. We have gone out of our way to include a big sampling of ethnic bakeries (Michigan is outstanding in the variety of its ethnic bakeries) and to search out the best bakeries in popular vacation areas.

In the end, the best part about getting interested in better bread and baked goods is that you may be led to expand your own horizons by sampling other bakeries (they can be in unlikely places, such as the 24-hour Shell gas station in Homer, Michigan), and maybe even by baking more yourself.

Bakeries are arranged by region, starting with Metro Detroit, followed by the rest of the Lower Peninsula (page 237) and the Upper Peninsula (page 281).

METRO DETROIT

DETROIT — EASTSIDE

1 Bommarito Bakery Dolceria Palermo

Tuesday through Saturday 8 to 8.
21830 Greater Mack at Avalon, across Mack from Meldrum Bros. Nursery in St. Clair Shores. From I-94, take Vernier exit, go 1/2 mile east on Vernier to Mack, then left on Mack to bakery. (313) 772-6731.

The food-loving eastside Italians in Detroit's Eastern Market produce business mention Bommarito's right off the bat when asked about Italian bakeries. Their cannoli are deemed outstanding. These puff-pastry cylinders are filled the traditional way with cooked-down whipped cream flavored with cinnamon and chocolate chunks. The ends are dipped in toasted almonds. It's quite an affair for just 75¢. The same cream filling is used for *cassata*, rich

Metro Detroit BAKERIES

cakes made with or without rum.

"The original Italian bakery, family owned and operated since 1925," proclaims the sign behind the counter of this big bakery and Italian food store. Founders Jim and Rose Bommarito, whose portraits loom large over the bakery counter, came from Sicily to Detroit during the great auto boom. Today their son-in-law, Sam Valenti, and granddaughters Frances Cottone, Roseanne Valenti, Christine Corrado, and Grace Adams run the bakery, now at its third location. Grace's husband Eric is the baker; he first started working here at the age of 14.

Italian bakeries have traditionally supplied almost everything that's a must for a real Italian wedding, except for fresh fruits and the wedding meal itself. That means Bommarito's carries confetti (colored Jordan almonds), *gelati* (ice cream) and lemon *granita* (ice) made in the store, along with traditional butter and almond paste cookies and Italian angel wings (made with sour cream and butter, they're $3 a half pound), and wedding cakes so complex they're like architecture, with stairways and arches connecting as many as five or seven cakes. "Italians have always been big on *fou fou*," explains Chris Corrado. For examples, just check out the cake photographs in the album in the center shelf display.

Bommarito's other famous specialty is the sub sandwich, a delicious and satisfying affair of Polish ham, hard salami, provolone, lettuce, onion, and peppers on a chewy bun that holds in all the juice from the homemade Italian dressing. It's a generous meal for just $2.19 ($3.19 with turkey; also available with roast beef and chicken). (Subs keep well enough for lunch the next day, incidentally.) For evening parties, where the six-foot sub is a favorite. Sub rolls can be ordered ahead of time. The same bread dough, crusty on the outside, chewy in the center, is used in various rolls (some with softer crusts), square loaves ($1/lb.), bigger baguettes almost two feet long ($1.39), and various rolls. For health-conscious people who like to have a slightly sweet morsel with after-dinner coffee, there are simple sesame cookies.

Typical American pizza is made here at lunch and dinner, sold by the slice for 79¢. But for a real treat, Corrado suggests ordering Italian spinguini (pronounced SPIN-june-ee) an hour ahead. (A $12 half tray feeds six to eight. It's a bread-dough pizza topped by parmesan cheese, olive oil, bread crumbs, and lots of onions. To be authentic, it should have some anchovies, too.

The grocery section has many easy-to-prepare foods that are tasty, often healthy, and reasonably priced for modest budgets of regular folks. There are imported pastas in uncommon shapes; the usual Italian cheeses, prosciutto, hams, and salamis; crusty hard rolls that come out of the oven about 10:45; and, for about $2.50 a pound, frozen ravioli, gnocchi (potato dumplings), and cappelletti (little cheese-filled dough hats) made at Mrs. Turri's Italian Foods on Detroit's east side.

The Bommarito clan has decided to scale down their business and keep it at a size where the family can run it without much extra help. A foray into mass-production supplying subs to the K Mart lunch counters meant "the business was running us," says Corrado. "Pride goes down when you become so involved in trying to produce high volume. Now we do wholesale-retail, but our wholesale customers pick up from us. We only have one truck. Wedding cakes are delivered by my dad or my brother. We know who our customers are."

2 Josef's French Pastry Shop

Tuesday through Saturday 8-6, Sunday 8-1:30. Closed Monday.
21150 Mack on the corner of Brys in Grosse Pointe Woods, almost in St. Clair Shores. Look for the dark purple awning. From I-94, take the Vernier exit, go east on Vernier, then north (left) onto Mack. Shop is a few blocks past Farmer Jack. (313) 881-5710.

Josef's rules the top-of-the-line market of Detroit's east side from its elegant, friendly shop on Mack Avenue, where that major artery becomes a well-manicured boulevard of service and retail shops catering to the affluent Grosse Pointes. Several tables by the front windows make this a pleasant place for a snack or lunch. Despite the setting, this isn't particularly pricey; a danish and coffee (in a styrofoam cup) are under $1.50. For a quick lunch, there's pizza ($2 a slice), quiche ($2.25), and pasta salads ($5.50/ lb.) However, don't hope to take anything out to enjoy at one of the Grosse Pointes' beautiful parks on Lake St. Clair; their parks are for residents only, and always have been.

Discriminating lovers of baked goods give Josef's high marks for both quality and eye appeal, and, all things considered, the prices aren't bad, either. Josef's doesn't just make the beautiful French pastries its name suggests, though they are indeed excellent — not over-sweet, with lots of fresh fruit, semi-sweet chocolate, and whipped cream that has layers of flavor. Brass-trimmed showcases set off pastries, tortes, morning sweet rolls, and cookies like jewelry trimmed with fruit and chocolate gemstones.

Refrigerated pastries (all $2.10) are fairly light affairs like mandarin oranges on a chocolate shell with a Bavarian cream filling, and kiwi and strawberry slices on flan tartes. Mousses, custards, butter creams and whipped creams, and fresh fruits, locally grown when in season, come in many beguiling flavors (including chocolate raspberry, white chocolate mousse, and lemon) in roll cakes ($5.45-$6.10, serving 6) and tortes ($10.45 to $15.45 for 8 slices). A big variety of cookies are elegant and delicious. A special treat are florentines (75¢), lacy-crisp continental favorites made of cream and sugar dipped in semi-sweet chocolate. Cream puffs shaped like a swan are $1.50. So are excellent chocolate eclairs.

As for breads, Josef's doesn't just do the fancy stuff. Jewish ryes

Josef Bogdosian of Josef's French Pastry Shop in Grosse Pointe Woods, presides over a big busy bakery that turns out delectable classic pastries with custards and cremes, and often semisweet chocolate and fresh fruit. His own favorite? Chocolate cake with chocolate icing.

and pumpernickels are hearty, with the chewy, flavorful crust created by steam in the oven and by multiple risings that aren't hurried. They make attractive rolls, too. Brioche ($2.25) is baked for weekends. Dark-light braids of rye and pumpernickel bread could be the centerpiece of a beautiful party bread arrangement.

Josef Bogdosian became involved in baking when he was waiting to be inducted into the army in the 1960s. He took a temporary job at Ranier's Pastry Shop on Seven Mile at Livernois. But his induction notice never came, and baking turned into his career. After working at an eastside French patisserie, he established this bakery in 1971. With 16 to 18 full-time bakers, he has quite an array of specialists at work each night. Day-old goods are donated to a soup kitchen.

☛ EXACT PRICES have been given to provide the best possible relative price comparison information. **It is expected**, of course, that **prices will increase** over the life of this book.

DETROIT — DOWNTOWN AND MIDTOWN, including HAMTRAMCK

3 Astoria Pastry Shop

Monday-Saturday 8 a.m.-11:30 p.m., Sunday 9 a.m.-11 p.m.
541 Monroe Street, across the street from Trappers Alley in Greektown. (313) 772-6731.

The spiffy new location of this longtime Greek pastry shop has definitely been designed with an eye to the huge amount of visitor traffic in Detroit's most popular visitor destination. Now it offers ice cream cones, and quite a few tables so you can sit down and enjoy a cup of coffee with sweets. The spinach pie ($1) makes a nice snack if you don't feel like buying an entire meal at a nearby restaurant. All the traditional honey-nut pastries of Greece and the Middle East are here, some in pure form and also with a new twist, like chocolate baklava (80¢). If you plan to buy these in quantity, you'd do better on price by going to an Arab pastry shop in East Dearborn (see pages 229, 232, and 236), where competition keeps prices lower. But Astoria offers a much wider range of things, including American standards, lots of kinds of macaroons, and Italian favorites like toasted biscotti (some dipped in chocolate and walnut) and cannoli.

Greek breads (about $1 a loaf) are on hand, crusty and hard on the outside, soft and sponge-like on the inside, perfect for sopping up salad oils and pan juices. With olives, pan-fried kasseri cheese dredged in flour, sliced fresh tomatoes, and cold, cold retsina wine, it's the basis of a simple, delicious meal enjoyed by many native Greeks. If it's bread you want, you might consider looking in at the Monroe Grocery and Bakery a few doors down at 573 Monroe. Now part grocery, part party store, it has decorative arrangements of cans of olive oil and big loaves of bread stacked up on shelves — things that give an idea of an old-fashioned Greektown grocery in the old days, when Greeks really lived on Monroe Street and the vanished neighborhood around it.

4 New Palace Bakery

Monday through Saturday 5 a.m. to 7 p.m.,
9833 Joseph Campau between Yemans and Evaline. Though surrounded by Detroit, Hamtramck can be surprisingly hard to reach,

surrounded by rail lines and old industrial sites. It's just a mile northeast of Detroit's New Center. From Woodward north of Grand, take Holbrook east (right) to Joseph Campau, then left (north). (On-street parking is limited; get a spot where you can and enjoy the walk down this bustling street of small shops.) From I-75 south-bound, exit at Caniff and take Caniff left to Joseph Campau, then right; from I-75 northbound, exit at Holbrook, go right on Holbrook, then left on Joseph Campau. Friday to 8. (313) 875-1334.

The Polish industrial enclave of Hamtramck was developed in a burst in 1914 to house workers at the then-new Dodge Main plant. Today it's an amazingly lively relic of bluecollar neighbor-hoods and shopping districts from the 1930s and 1940s, when streetcars were the main form of everyday transportation and street life was vibrant.

Hamtramck has everything required to keep good ethnic bak-eries going: a big market of immigrants familiar with what their homeland's food is really like (Polish food is appealingly homey and far more interesting than that of neighboring Germany), plus a supply of skilled immigrant bakers willing to work a baker's long hours. Hamtramck has a lot of old Polish-speaking people (their children have mostly moved to the suburbs); it also has many re-cent Polish and Albanian immigrants to freshen the Central European culture. It also doesn't hurt that Hamtramck has low rents and an area-wide reputation as a fun place to with good restaurants and bars.

The New Palace, Hamtramck's oldest and largest bakery, offers the most variety. Owner Barbara Matoski says everything is made from scratch, even the doughnuts, and that's why the frostings and doughs on cakes and cookies aren't sugary sweet, as they are at many bakeries that now use standard American mixes. For $2.90, try the New Palace's sour cream coffee cake with cherries or nuts and raisins, she says, and you'll notice the difference. Coffee cakes, including the excellent danish-type logs swirled with cinnamon, poppyseed, or almonds, are made for the weekends only.

The big sellers here and at every real Polish bakery are the rye bread ($1.30 for a 20-ounce loaf); onion rolls and kaiser rolls (plain, or with poppyseed or sesame), both made fresh daily; spe-cialty cookies like angel wings (a very thin dough fried, then pow-dered with sugar); kolachky (little pastry bow ties filled with fruit jams, $4.50/lb.); and, of course, paczki (pronounced PUNCH-key), the famous Polish fried bread (40¢ apiece). They are traditionally made on Shrove Tuesday to use up the last of the fat banned during Lent. Paczki have become such an area pre-Lenten tradition that now every supermarket promotes Shrove Tuesday as Paczki Day; lines form early here. Many Polish bakeries, including the New Palace, use a richer dough just before Lent.

Once-a-week specialties include rye hard rolls (**Mondays**); Polish bagels (softer because of butter, they come in onion, cheese, potato, salty, and plain; 30¢, on **Tuesdays**); individual strudels, without the buttery crisp pastry (50¢ on **Wednesdays**); salt sticks, onion pillows, and whole wheat rolls on **Thursdays**; and Hungarian horns (danish-like affairs with poppyseed, almond, or cheese filling, 50¢ on **Fridays** and **Saturdays**).

To add to the atmosphere, a good many of the counter staff are young women who have recently arrived from Poland. Sometimes you can hear so much Polish, you'd think you were in Warsaw.

Competition thrives in immigrant neighborhoods, and the customer benefits. You can see for yourself by stopping at various Hamtramck Polish bakeries on trips to Detroit musical events and museums. Start-up immigrant businesses are always angling for an edge; when they draw on the same customer base, that makes for innovations and/or lower prices. Each bakery makes a slightly different paczki, for instance.

Other Hamtramck bakeries are the **New Deluxe Bakery**, 11920 Conant at Eldridge (Conant parallels Joseph Campau eight blocks east of it); the **New Martha Washington Bakery**, 10335 Joseph Campau at Caniff; and **Oaza Bakery & Deli**, 9405 Joseph Campau between Caniff and Holbrook. Tables and deli foods make the Oaza (pronounced oh-A-za) a good stop for sampling Polish foods.

Benches in the little **park** on Joseph Campau at Belmont let you have coffee and baked goods or deli takeout with the pope — an imposing statue of the first Polish pope, that is. The fence and gates are from the old Dodge Main plant that gave birth to Hamtramck. . . . The **Polish Art Center**, 9539 Joseph Campau near Norwalk, has many kinds of folk art, books, and imported sweets. Open Monday through Saturday 9-6, Friday to 7. . . . In the old socialist co-op at 2934 Yemans just east of Joseph Campau, **Polonia** restaurant (one of several Hamtramck eateries that are good, pleasant, and cheap) has a new folk dance coffeehouse (Polish, Armenian, Chaldean, Albanian, Romanian) upstairs Fridays from 8-12.

5 T.J.'s Take-Away Cafe at the Traffic Jam

Monday-Friday 11-3. When takeout is closed, bread can be pur-
chased from the restaurant bread cart. Restaurant closes Tuesday
through Friday at 10:30. Saturday 5-11. Closed Sunday. Lunch only
on Monday.

On the southeast corner of Canfield and Second, between down-
town Detroit and the Wayne State campus. From Woodward, turn
southwest onto Canfield at the Whitney Restaurant in the elaborate
1890s mansion. T.J. is in 2 blocks. (313) 831-9470.

The Traffic Jam is far more than a restaurant. It makes award-
winning cheese, bakes its own breads, and finally, after years of
legal hassles, it makes its own beer. Now, like an increasing number of successful restaurants, it has opened a regular takeout arm,
at midday only; after three o'clock bread is available from the
restaurant's bread cart. Breads you may hear people rave about —
potato dill or walnut rye, for instance — probably aren't available,
however. That's because the owners and staff are ideologically
committed to improvisation and surprise. "Everything changes,"
says co-owner Richard Vincent. "The only constant is that we're
here." You can expect, each day, three to five different breads,
several kinds of giant $1.50 cookies like lemon crumble or white
chocolate cashew crunch, and sandwiches that are cheaper
($3.50) and faster than at the sit-down restaurant.

With this menu philosophy, you might expect irritating incon-
sistencies in quality, but that's never considered a problem by the
Traffic Jam's many fans.

Breads (about $2 for a one-pound loaf) may include a spinach-
cheese bread with homemade cheddar cheese; a wholegrain sourdough incorporating fermented grain from the brewery; poppyseed and honey buns; or a jalopeño cheddar bread that makes a
fantastic pizza base even with ordinary pizza sauce. There's always
a quick bread for $4 to $4.50, like Michigan dry cherry-chocolate
chip or macadamia nut rum.

OAK PARK/ SOUTHFIELD/ BIRMINGHAM

6 Ackroyd's Scottish Bakehouse

Monday through Friday 9-6, Saturday 9-5.
300 Hamilton Row in downtown Birmingham. Hamilton Row runs
between Woodward and Hunter just north of 15 Mile. Park in the

structure off Hamilton. (313) 540-3575.

Canadians, Scots, and Irish are an important part of the great ethnic hodgepodge that came to work in Detroit in the auto boom of the early 20th century. Al Ackroyd, from Windsor, catered to fellow Canadians and Britons in his eastside grocery in the 1950s by selling meat pies from a local bakery. Then he learned how to make them himself from a Scottish master baker.

Today baking is Ackroyd's entire focus; the grocery is long gone, along with the considerable populations of Scots and Canadians who once lived on Detroit's east side and in Highland Park. At his longtime Redford bakery Al Ackroyd makes traditional breads of the British Isles, such as Irish soda bread, oatmeal bread, and Scotch homemade bread, plus scones (plain, raisin, cranberry, and fruit; $1 each). Two-thirds of his customers are still first-generation Irish, Scots, and English.

At the Birmingham store, his son Allan caters to a rapidly growing non-ethnic market with meat pies that are ideally suited

Chris Corrado is the granddaughter of Jim and Rose Bommarito who founded Bommarito's Italian Bakery on Detroit's east side in 1925. She and her sisters, brothers, and father continue the personal approach of Detorit's oldest Italian bakery.

to juggled contemporary lifestyles. The pasties here are smaller and not as heavy as the Upper Peninsula pasty, with peas, carrots, but no rutabagas and with a puff pastry crust that uses vegetable shortening, not lard. At 80¢ each, the pasties, sausage rolls, pork pies, and broccoli-cheese turnovers are priced to be bought in quantity for quick meals (one to one and a half are a good lunch) or the freezer. Sausage rolls come in appetizer size, the chicken pot pie ($4.65) and steak & kidney pie ($9.50) serve four.

Allan also makes cookies and pastries, including a best-selling butter shortbread and a number of variations on tarts and pastry squares, often involving currants and raisins.

All items are available at both stores.

7 Baking by the Auers

Tuesday-Saturday 7 a.m.-6 p.m.
29207 Southfield Road between 12 Mile and 13 Mile in Southfield. On west side of street, in Southfield Commons, closer to 12 Mile than 13 Mile. From I-696, take Southfield Road exit, go north about 1 1/2 miles. (313) 424-8660.

This big, successful production bakery made its name with French breads, produced in many forms: the long baguette ($1.50), a half-size version good for subs, a four-ounce loaf, and an epi ($1.75), scored to resemble a grain of wheat and be pulled apart. Now the bakery has grown so large that it regularly offers 20 kinds of bread, and even more on Saturday. (But come early on Saturday for a complete selection; they sell out fast.) These breads are both delicious and beautiful to look at; they make a great-looking party spread without being full of calories. The onion bread is especially popular at Bonnie's Patisserie, which carries the Auers' breads. Baker-owner David Auers, who studied cooking in France, is now assisted by a pastry chef who's French. The volume of croissants sold here is such that prices are quite reasonable: 75¢ for sandwich-size, 35¢ for the mini croissant.

8 Bonnie's Patisserie

Monday-Saturday 8:30-6.
29229 Northwestern Highway in the northwest corner of South-field. Just northwest of 12 Mile Rd. in a remodeled house. (It's also north of the Waldenbooks in Franklin Plaza.) From I-696, take the Northwestern Highway exit and head west. (313) 357-4540.

Connoisseurs of sweets in metro Detroit give high marks to
Bonnie's inventive pastries and exclaim at length about the
Schaum Torte (foam torte), a meringue-bottomed affair with
chocolate, strawberries, and whipped cream. A $3 portion is
plenty for two. Alas, humidity is its enemy, and it's not available in
summer. Bonnie's German poppyseed torte and toffee torte also
enjoy claims to local fame. (They're $20 for the eight-inch size
that serves eight to twelve.) Only the carrot cake and chocolate
cheese cakes are available by the slice. There are also things like
white chocolate brownies, and many kinds of giant cookies and
tartes from $1.25 to $2.50. Among the morning pastries, favorites
include sticky buns ($1 on Tuesdays and Thursdays) and cream
cheese danish ($1 on Wednesday and Saturday). Breads are from
Baking by the Auers.

Full-line catering has been a big part of Bonnie Fishman's business ever since it opened in 1979. For the past three years that
has expanded into a lunch business featuring sandwiches (the
turkey breast is always fresh-roasted), salads, pastas, and hearty
stews and soups in winter. Bakery customers are always welcome
to sit down for coffee.

Bonnie's is quite close to the Star Bakery's suburban outlet,
which makes this area a handy stop for some of the best breads in
metro Detroit. It's a relief to find a friendly little spot like Bonnie's so close to the glassy, cold, and impersonal-looking office
monoliths of corporate Southfield just east of here.

9 Le Petit Prince

Tuesday-Saturday 7-7, Sunday 7-2.
*In Birmingham on 124 West 14 Mile at Pierce, between Green-
field and Southfield and south of Woodward. In a neighborhood
shopping strip next to a grocery and drug store. (313) 644-7114.*

When they were visiting friends in Birmingham in the 1970s,
Pierre and Paulette Diderjean, a baker and pastry chef from
France, noticed a glaring void in this affluent suburban market.
There was no good French bread. They decided to fill the gap and
soon thereafter opened Le Petit Prince, bearing the same name as
their previous bakery on the Riviera. The crusty long baguette,
soft inside, elicits raves, and it's only $1.10. Other celebrated
items are a croissant filled with homemade almond paste ($1.50)
and the beautiful, bite-size gateaux de soiree — miniature decorated French pastries in 36 varieties, including eclairs, cream

puffs, and many tartes. (They're 80¢, or $9 a dozen.)

Everything here is French: cakes, meringue desserts, dinner rolls, and beautiful cookies ($11 a pound in heart, crescent, and other shapes). Only butter and cream are used — no substitutes. Everything tastes as good as it looks, and it looks marvelous. Despite its high French standards and its Birmingham location, this place is also friendly.

10 Modern Bakery

Open daily including Sunday, 6 a.m. to 8 p.m.

13735 West Nine Mile, 1 1/2 blocks west of Coolidge in Oak Park. South side of the street, across from post office. From I-696, take Coolidge exit, go south a little over a mile, turn right onto Nine Mile. (313) 546-4477.

Oak Park is blessed with three good Jewish bakeries — the Star at three locations, Zeman's kosher bakery in the retail strip at the northeast corner of Greenfield and Ten Mile, and the Modern Bakery here. It produces 200 varieties of baked goods, including all the standbys — challah (sweet egg bread prized for breakfast toast with jam), pumpernickel, corn bread, babkas, coffee cakes, crescent-shaped rugelach and other little cream cheese pastries bought by the pound for bar mitzvahs and other festive occasions (in this category the Modern Bakery is said to excel), prize-winning chocolate chip cookies, seven-layer cake, and much more. Prices: $2.50 for most two-pound loaves of bread, 35¢ for a kaiser roll, $5.25 per pound of rugulach. For something pleasantly light and airy and slightly sweet without being rich or sugary, try the long sticks of kichel, also $5.25 a pound.

For 40 years baker Martin Weiss has been here. Now the center of metro Detroit's Jewish population has moved west, and he has decided to not to open branches but to focus on wholesale sales from this single location. Thus it is that anyone who has eaten a sandwich at Zingerman's celebrated Ann Arbor deli is already familiar with the good rye breads from the Modern Bakery without realizing it.

To achieve some of the goodness of fresh, hot bread, you can do what Zingerman's does to its rye bread from the Modern Bakery: double-bake it. Heat the oven to 325° or 350°, and bake the bread 20 minutes (that restarts the baking process and releases more of that delicious fresh-bread smell), then slice while hot. That also makes a crustier crust.

11 Star Bakery

♦ *Bakery in* **Oak Park**

26031 Coolidge, in an older strip mall on the west side of the street north of Lincoln between 10 Mile and 11 Mile. From I-696 Coolidge exit go north to bakery. Monday through Saturday 6 a.m.-7:30 p.m., Sunday 6-6. (313) 541-9450.

♦ *Outlet shop in* **Southfield**

29145 Northwestern Highway on southwest corner of Twelve Mile in Franklin Plaza strip mall next to Waldenbooks. Monday through Saturday 7 a.m.-9 p.m., Sunday 8-8. (313) 352-8548.

♦ *Outlet shop in* **Southfield/Oak Park**

15600 West Ten Mile at Greenfield, in the New Orleans strip mall at the intersection's northwest corner, on the dividing line between Southfield and Oak Park. Monday through Saturday 6 a.m.-7:30 p.m., Sunday 6-6.(313) 559-4808.

The Star's rye breads are regarded by many fans and critics of Detroit-area Jewish bakeries as the best around — as good as the best Jewish bakeries in New York, some say, and better, perhaps, than anyplace else in the U.S. Good sourdough rye breads are the basis of any good Jewish bakery or deli. Like other European-style sourdough breads, they're made without fats and sugar and without much yeast, sometimes only a little to get the starter going. These "lean" breads rise mainly through the chemical action of a naturally fermented sour starter made mostly of flour and water, and sometimes potato, with just a little yeast to get it going. There's a good deal of judgment and intuition in dealing with the sour — how much to use, how to feed it, how long to let it develop. Three long, slow risings mean it can take up to eight hours to make from start to finish. That goes against all the "improvements" of modern production-line mass baking involving fast-action yeasts and self-rising dough placed immediately in pans by automatic dividing machines. (Add even a little egg and butter, and you get a soft crust and a moist interior; more makes bread richer and more cake-like.)

The slow, deliberate process is what develops a good deal of sourdough bread's taste and texture. (Taste is also developed by the sour starter itself and by steam applied in the oven on the crust, which permeates inward through the bread. Time spent mixing and kneading the bread affects the bread's gluten structure and thus its texture. More mixing makes chewier bread.)

"The time! You haff . . . to take . . . the time!!!" Benny Moskovitz emphatically states. Born and raised in Czechoslovakia, he's the 65-year-old-owner and baker at the Star Bakery. "It's a *slow* process," Moskow says. "This bread here'll take weeks and months [to develop the taste of the sour] because of the handling. You cannot give the bread a taste by putting *drrruggs* in it," he says, referring to the chemicals added to fast-rise breads.

Fans especially praise the moist texture and full-bodied taste of the Star's corn rye, baked in round or long loaves, with or without lots of caraway seeds. (Despite the name, there's no corn in it, just a mixture of wheat and rye flours. "Corn" is a direct translation of *kern*, the German and Yiddish word for kernel or grain.) Other favorites are raisin pumpernickel (baked only on Fridays, Saturdays, and Sundays) and pumpernickel health bread (made with wheat berries and cracked rye and wheat on the crust).

Kaiser rolls and onion rolls are another mainstay of Jewish baked goods. Some hold the Star's kaiser rolls to be the best in town. A fresh kaiser roll is one of the great joys of everyday life, aficionados maintain. This crusty classic, soft inside, depends on egg, egg white, and steam for its special character. Here they typically come out of the oven at six each morning and stay warm for a couple hours.

Benny Moskow, the Star Bakery's baker-owner, comes direct from the Old World school of making traditional sour rye breads the slow-rise way, with only enough yeast to get the sour starter going.

Of course, like any full-line Jewish bakery, the Star offers seven-layer cakes with cream fillings, egg-rich braided challah, danish, cupcakes, coffee cakes, cookies, and cakes in traditional and common American guises. Jewish bakers have never been bound to tradition, instead picking up on American classics like brownies but doing them the Jewish way: not too sweet but with the best ingredients.

The Star's chocolate babka, eaten fresh, is "to die for," says an otherwise quite sober Jewish chocoholic. "Babka" makes it "grandmother's" coffee cake, rich with butter and egg and light from yeast and eggs, swirled with a mix of walnuts, almond paste, and semi-sweet chocolate, and drizzled with more chocolate.

Retail prices here are unusually low: $1.25 for a plain 20-ounce loaf of rye, white, and French breads, 10¢ extra for seeds, $1.40 for most egg breads. Big two-pound loaves are $1.85 and $1.95. Kaiser rolls are 30¢ each, a chocolate chip butter horn 55¢, and the fabled chocolate babka is about $4.50, sold by the pound.

For a really interesting outing to Oak Park, stop at the Jewish bakeries, nearby Saad's pastries, and two other unusual shops. Borenstein's Book and Music Store, run by outgoing Orthodox Jews, stocks "everything for the Jewish family," books, recordings, gifts and art, even comedy routines. It's in Greenfield Center at the northeast corner of Greenfield at 10 Mile, alongside Zeman's kosher bakery and a very good Middle Eastern restaurant, the Pita Cafe. Then drive north half a mile, over the freeway, to the big shopping center on the northeast corner of 10 1/2 Mile Road, dominated by the prototype K Mart that kicked off the retailing giant's updated look. At the west end of the L of small shops by K-Mart is Book Beat, a combined gallery, photography and art bookstore (one of the best in the U.S.), and a delightful children's bookstore. It also has a compelling, artfully displayed range of handcrafts — pins and creatures by Tracy Gallup, papier-mache by Mexican masters of the craft, Day of the Dead figures, and much more. If that meshes with your interests, you could easily spend hours here — spelled with a break at the outstanding deli a few doors down.

12 Saad's Pastries

Open daily 9 a.m.-9 p.m.
  24711 Coolidge just south of I-696. On the west side of Coolidge in a small retail strip, next to Arabic Town Grocery. (313) 545-1640.

When Oak Park was built up after World War II, it was mostly Jewish. Now its Jewish population is largely elderly, or Orthodox, or very recent Russian emigrants. The many Jews who have moved upward and outward to West Bloomfield Township, the current center of metro Detroit's frequently shifting Jewish community, have been replaced by a melange of ethnic groups that's most heavily African-American and Chaldean. Chaldeans are Assyrian Arabs from Iraq who are Roman Catholic and whose native language and foodways are Arabic; metro Detroit is the center of Chaldeans in the U.S.

Saad's appeals to Oak Park's Chaldeans but describes itself as a Lebanese and French pastry shop. All the honey-nut pastries found in the Arab part of Dearborn are here as well, along with good spinach and meat pies. Something not so common is an Egyptian pastry called King of the Breads in English, though it's not very bread-like. It's round like a pie, $2 a slice, and looks awfully rich, what with the glistening sweet pistachio topping. But it turns out to be mostly a refreshing milk pudding flavored with orange water — surprisingly pleasant to an American palate.

Flanked by a large Middle Eastern grocery and a video store with tapes in many languages of the Middle East, India, and Asia, this makes for convenient one-stop shopping for area Arabs. Prices are lower, however, in the very competitive Arab shopping district along Warren and Schaefer in Dearborn.

SOUTHWEST/WESTSIDE/DEARBORN

13 Ackroyd's Scotch Bakery

Monday through Friday 9-6, Saturday to 5.
25566 Five Mile at Beech-Daly in Redford Township. On the northeast corner one door down from Beech-Daly. Take I-96 to Beech Daly, go north 1 mile. (313) 532-1181.

Well known for meat pies and breads of the British Isles, and patronized largely by Canadian, Scottish, Irish, and British immigrants. See description of Ackroyd's Scottish Bakehouse, page 222.

☛ EXACT PRICES have been given to provide the best possible relative price comparisons. **It is expected**, of course, that **prices will increase** over the life of this book.

---

14 Afrah Pastry

Open daily 8 a.m.-11 p.m.

12741 West Warren at Appoline, a few blocks east of Schaefer, in the northeast corner of Dearborn. (313) 582-7878.

Not as big or well-known as Shatila, this newer pastry shop in Dearborn's thriving Arab shopping district on West Warren is well regarded by locals for its typical Middle Eastern pastries — numerra (a sweet farina square that many non-Arabs enjoy) and beautiful honey-filo-nut pastries like pistachio-filled bird's nests and baklava. Most things are 60¢ or so; sold by the tray, the price goes down considerably. (In Mediterranean cultures, it's never considered rude to ask for a better price.)

There are tables for sitting and having thick, cardomon-flavored Arabic coffee with pastries. (They're a terrific combination.) And unlike Shatila, Afrah is in an more interesting area that makes it a nice after-dinner destination if you like to walk and browse. The Coffee and Nut Gallery, which sells spices, dried coffee, chick-peas, rice, and more, is right next door. Warren is becoming more widely known as a restaurant area, and lately an increasing number of retail shops selling clothing and jewelry are opening, as ever more people emigrate from the war-plagued countries of the Middle East. It's hard to believe that this vibrant shopping district on Warren west of Miller was half empty 15 years ago. Arabs like to shop at night, and competition keeps prices down and hours long. In metro Detroit and elsewhere, immigrant neighborhoods are an urban bright spot in areas abandoned by Americans focused on suburban life as a deceptively easy solution to urban problems.

15 Arabian Village Bakery

Daily including Sunday, 9 a.m.-9 p.m.

10045 West Vernor at Dix in Dearborn's South End, just east of the Ford Rouge plant. Directions from I-94. Eastbound take the exit to Michigan and Wyoming, go south on Wyoming 2 miles to Vernor, then right on Vernor. Westbound, take the Michigan Ave. exit, go east on Michigan to Wyoming, then south to Vernor, and right. (313) 843-0800.

One of several Middle Eastern groceries along Dix and Vernor, the Arabian Village also is a home-style bakery catering to local residents and to the crowds who come to the nearby mosque on Saturday. Newcomers' budgets are very limited, and prices haven't gone up in a long, long time, so don't be surprised to find occasional gristle in the meat pies. Everything's quite tasty, though maybe not to mainstream American tastes. *Zahtor*, for instance, a popular breakfast bread, is spiced with sesame, thyme, and sumac, sometimes with kassari and mozzarella cheese on top. Three round pieces are $1. Some non-Arab Americans enjoy it for breakfast with tea.

Meat pies and lemony spinach pies ($1 each) are in a simpler, chewier bread pocket than familiar Greek spinach pie in filo dough. If you're eating on the run, ask for a squirt of hummus on your meat pie. *Kaak* (spice cookies, 3 for $1) are attractively stamped with decorative molds. There's just one display case (most customers already know what's available) but questions are encouraged and samples given freely. (Famously hospitable, most Arabs treat warmly any non-Arabs who show friendly interest.)

Tabooli, stuffed grape leaves, and hummus are also available.

Other Arab bakeries are more upscale and modern; here's where you get a sense of life in an immigrant neighborhood, Members of the Homayed family who run it are bilingual and love to field questions about Arab culture and comparative religions.

Dearborn's South End, at the gates of Henry Ford's famous Rouge plant, once was home to autoworkers of over 50 nationalities and all their taverns. Today their children have moved to neighborhoods of newer or bigger homes. Meanwhile, the small original group of Middle Easterners has formed the nucleus of what has become the largest concentration of Islamic Arabs in the United States, nearly all Yemeni or refugees from Lebanon and Palestine. The South End is their port of entry; when they earn more money, typically they move elsewhere, often to the more substantial Dearborn neighborhood along West Warren. For an Old World atmosphere, the South End can't be beat, especially in summer, when many men like to wear long, cool gowns on the street. Shop-owners pull out little prayer rugs from behind the counter when they hear the call to prayer from the minaret of the nearby mosque.

A nearby glimpse of the Middle East can be yours weekdays at ACCESS (Arab-American Community Center for Economic and Social Services), a sort of contemporary settlement house on Saulino Court just north of Dix. Its halls and public rooms are full of interesting displays on Arab food, art, language, and religions; all are welcome. Open weekdays 9-5. (313) 842-7010.

16 Chamberlain Bakery

Monday-Friday 8-5, Saturday 8-12.

In Southwest Detroit on Chamberlain at Springwells about 4 blocks north of Fort and a mile east of the Ford Rouge plant. From I-75, take the Springwells exit, go north on Springwells. After you pass McDonald's and Wendy's and go under the railroad viaduct, turn immediately left onto Chamberlain. Bakery is on the corner, attached to an old house. (313) 842-8854.

Honors for best Old World sour rye in a non-Jewish Detroit bakery easily go to the Chamberlain Bakery, tucked away in a residential neighborhood on Detroit's southwest side. Much of its business is wholesale. Chamberlain bread is available at R. Hirt's in the Eastern Market, the Westborn Market in Dearborn, and the Merchant of Vino. But, of course, visiting the bakery itself gives a taste of authentic atmosphere — and freshness is insured.

Bread's the only thing actually made here — all by hand— and the two sour ryes are what most people come for. The Old Country rye is 97% rye flour; it comes only in a two-pound long loaf ($2.10). Sour rye, 80% rye, comes in a two-pound round loaf (also $2.10) or a 20-ounce long loaf. There's also a 20-ounce half rye, French bread, pumpernickel, and a delicious, dense white egg bread loaded with golden raisins ($2.60 a 22-ounce loaf). Some people think it's as even better than the sour rye.

A Lithuanian immigrant opened the bakery next to his house in this then-new autoworkers' neighborhood in 1924; one of the neatest things about visiting such places today is getting a look at the room-sized brick ovens. The bakers and their recipes are part of an unbroken East European tradition, but the Chamberlain Bakery's owner today is a former customer and not a baker at all. One day, some dozen years ago, he came in and found his favorite bread sold out. "What do you have to do to get a loaf of bread around here?" he asked. "Buy the place?" Upon hearing that the bakery was actually for sale, he decided to buy it and manage the marketing side from the office of the company he owned.

17 Luna Bakery

Monday through Saturday 8 a.m.-9 p.m., Sunday to 7.

In southwest Detroit at 5620 West Vernor at Junction, across from Holy Redeemer Church. From I-94 or I-75, take the Livernois exit, go south or north respectively to Vernor, then east on Vernor toward downtown. (313) 554-1690.

If you enjoy something slightly sweet with coffee or milk, but if greasy doughnuts or over-rich coffee cakes turn you off, a trip to a Mexican bakery may be well worth your while. Mexican sweet breads are light but not vacuously puffy, simple, and not too sweet. They come in many attractive shapes that look terrific together on a serving plate. They are meant to be eaten at breakfast, after meals, and as snacks.

This busy bakery in the heart of the West Vernor retail district is a friendly place to learn about Mexican sweet breads. A counter person is happy to assemble a sampler box of cakes and breads that are mostly about 40¢. The hits of our sampling included the following:

◆ yoyo — two cakey hemispheres, denser and more satisfying than some Mexican sweet breads, joined by strawberry filling.

◆ vanilla cupcake — more interesting than you'd expect.

◆ oatmeal bread — more of a cookie, really, with raisins.

◆ apple turnover — similar to American pastries, but with a nice, brown crust and a somewhat less rich dough.

◆ guayaba — a yellow, rounded bread with raisins.

◆ oido (ear) — an ear-shaped crispy pies of sweet puff pastry.

A delicious and satisfying combination for breakfast or mid-morning snack with coffee is to spread labne (a thickened yogurt sold in Middle Eastern and natural food groceries) on Mexican pastries.

18 New Yasmeen Bakery and Deli

5:30 a.m.-8:30 p.m., daily including Sunday. (313) 582-6035.
13900 West Warren at Horger, 3 blocks west of Schaefer on the northeast side of Dearborn. On north side of street; look for illuminated green awning. From I-96, take Schaefer exit, go south 2 1/2 miles, then west (right). From I-94, take Lonyo exit, go north a mile on Lonyo, then west on Schaefer a little over a mile.

New Yasmeen's pita bread has become a familiar staple at many metro Detroit groceries, and its *fatiya* or spinach pies are considered the best around. Lebanese spinach pies are much simpler and healthier than their Greek counterparts in filo dough that's flakey with butter. Fatiya dough is plumper and more substantial, and the spinach filling is deliciously lemony. One and a half or two pies make a handy, satisfying lunch for $1.50 or less. Meat pies,

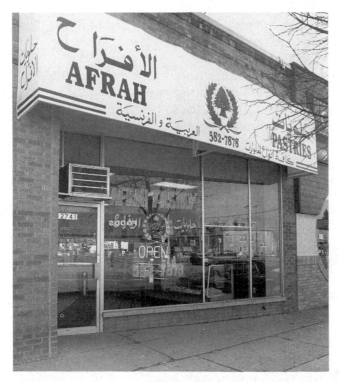

Afrah Pastries is one of many Arab stores started by emigrants from war-torn Middle East that have transformed Dearborn's West Warren from a retail street of half-empty storefronts into a vibrant, ever-expanding shopping district that's a boon to lovers of Middle Eastern restaurants and food.

filled with a ground lamb mix, come in the same plump triangular pockets (both are 75¢), while the same dough in is used for round, 10" open pies topped with cheese, meat, or thyme mixed with sesame and oil ($1.25 each).

Now the bakery has moved and expanded. It has a deli and a large area with tables, and it stays open until 8:30. "It's the talk of the town," says an enthusiastic Dearborn resident. Now it's easy to stop for a quick meal for less than half of what you'd pay at a nearby restaurant, and go home with an array of breads, spreads like hummus, and salad fixings like tabooli and fatoush so you wouldn't have to cook for days. Big refrigerator cases of deli items like stuffed grape leaves, and several kinds of olives and cheese mean you can put together a fast, quick, and varied meal, topped off with sweets like date fingers or sesame pistachio cookies or sponge cakes.

Like nearly all Middle Eastern breads, the pita bread is made without preservatives. It also freezes well; just take it out five or ten minutes before you want to use it. Buy them here at the store, and you get 1 extra, 11 in all, for 75¢. Many people buy 10 bags at a time.

The helpful, friendly staff is happy to provide samples and advise non-Arabs about what to eat with what and when. Labne, for instance, is a thickened form of yogurt that makes a terrific, healthy breakfast when spread, with or without jam, on date-filled bread rings, raisin bread ($1 a loaf), and other breakfast breads. (Watch out and ask first! A fair number of those beautiful-looking breads are flavored with cardamom, which many Americans find a strange taste.)

New Yasmeen is run largely by four members of the Siblini family from Loubieh in south Lebanon, too close to Israel for its own good. Their father and grandfather were also bakers. Ibrahim, the middle son, was the first to come to Detroit, to study engineering. On a visit, his older brother Mohamad saw the opportunity offered by the burgeoning Arab population and the increasing popularity of healthy Middle Eastern food to someone willing to start a good-sized, aggressively run bakery. He started New Yasmeen in 1985. Now his extremely pleasant sister Amane and her husband manage the store at night. The younger Siblini brother Hussein is the retail manager. Though Hussein has a degree in engineering from Wayne State, he's decided to join the family business. "The bakery is ours," he says, echoing the words of immigrant bakers from all over the world. "With it you can be your own boss."

19 Redford Italian Bakery and Pizzeria

Tuesday through Friday 9-6:30, Saturday closes at 5:30.
26417 Plymouth between Inkster and Beech Daly in Redford Township. From I-96, take Beech-Daly exit, go south on Beech-Daly to Plymouth, then right (west). Bakery is across from Long John Silver. (313) 937-2288.

The Redford Italian Bakery has three things to recommend it: big loaves of Italian bread, Etruscan pizza, and a courtyard sculpture garden that's an amazing work of folk art.

Unlike some other area Italian bakeries that have grown into delis and specialty groceries, this is a ma-and-pa operation. Owners Silvio and Rita Barile, who live right next door, make Italian bread that's crusty on the outside and moist in the middle. As native Italians, they're familiar with the real thing. They also make carryout pizzas and an award-winning sausage subs, up to closing at 6:30. There's regular pizza with tomato sauce, but Etruscan pizza is something different: there's no sauce to cover up the flavor of olive oil, garlic, and vegetables that are on it.

**Silvio Barile of the Redford Italian Bakery works in two plastic media —
dough and concrete. The courtyard behind his bakery, and his own back
yard, are filled with creations like this patriotic monument.**

Customers are welcome to buy pop and sit outside in the courtyard, surrounded by some of Silvio's elaborate sculptural creations
in Kwikcreke. All it took was patching his driveway to reawaken
an old childhood fondness for making clay figures. As a baker, of
course, he works in a plastic, clay-like medium all the time. His
first creation was a little dog; his latest, a statue of Columbus that
took 65 hundred-pound bags of cement.

20 Shatila Bakery

Monday-Saturday 8 a.m.-11 p.m., Sunday 8-7.
6712 Schaefer south of Warren in the east part of Dearborn.
Opposite L'Opera banquet hall. From I-94, take Michigan Ave. exit
on the east side of Dearborn, go west on Michigan, north on
Schaefer. (313) 582-1952.

Generous hospitality and entertaining at home are hallmarks of
Arab culture, which means there's a strong demand for pastries.
For years the big name in Middle Eastern pastries has been
Shatila. The big, super-modern retail shop is small potatoes compared to its three-story factory on Warren from which baked
goods are trucked to Metro Airport and shipped all over the U.S.
Along with an extensive variety of traditional honey-nut-filo pastries with walnuts and pistachios, Shatila makes many kinds of
beautiful French pastries with whipped cream — not a surprise
considering how completely French ways dominated Lebanon for
most of the 19th and half the 20th century. The French pastries,
based on light sheet cake, are good, but they mostly taste the
same — the differences are for appearance only.

There are tables, so you can sit and observe the goings-on in
this busy, popular place, where neighbors meet in line. But it's big
and rather impersonal compared to family-run spots like New
Yasmeen and Afrah and El-Masri down Schaefer a block north of
Michigan at 5125 Schaefer. Most businesses here are run by
Lebanese; El-Masri is Palestinian, owned by a family from the West
Bank village of Nablis. Nablis is famous for its *kanify*, a pizza-like
affair of sweet cheese, and El-Masri offers the real thing. One
word of advice: the serving-size slice is meant for more than one.

☛ EXACT PRICES have been given to provide the best possible relative price
comparisons. **It is expected**, of course, that **prices will increase** over the life
of this book.

OUTSTATE Bakeries

ANN ARBOR/YPSILANTI AREA

1 Benny's Bakery

Tuesday through Friday 5:30 a.m. to 2 p.m., Saturday 5:30 to noon.
111 West Michigan (U.S. 12) in downtown Saline, about 8 miles southwest of Ann Arbor. From U.S. 23, take U.S. 12 exit west into town. From I-94, take Saline-Ann Arbor Rd. exit south past Meijer to Saline. Bakery is just west of the main light downtown, on the south side of Michigan. (313) 429-9120.

Benny Galimberti is a native of Italy, from a small town near Milan, but his pleasant bakery is geared to Midwestern small-town tastes, without any Italian specialties at all. The most ethnic Benny gets is a very good soft German pretzel made on Saturdays (one bakery supplier says it's the best in Michigan) and loads of traditional German Christmas cookies for the holidays. With seven tables and a counter, Benny's is a great morning coffee stop for locals and visitors alike. Ann Arbor bicycle enthusiasts love it, and so do people who work in Saline. Locals go for white bread and French bread (real bargains at 70¢ a loaf) and whole wheat (80¢). Benny also makes salt-rising bread he keeps in the freezer for those older customers who know enough to appreciate a bread with character. Breakfast favorites include donuts, danish made with margarine (40¢), butter croissants (60¢ on Fridays and Saturdays only), and weekend coffee cakes like the popular one with pecans and maple-flavor icing ($2.25 for 12-16 ounces). "I don't eat much of that stuff," Benny says. He bakes hard-crust, Old World breads for himself, but his customers won't buy enough of them to carry at the store.

2 Depot Town Sourdough Bakery

Monday, Wednesday, Thursday and Friday open 8-5:30. Breads also sold at the Ypsi Food Co-op next door (open daily 10-7 at least, except Sunday noon-5), the Ann Arbor Farmers' Market (Saturdays only), at Ed's honey stall at the Ypsilanti Farmers' Market in the railroad freight house just north of Cross on the west side of the tracks.

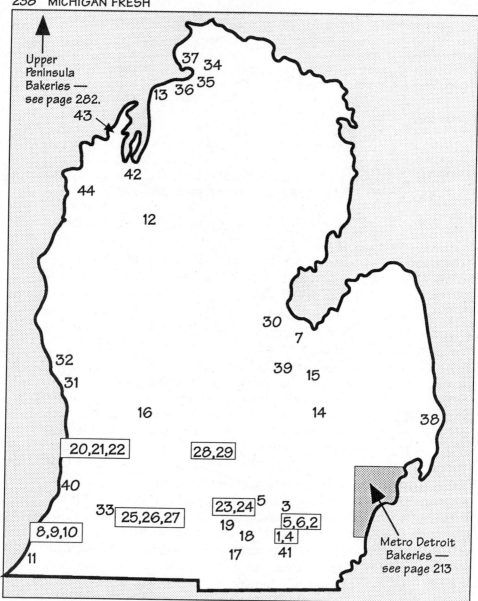

Upper
Peninsula
Bakeries —
see page 282.

Metro Detroit
Bakeries —
see page 213

Outstate
BAKERIES

(313) 487-8110.

310 North River in Ypsilanti's Depot Town, in the Millworks Building shared by the Ypsi Food Co-op. Depot Town is a very old commercial subcenter, mostly along Cross Street where it crosses the Huron River and the train tracks. From I-94, take the Huron Street exit north past downtown, turn right onto Cross, right onto River as soon as you cross the tracks.

This small bakery is unusual in many ways. It makes only traditional-style sourdough breads, only from whole grain flours that are stone ground right here from organically grown wheat and rye berries. (Stone grinding lets bakers vary the coarseness of their flour as they like.) It's a nonprofit business run by a collective of four, with some volunteer help, under the guidance of the community members at quarterly meetings. Its home is a very old brick building that goes all the way back to the 1830s. The adjoining Ypsi Food Co-op (open much longer hours; see above) carries the bread, plus cheese, peanut butter, some salads, and such that would make for a nice picnic in pretty Riverside Park. (The park is a pleasant walk west across the Cross Street bridge past Depot Town's interesting antique shops. Don't miss Miller Motors, the world's only surviving Hudson dealership, at the corner of Cross and River.)

Over four-fifths of the bakery's weekly production of some 600 loaves is sold wholesale to area co-ops and food stores like Zingerman's and the Produce Station. So what customers see here is not a retail sales room, but bakers at work. The staff enjoys having customers watch and ask questions; they like to show off the brick oven they built.

People who appreciate good traditional breads but aren't organic purists will find a lot to enjoy about these flavorful, chewy, substantial breads — the kind that make a satisfying meal with a little cheese, hummus, peanut butter, or apple butter, and some fresh fruit. Considering the special ingredients and time involved, the prices are quite reasonable, too: $2.25 for 28-ounce loaves of whole wheat or rye, $2.50 for whole wheat with sesame, $3.25 for whole wheat-cinnamon-raisin bread with walnuts, and $2.75 without the nuts.

The Depot Town Sourdough Bakery has been selling bread since June, 1990. A spinoff project of Ann Arbor's Wildflour Community Bakery, it's the realized dream of Tom Kenny. He was so impressed with a bread a customer brought in from the Baldwin Hill

Bakery in Massachusetts, made with desem, a Flemish-style sour leavening agent made simply of fermented flour, water, and salt, that he decided to try and make a similar bread here. The night before baking, the desem (DAY-zem) starter has to be mixed and punched hourly for 12 hours (a timer turns the mixer on), then allowed to rest. ¢

3 Dexter Bakery

Tuesday to Saturday 5 a.m.-5 p.m. (313) 426-3848.

8101 Main St. in downtown Dexter, about 8 miles northwest of Ann Arbor. You can take the freeway route (I-94 to Baker Rd. exit, north on Baker into town, left onto Main at light. Bakery is at 2nd light). But other ways are nicer. The direct route from Ann Arbor: take Huron (Business Route I-94) west from downtown, go right at the forks onto Dexter Rd., continue to Dexter. Everybody's favorite scenic route from downtown Ann Arbor: go north on North Main to Huron River Dr. (look for it to the left just before the freeway), wind out on Huron River to Mast Rd. (just past Dexter-Huron Metropark), left into downtown Dexter.

Few small-town bakeries manage to do so many things well and satisfy so many kinds of customers — a steady stream of tradesmen, retirees, bicyclists (the ride from Ann Arbor along Huron River Drive is exceptional, and the Ann Arbor Bicycle Touring Society descends en masse on Saturday morning), and locals who meet for their regular kaffee klatsch. Strangers may be invited to join the coffee klatsch — there's only one large table — and chat. Demand for morning sweet rolls often seems to overshadow everything else in small towns. Here, though sweet rolls are produced in beguiling variety, including walnut crisps, French crullers, 40¢ muffins, chocolate crullers, and a very popular 65¢ apple nut roll, there's enough demand to produce some good breads. And there are some exceptional specialties like chewy date-filled cookies that are refreshingly unsugary, and salty cheese pockets made of pretzel dough stuffed with processed cheese. (It tastes a lot better than it sounds.) The most popular breads, all $1.40 or $1.50 for a one-pound loaf, are English muffin bread, with or without raisins; sourdough white; and salt-rising bread, tricky but flavorful and delicious toasted. Soft German pretzels are made on Saturday, but 35¢ sticks of the same dough are made all week.

4 The Great Lakes Pretzel Company
& The European Breadery

Monday-Thursday 10-4:30, Friday & Saturday 7-3.

204 West Michigan Ave.(U.S. 12) in downtown Saline, west of the light on the north side of the street. See Benny's Bakery for freeway directions. (313) 429-3546.

Owner-baker Earl Spears makes pretzels and breads using German recipes and Old World methods, for traditional products not often found in the United States. Assimilation and World War I have caused Germans to lose touch with more of their culinary heritage than many ethnic groups. Spears enjoys testing recipes from old-timers who stop by, and tracking down their European origins. His customers include German fraternal organizations.

In Germany, every region has its special pretzel. Spears makes three kinds. The Bavarian pretzel is softest. The Swabian pretzel has a crispier outer shell. His beer pretzel, made with beer instead of water, has a malty flavor. Germans sometimes spread pretzels with margarine, but never mustard, an American innovation. Hand-size pretzels are 45¢, sticks 32¢.

In deciding where to set up his business, Spears researched not only potential nearby markets but the water supply, since bread is, on the average, 42% water. Here in Saline he found an artesian well, inspected monthly by the state agriculture department, that provides the untreated water Spears wanted to produce as natural a product as possible.

Spears also produces 14 kinds of bread: an Eastern European-type multigrain bread, a popular French bread, and several kinds of rye bread: sourdough, cheddar-dill, and a Berlin-style onion-dill bread. Most breads come in one- and two-pound loaves and sell for $1.35 to $2.60. An unusual and pretty specialty are *laugenwecken* ($1.44/dozen), dinner rolls stamped so that the baked roll has a daisy-shape of white showing through the crisp brown crust.

5 The Moveable Feast

◆ *Kerrytown shop. Monday-Friday 8:30-7, Saturday 8:30-5. In the Kerrytown Shops (front north corner of food building, facing North Fifth Avenue). Kerrytown is between North Fifth and North Fourth just south of Kingsley. Closest easy-to-find parking access: in lot at Catherine and Fourth. (Take Catherine 1 block east of Main.)*

To be sure to find a parking space: go to structure just west of Main, entered from First or Ann. Walk to market along Miller/Catherine. (313) 663-3331.

◆ *In downtown* **Chelsea** *at 107 Main two doors north of Middle and south of the tracks. Parking lot just north of here at tracks. From I-94, take M-52 north into town. Call (313) 475-3611 for hours.*

◆ *Restaurant bakery counter at* **326 W. Liberty** *just west of downtown Ann Arbor, open Tuesday-Friday from 11 a.m. until sold out. Call for late-afternoon availability. A more limited range of takeout breads and baked goods. (313) 663-3278.*

Other bakeries in and around Ann Arbor may produce pastries and breads that look as good. But when it comes to the essentials of taste and texture, the standards set by the careful perfectionism of co-founder Ricky Agranoff pay off, even after she has retired from her ownership role. Since 1990 the bakery, now owned solely by Pat Pooley, has been gradually and deliberately expanding into new areas. Baker Greg Uhlein has been happily transplanted to the Midwest from heading the kitchen at Washington's Blair House residence for Presidential guests. (He and his wife love living in the country, in rural Jackson County.) He has been developing new breads, pastries, and products like low-fat

The Dexter Bakery northwest of Ann Arbor caters to a most diverse clientele for a small-town bakery. Both burly tradesmen and lean Ann Arbor bicyclists are tremendously fond on morning pastries.

muffins to augment the classic sourdough French-style bread, flakey butter croissants, and rich pastries on which The Moveable Feast's reputation is based. Baking for the explosion of Ann Arbor coffeehouses has been a boon to the bakery's wholesale business.

Among some 20 kinds of bread made here, Uhlein's favorite new additions are a cider-oatmeal bread made with white raisins ($3 a one-pound loaf), a terrific light cracked wheat, very popular for toast ($1.75 for a one-pound loaf), and a dense, Old World pumpernickel ($2.10 for 20 ounces). Along the lines of the new-old slow-fermentation sourdough breads being popularized by Chez Panisse's bakery in Berkeley, California, are a really sour sourdough round in which the sour starter is flavored with onion. (It's $2.25 a 19-ounce loaf.)

The white sourdough used in The Moveable Feast's locally famous baguette ($2.05) spends four hours rising in a warm room before being baked the next day. It reappears in other interesting forms: a 19-ounce oval loaf with poppyseeds and sesame ($2.55), three-ounce bread sticks (75¢), and an epi (also $2.55), in which a pull-apart loaf is scored in a pattern that resembles wheat.

Another old standby, an outstanding all-butter croissant, is produced in such volume that it only costs a dollar (up to $1.50 when filled). That's a great bargain for a croissant made by hand (using no shortcuts whatsoever) with fresh dough each day.

On the fancy pastry side, a chocoholic's dream, the Gateau Nancy, a super-rich flourless chocolate cake with rum and brandy filling and glaze, is available in individual-serving sizes (a slice-size bar for $2.50, a two-bite finger for 75¢) at the retail store. But not everything is so heavy. Uhlein recommends a wonderful lemon curd/cream cake like the one made at the Blair House (six servings for $15) and three-bite fingers (95¢) in which a lemon pastry is filled with almond cream frangipane and pureed raspberries, then coated in chocolate.

Breakfast pastries are also produced in such volume that prices are surprisingly affordable for such quality. Danish are 85¢; an excellent almond tea ring, inspired by Sanders' popular coffee cake, appears in individual sizes, large ($1) and small (60¢).

Both the Moveable Feast's Kerrytown shop and new retail outlet in downtown Chelsea have tables, coffee, and a variety of takeout pâtés, pasta and vegetable salads, and other lunch and dinner items.

6 Wildflour Community Bakery

Monday through Friday 7-6, Saturday 8-5.

208 North Fourth between Ann and Catherine, a block south of the Farmers' Market on the northeast side of downtown Ann Arbor. From Business Route I-94 (Huron) a block east of Main, go north on Fourth. Park in the lot at Catherine and Fourth, or in the big structure two blocks west off West Ann. (313) 994-0601.

Ever since 1975, Wildflour Community Bakery has been a fixture next to the People's Food Co-op on Ann Arbor's alternative cultures block of North Fourth Avenue. Outsiders might think this bakery offers only wholegrain, organic, whole wheat bread that's heavy as a brick, bland, and eaten more for its politically correct healthfulness than for its taste.

So it may be a surprise to discover a huge variety of healthy breads here, from dense to light and everything in between, plus a number of satisfying sweet treats. Most, including some terrific whole wheat burger buns, win compliments from mainstream eaters. And the prices are rock-bottom, considering the quality of ingredients. The basic, 20-ounce whole wheat loaf has been the same price for eight years — $1.30. Most other breads are $1.65 to $1.80 a loaf.

The six-person production collective, run with the input and volunteer labor of the larger local natural foods community, has successfully achieved its goal of providing high-quality basic foods at a low cost — quite a feat in a town where people are accustomed to paying top dollar for good food. Wildflour's six bakers, like all bakery crews, have learned to work together intimately on a daily basis, while the relatively expensive and much larger food co-op next door has been less harmonious and practical. Wildflour also manages to have time and money for its successful "Rolling in Dough" program, in which a baker kneads and bakes bread in school classrooms and discusses sustainable agriculture and cooperation while the dough is rising.

Popular Wildflour favorites include variations on basic whole wheat bread (cinnamon-raisin, herb-onion, seven-grain) and sprouted grain and sesame-sunflower breads. The last two are yeasted whole wheat breads with sprouts and soy flour added to complete the protein.

Numerous specialty breads and rolls appear on Wildflour's weekly baking schedule, printed for customers. Of them, the essene breads are the most unusual, made by only a handful of American bakeries, none in the Midwest. This unleavened, flowerless, fatless bread is named after one of the tribes of Israel, which baked it on hot rocks. It's made of carefully sprouted wheat or rye berries, ground up into a sticky dough, then baked a long time at a low temperature. Fruits and nuts are often added. The result is a dense, nutritionally rich bread with a dry crust and moist, chewy inside, made sweet by the sprouting proces. For people who can't eat wheat, Wildflour also makes spelt bread from a grain mostly used to feed cattle in this country.

Wildflour's range of healthy, inexpensive fast foods are most welcome in a town that has become so expensive. Big bran or fruit muffins (60¢) and whole wheat bagels in several flavors (50¢) are made daily. Organic fruit is used in the oatmeal and barley fruit bars. For the cheapest lunch in town, whole wheat rollups, baked with chopped vegetables, tomato sauce, and cheese inside, are available every day from 11:30 to 1 or so for $1.25. On Saturday, there's whole wheat pizza after 10 a.m., also $1.25 a slice.

Committed co-op bakers are happy to share their accumulated wisdom and recipes. *Uprisings,* a fat, user-friendly book about whole grains in baking, has recipes from 32 cooperative whole grain bakeries. It's $10 at Wildflour, or at the co-op next door, which opens on Sundays and evenings when the bakery is closed.

BAY CITY

7 Barney's Bakery

Tuesday-Friday 6 a.m.-5:30 p.m., Saturday 6-4.

In the south-central part of Bay City's east side, at the corner of 16th and Van Buren. At I-75 exit 162 where U.S. 10 joins I-75, take Business Route I-75 into town across the Saginaw River bridge. At the second light, turn right (south) onto Madison. In four blocks turn left onto 16th and proceed 3 blocks to the bakery. (517) 895-5466.

Bay City is an amazing fossil, a once-bustling city that has survived the loss of most of its industrial powerhouses with more grace than would seem possible. A good deal of the credit goes to extremely stable eastside Polish neighborhoods like the one Barney's Bakery is in. Poles from Saginaw and farther come here to buy fried *paczki* ($3.25/dozen), here made with raisins and available year-round, not just in the weeks before Lent. To call them jelly donuts is a disservice; they're made with a different dough than normal American yeast-raised jelly donuts. (For huge portions of good Polish food, ask for directions to Krysiak's House restaurant.)

Owner-baker Daniel Zielinski's grandfather came from Germany and worked for other bakers before starting Barney's in 1929. Many of the recipes he brought from Europe are still used here — for instance, a rich, eggy streusel coffee cake with raisins and crumbs on top ($1.90). Most things at Barney's are still made from scratch. A brick oven helps make for a nice, thick crust on the breads: rye, dark rye, sour rye, poppyseed, and potato bread, from $1.15 to $1.40 a loaf. Some breads are made now in very small quantities, to accommodate a dwindling number of older customers who appreciate Old World breads. The holidays bring on a number of traditional favorites — stollen, and cookies like lebkuchen, springerle, and pfeffernüsse.

Don't leave Bay City without driving — or, better, walking a few blocks — down Center Street (M-25), the Victorian show street of elaborate mansions from Bay City's lumber boom days. It runs from downtown east to the beautiful early 20th-century neighborhood on and north of Center at Park. Two blocks north on Park — that's about a mile east of downtown — Carroll Park at the end of Fourth and Third Streets would be a nice place to sit and enjoy coffee and bakery rolls.

BENTON HARBOR/ST. JOSEPH AREA

8 Bit of Swiss Pastry Shoppe

Open April-December, Tuesday-Saturday 8 a.m.-10 p.m.

Behind Tosi's restaurant between St. Joseph and Stevensville. From I-94, take exit 34 (the southernmost of all the exits around Benton Harbor/St. Joseph, where Schuler's is) and go north on Business Route I-94 (the Red Arrow Hwy.) less than a mile to Glenlord Rd. Turn left (west) on Glenlord, left again onto Ridge Rd. Tosi's is in about a block. (616) 429-1661.

Bavarian cream cakes and European-style tortes and fancy pastries are the chief specialties of this 25-year-old bakery and pastry shop that caters to the affluent resorters and old money in and around St. Joseph. Ingredients are first-rate, and prices much lower than in comparable shops in big metropolitan areas. Cherry brandy slices, Linzer tortes, Napoleons, and many more cakes and pastries are available by the slice or in individual portions, for $1 to $1.50. There's also a full line of morning pastries and sweet rolls, and cookies — and a few tables for customers who want to sit and have coffee.

If you've eaten at Tosi's, the wonderful Northern Italian restaurant in front, you've been served breads baked here in Tosi's bread basket. A chewy, crusty light rye ($1.50 a loaf) is the specialty of the house; sourdough, six-grain, and herb breads are somewhat more.

9 The Flour Shop Bakery & Pizzeria

Tuesday-Thursday 7 a.m.-9 p.m., Friday & Saturday 7 a.m.-10 p.m., Sunday 3:30 p.m.-9 p.m. Monday closed. Pizza only after 4 p.m.

In Stevensville, 6 miles south of St. Joseph, on John Beers Rd. at Cleveland Ave. From I-94, take exit 22 (Stevensville/Grand Mere State Park). Go east across Red Arrow Hwy. on John Beers Rd. through downtown Stevensville, continue east a mile, past the high school, up to but not through a busy commercial intersection. Bakery is in a small retail strip on the left. (616) 429-3250.

At Alpen Rose bakery restaurant in Holland, Hermann and Louise Schwaiger have opened an Austrian konditorei. He came to the U.S. to head the kitchens at Mackinac Island's Grand Hotel.

Debbie Nixdorf has been a baker her entire working career, mastering cake decorating at area grocery store bakeries and learning about European-style pastries at A Bit of Swiss nearby. Now she, her husband Klaus, and her brother (a former pizza store manager) have teamed up to transform an existing pizza shop into a general-line bakery that sells the usual morning sweet rolls and cookies, plus pizza baked in an old-fashioned brick oven, and a number of European-style specialties made with light whipped cream and light, silky butter creams. Of the many-layered tortes, German chocolate torte, layered with Bavarian cream custard, is generally on hand; it's $1 a slice, or $11 for an eight-inch cake. Black Forest, hazelnut, and other special tortes should be ordered four or five days ahead. Delicious additions to any picnic on a nearby beach would be lemon-poppyseed muffins (49¢) or carrot-raisin muffins (59¢) or eclairs filled with real custard and topped with a nice semi-sweet chocolate ($1) or cream cheese strudel sticks (59¢) made with blueberry or apricot filling.

Special-order cakes, creatively designed by Debbie, are a big part of the Flour Shop's business. It's fun to look through the photo album of every cake made here since the shop opened. The ovens are so constantly used in the daytime with cakes and pizza that there's only been time to do two kinds of bread: a crusty Italian ($1.30 a one-pound loaf) and a light rye ($1.50). More bread is planned when the Nixdorfs add a night baker to their crew.

10 Golden Brown Bakery

3 coffee shop locations in Benton Harbor/St. Joseph area also offer soups, sandwiches; main bakery and cafeteria is in South Haven. All may close earlier in winter.

◆ *In* **downtown St. Joseph**, *at 113 Main (U.S. 33), across from the courthouse in a row of low shops that also includes Baskin Robbins.* **Open** *Monday-Saturday 6:30 a.m.-6 p.m. (616) 983-2002.*
◆ *In* **suburban Fairplain**, *just south of Benton Harbor, on Colfax at Napier (southwest corner, toward St. Joseph).* **Open** *Monday-Saturday 6:30 a.m.-6 p.m. (616) 925-2730.*
◆ *In* **Watervliet**, *about 10 miles east of Benton Harbor, just north of I-94 Watervliet exit. At 319 North Main.* **Open** *Monday-Saturday 6 a.m.-4 p.m. (616) 463-4731.*

Founded in 1938, this successful resort-town bakery keeps up with changing food trends and now wins good comments in the area for its dense, satisfying 6-grain bread ($1.59 a one-pound loaf) and even heavier 3-seed bread ($3.79 a two-pound loaf). Both consist mainly of wheat flour. The six grains are barley, oatmeal, cornmeal, crushed rye, millet, and sesame; the three seeds, poppyseed, sesame, and raisins, are on the crust and inside, too. In all, some 20 kinds of bread, all raised with yeast, are made, though not every day.

Other favorite items are cheese danish (70¢) and lots of things featuring South Haven's leading fruit crop, blueberries. They're fresh in season, and held frozen for use throughout the year in oversize blueberry muffins (80¢), coffee cakes ($4 for 22 ounces), and more.

11 Harbert Swedish Bakery

Open from Easter to Thanksgiving on a changing schedule. From Easter to Memorial Day, open Friday through Sunday 7:30 to 6, Sunday to 4:30. In June: same hours, also open Thursday. From July 4 weekend through Labor Day weekend: open Wednesday through Sunday. After Labor Day up to Thanksgiving: open Friday through Sunday.

In Harbert, one of the little Lake Michigan resort towns a third of the way north between New Buffalo and St. Joseph. at 13746 Red Arrow Highway at the intersection of Harbert Rd. From I-94, take the Sawyer exit (exit 12), go west to the Red Arrow Highway (not east to the town center of Harbert), then south about 2 miles to Harbert. (616) 469-1777.

It's worth figuring out the tricky seasonal schedule to plan a stop off I-94 to Chicago at this authentic Swedish bakery. There's been a bakery at this place for over 80 years, going back to when Harbert was largely Swedish, a logging camp turned farm town and resort for Swedes from Chicago. (Carl Sandburg's goat farm was nearby.) For the current baker owner, a former Chicago upholsterer of Swedish descent, taking over the bakery and continuing to bake high-quality traditional ethnic baked goods is the fulfillment of a longtime dream. There are round limpa bread (a Swedish rye bread lightly and pleasantly flavored with cumin, fennel, and orange), Swedish rye ($1.40 for a 24-ounce loaf), many kinds of sweet rolls including Danish (85¢), soft pretzels, kaiser rolls, bran muffins, eclairs, pies, tortes, cookies, and Bohemian kolachys (a rich egg bread flavored with lemon).

This is a cheerful, cozy place, paneled in knotty pine, with lace curtains. There are a few inside tables for coffee drinkers, and a picnic table for frequent bicycling customers.

CADILLAC

12 Hermann's European Inn & Cafe & Chef's Deli

Deli & bakery hours: Monday-Thursday 7 a.m.-7 p.m., Friday & Saturday 7 a.m.-8 p.m. 214 N. Mitchell in downtown Cadillac. From the junction of U.S. 131 and M-115 south of town, take U.S. 131 north into town. (616) 775-9563.

One of the beneficial spinoff effects of having big, expansive resorts in Michigan is that they recruit chefs trained in Europe according to more rigorous standards of quality, and that eventually a good number of those chefs start their own restaurants, sometimes with an in-house bakery. That's the story behind Hermann's Cafe and Deli in Cadillac. Austrian chef Hermann Suhs came to the U.S. in 1978 as executive chef at the Grand Traverse Resort. Six years later, he started his own place in downtown Cadillac. Now it's not only a restaurant but a deli/bakery and seven-room inn.

Hermann's initial training was in making Viennese pastries. His Sacher Torte (usually served in the restaurant only) is the real thing — he actually worked at the Hotel Sacher. In the European tradition, using anything but real whipped cream and real butter in pastries is close to sacrilege. But vacationers may consider Hermann's breads the most valuable find of all. Good bread can make the simplest picnic or cookout memorable, and, oddly, really good bread is hard to find in the Grand Traverse area. Hermann's sourdough French breads and his rye breads have a good, hard crust. The French breads come in many useful forms: small hard rolls (35¢), bratwurst and sub buns (60¢), baguettes ($1.20), and a one-pound sandwich-size loaf ($1.50, like most breads here). Other breads include dill, vegetable bread (with carrots, oniions, and celery), raisin bread, and cinnamon bread.

Butter croissants come plain (95¢) or flavored with raspberry, strawberry, chocolate, blueberry, and strawberry-cream cheese ($1.19). Dessert pastries include custard eclairs and Napoleons (puff pastry filled with fondant, vanilla mousse, and custard). Baked goods and coffee may be enjoyed in the deli area, or on the sidewalk cafe outside. The adjoining restaurant features special menus on Friday ethnic nights.

CHARLEVOIX

13 Stafford's Weathervane

Open at lunch and dinner year-round.
    On the Pine River Channel just off Bridge St. (U.S. 31) in down-town Charlevoix. (616) 5437-4311.

See Stafford's Bay View Inn, page 274. There's also a possibility that bread from Tapawingo restaurant in Ellsworth may be sold at their new cafe across the street at the Weathervane Terrace Hotel.

FLINT

14 Balkan Bakery

Open Sunday 7-noon, Monday-Thursday 8-4:30, Friday 8-1. Closed Saturday.
    Dayton Street at Delmar, just to the west of Forest Hills across from the Civic Park. From I-475 take the Hamilton North exit. From I-75 take the Pierson Road exit. (313) 235-3431.

The claim to fame of this modest old Yugoslavian bakery is its "Mother's Bread," a hefty 20-ounce unsliced loaf that sells for just $1.55. It's an old-fashioned Vienna-style hearth-baked bread without shortening or preservatives, available either plain or with poppyseeds or sesame seeds. The crust is wonderfully thick and crunchy, enveloping a soft, somewhat moist white bread. It's great when reheated ten to twenty minutes in a slow (325°) oven. Eat it the way they do in Eastern Europe — break off chunks and use it to sop up juices of stews and salads.

People come from miles around to buy Mother's Bread. A Delta commercial pilot from Georgia fills his empty suitcase with 20 loaves to take back home. But the Balkan Bakery is content to keep a low profile. A sign at the cash register proclaims that neither checks nor $20 bills are accepted. It's in a neighborhood of smallish autoworkers' homes that was quickly built by General Motors around 1916 to house the flood of workers coming to the boom town of Flint during the heydays of Buick and Chevrolet. Back then these five- and six-room homes cost as little as $3,500. It's interesting to see how the once nearly-identical homes have evolved into very different appearances over the decades.

The Balkan is presided over by Barbara, whose family has owned

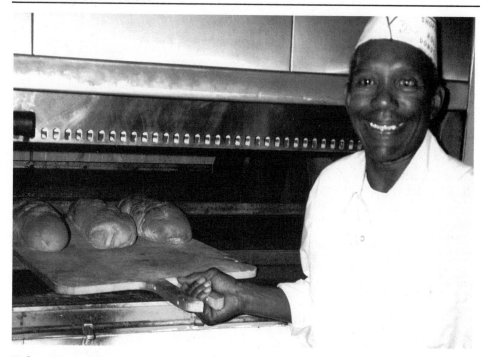

Baker Roosevelt Seabron takes out some of the Balkan Bakery's famous Mother's Bread. The hefty loaf's wonderful crust draws customers from well beyond Flint.

it since 1941. They bought it from another Yugoslavian family which had started the bakery in the 1920s. Her two bakers, Roosevelt Seabron and Bob Dowd, have been with her over a quarter century, working from midnight often to noon the next day. Their baking methods are the opposite of modern automated bakeries. Intuition takes the place of instrumentation. They know, for example, that a hot day will speed up the baking and a cold day will slow them down.

Balkan sticks to the basics — no fancy decorated cakes here. Potato bread ($1.40 for a one-pound loaf) is popular. The small crew makes pies and doughnuts, corn bread and cookies. The cookies, 30¢ each or $2.20-$2.40/dozen, are the classic varieties: ice box, peanut butter, sugar, oatmeal, chocolate chip, molasses, and raisin.

Balkan sticks to the basics — no fancy decorated cakes here. Potato bread ($1.40 for a one-pound loaf) is popular. The small crew makes pies and doughnuts, corn bread and cookies. The cookies, 30¢ each or $2.20-$2.40/dozen, are the classic varieties: ice box, peanut butter, sugar, oatmeal, chocolate chip, molasses, and raisin.

FRANKENMUTH

15 Zehnder's

730 South Main Street in Frankenmuth. (517) 652-3992. Open 8-9 daily.

Zehnder's may be best known for its fried chicken dinners, but the huge Frankenmuth restaurant also has one of the most extraordinary bakeries in the state. The restaurant began back in 1927, but the full-line bakery was started in 1977. The gleaming, expensively-equipped facility is a European-style bakery. Even the sizable display cases were imported from Europe. Great care has been taken to create authentic European breads and pastries. An entire room with its own special oven and preparation area is devoted to tortes. In another area is the busy five-person cake crew, operating under the watchful eye of 40-year veteran Harvey Menzel. Everything is made from scratch, and the scale is such that the ingredients are exceptionally fresh. The apples in apple pies are peeled right before making the filling, the lemons for the lemon meringue pies squeezed just before adding.

There's a Germanic efficiency and bustle to this big operation, which you can observe through a window at the base of the stairway going down to the retail sales room. Sitting on colorful tiled floors are the huge ovens that can bake 1,000 loaves an hour. This is a scale you might expect from a wholesale bakery, but everything baked at Zehnder's is sold here or by mail order. The volume is needed to meet the demand of the complex's million-plus visitors a year. A big spiral mixer mixes huge batches of bread dough, which is hoisted over to a divider hopper, where loaves are automatically molded. By far the most popular product here is the stollen, a very tasty fruit bread full of candied fruit, coconut, raisins, and nuts. Next in popularity is backofen bread, a white bread with a thicker crust which connoisseurs of toast prize highly.

While the breadmaking is highly automated, most of the other items — the pies and pretzels, the cakes and Danish pastries — are created with Old World handmade care. A popular new item are the tasty piecrust cookies with filling ($4.25 for a box of 6). The spacious sales room also features elegant chocolate truffles, hand dipped by Belgian-trained Ruth Rittmueller. Gift baskets, wines, and many tinned and bottled fancy foods are also for sale here.

GRAND RAPIDS

16 Ed's Breads

Tuesday through Friday 8-5:30, Saturday 8 to noon. Customers are welcome before 8, but all the baking may not be finished. (616) 451-9100.

1204 Leonard on the west side of Grand Rapids, just west of Garfield and across from Burger King. From U.S. 131, take the Leonard Street exit north of downtown, go west a mile. From downtown, take Division to Leonard, then west.

In this wonderful little bakery, the recent interest in breadmaking as a craft and a way to eat simply and healthily have combined with ethnic traditions. The result is a bakery that draws from two quite different but equally loyal clienteles: the Poles, Lithuanians, and Germans who make up most of Grand Rapids' west side, and food-conscious eastsiders and suburbanites who otherwise only venture west to visit John Ball Zoo and Park. Founder Ed Parauka worked on improving his Lithuanian and Polish grandmothers' breads and started this bakery when he had arrived at the point where he consistently got satisfactory results. Its philosophy has paid attention to nutrition without being a whole grains purist; white flours are widely used in combination with heavier flours.

The traditional dark East European breads made here are outstanding, especially the sourer doughs, like the fabulous Latvian rye and pumpernickel. The Polish rye is a staple among westsiders. Crusts, a hallmark of flavorful bread, are made hard and chewy by just the right amount of steam. (Getting it right in different kinds of weather is a matter of experience and instinct.) A successful new introduction is a 100% whole wheat loaf that's heavy but tall, not a leaden brick like so many 100% whole grain broads. (The secret at Ed's is mixing and kneading the dough for a very long time, to the point where it has speckles.)

Most breads are $2.25 a loaf, generally 2 1/4 pounds — quite a value compared to good bakeries in upscale locations. A nice, plumpish sourdough baguette is $1.50; health bread with many grains and some wheat berries is $2. In addition to the starring breads, Ed's offers excellent cookies, sweet rolls, and rolls. Hearty, satisfying cinnamon rolls ($1 for a huge one) are popular.

Special breads made once a week in smaller batches tend to sell out early; come in the morning or call ahead to order or reserve some. Here's the weekly schedule:

Tuesday: health bread. **Wednesday:** cream cheese-raisin (a big favorite), Latvian rye (so good you can eat plain cubes of it as a snack), oatmeal-honey, horseshoe rolls. **Thursday:** pumpernickel, sour French, potato bread. **Friday:** Lithuanian rye, oatmeal-honey, hotdog and hamburger buns, Parker House rolls. **Saturday:** bundukies (very popular bacon-onion rolls), buns, Parker House rolls.

Eventually a baker's long hours got to Ed and he became a salesman. His onetime assistant, Kathryn Kelly, and her husband, John, have been carrying on the tradition he developed, adding their own improvements without burning out; they have even managed to accommodate a baby daughter to a baker's schedule.

For a beautiful backroads drive to Grand Haven, continue west on Leonard. It turns into a delightful country road along the Grand River, passing many attractive farms and the picturesque old river villages of Eastmanville and Lamont. Continue on Leonard into Spring Lake, across the river from Grand Haven. An even prettier but more confusing way is to cross the Grand River at 68th Street in Eastmanville, then jig and jog along the river past its beautiful, lazy bayous and a park before coming into Grand Haven's south-west side. An Ottawa County map is most helpful for this.

HILLSDALE/JONESVILLE/HOMER AREA

17 A. J. Wedge

Monday-Friday 9-5, Saturday 9-3.

77 North Howell at Broad at the north entrance to downtown Hillsdale, across and uphill from City Hall. (517) 437-2888.

Most small-town downtowns in Michigan and the rest of the U.S. have taken a beating in the last 20 years. Hillsdale's is surprisingly healthy and lively. Among its surprises are a good used book store, a restored hotel, a wonderful old courthouse with an abstract sculpture outside representing the major regional rivers that originate in Hillsdale County (the Kalamazoo, the Grand, and the St. Joseph are three), and this cheerfully sophisticated little cafe, named after its owner and the wedge-shaped building it's in. It serves cappucino, café au lait, and iced coffee, and a nice line of rolls: individual-size pocket breads (white, whole wheat, and onion-parmesan) and chewy French bread rolls — all 40¢, and croissants (with fruit, chocolate or cream cheese $1.15, with ham and cheese $1.50). But it is the brownies that the owner really gets excited about: things like the Denver (87¢), involving butter cream, caramel, and nuts with chocolate fudge topping, and the Outrageous (78¢), topped with semi-sweet chocolate slivers.

18 Jonesville Pastry Shop

Monday-Saturday 7 a.m.- 2 p.m.
243 East Chicago (U.S. 12) in downtown Jonesville, 5 miles north of Hillsdale and 16 miles east of Coldwater. (517) 849-9864.

In this general-line small-town bakery, two labor-intensive specialties stand out: decorated butter cookies and salt-rising bread. The butter cookies are available all the time, and made into special shapes for various holidays, decorated with icing by hand, and ordered by the dozens as gifts. Co-owner Dale McKitterick says it's his cookie, and there's not another like it.

Salt-rising bread was developed before commercial yeasts were available; the bread is leavened by fermented milk and flour, to which salt has been added. McKittrick starts his bread on Sunday, lets it ferment three days, and bakes it on Thursday for the weekend. It's a coarse, dense bread with a tangy taste and strong smell that's released when toasted.

19 Joy Bakery

Open 24 hours, along with the Shell gas station it's in.
On M-60 at the west edge of Homer, 2-3 blocks west of M-99. From M-69 at Tekonsha, south of Marshall, take M-60 10 miles east to Homer. From I-94 at Albion, take M-99 south to Homer, stay on M-60 until you see the Shell Station. (517) 568-4668.

This is a very good small-town bakery in a strange but logical setting. Until five or so years ago, it was in Homer's quaint but by-passed downtown, until the owner-baker decided it made more sense to move to the 24-hour Shell station, so early-morning commuters could gas up and get their sweet rolls at the same time. Judy Krupka, the food-loving innkeeper at Homer's Grist Mill Inn, gets there early to be sure of getting just what she wants for the inn. The whole wheat, white, and cinnamon breads are terrific, and so are the prices — 90¢ a loaf, 35¢ for the excellent cinnamon rolls and other standard sweet rolls, and 40¢ for pecan rolls.

M-60, which goes northeast-southwest between Niles and Jackson, makes for an interesting alternative route part or all of the way to Chicago, provided that you take the time to explore the interesting small town centers that are usually just south of the highway. Concord, just east of Homer, is especially picturesque, and the Mann House, a state house museum portraying the lives of well-educated small-town leaders at the turn of the century, is delightful. Open April-October from Wednesday through Sunday 1-5. (517) 524-8943.

HOLLAND

20 Alpen Rose

Monday through Thursday 9-9, Friday and Saturday 9-10, Sunday 10:30-2:30 (brunch in main dining room only; ask staff to help with baked goods).

4 East Eighth at Central in downtown Holland. Plenty of parking lots along Ninth Street. (313) 393-2111.

Holland, the center of Dutch-American separatist culture, now has a remarkably authentic Austrian *konditorei* (a combined pastry shop and cafe) and an adjoining restaurant of the same name. They have become a cornerstone of downtown's renaissance after two huge malls vanquished most of longtime retailers.

Downtown's white knight is a locally well-known manufacturer who doesn't like to spread his name around on all his many projects. (Everybody knows who he is; if you really want to know, ask.) When he found out that Hermann and Louise Schwaiger, the executive chef and pastry chef at Mackinac Island's Grand Hotel, were thinking of starting an inn, he urged them to become his partners in a restaurant instead.

The cheery *konditorei* faces Eighth Street and the old Warm Friend hotel. The main entrance and dining rooms face Central Avenue. The whole interior looks as if it could be in a refurbished 200-year-old building in Salzburg; it's hard to believe that the elaborate architectural detail and stone floors are where a Woolworth's once was. Most of the decor — including Tyrolean-style furniture in bleached wood and lamps with simple linen shades — comes from Salzburg. The effect is completely unlike the typical German-American restaurant, without a beer stein, heraldic shield, or dark wood beam in sight.

The beautiful pastries are in the best Austrian tradition — never too sweet but rich with the subtle, layered flavor of whipped

Spring Ten Kley's successful Holland restaurant, Till Midnight, has now opened an excellent bakery next door. Here she sits on the outside sidewalk cafe and plans a catering order with a customer.

cream. Cakes and tortes are $2.25 to $3 a slice, but a sweet tooth can also be satisfied with smaller 75¢ pastries like a Linzer almond macaroon bar, brownies, cream cheese squares, and käse sahne (lemony cream cheese with whipped cream on almond sponge cake).

The rye and sourdough breads, chewy with body, are the perfect bases for easy picnic lunches in loaf or roll form. Louise Schwaiger's favorites include an apricot wheat bread with cinnamon swirl, good for toast; and tomato-basil, olive, rye, and sourdough breads. More kinds of breads, including brioche and croissants, are available on Saturday. Prices range from $1.50 for baguettes of French bread to $2.50 for a large loaf of hearty raisin pumpernickel that's the equal, in texture and flavor, to what's found in a good Jewish bakery.

21 Pereddies

Monday-Saturday 10 a.m.-9:30 p.m. Bread can sell out by 5.
447 Washington Square, southwest of downtown Holland between 18th and 19th Streets. Washington Square is a small, early 20th-century retail area on Washington Street, a major north-south street

parallel to Central. From the main north-south arterials of Central, College, or River, take any numbered street west to Washington, then turn south or north to 18th and 19th. (616) 394-3061.

Continuing the tradition of deli-bakeries in the old Detroit Italian neighborhood one of the founders grew up in, Pereddies makes crusty Italian bread. The same dough is used for baguettes, Vienna-style loaves slit down the middle (one pound is $1.50), and for smaller pannini and a fragrant foccaccia ($2.50) — a six-inch round topped with olive oil, garlic, basil, onions, and tomatoes.

It's only a short way to Kollen Park, Holland's main municipal park on Lake Macatawa. Go north on Washington to 12th Street, then west to the park.

22 Till Midnight Bakery

Monday through Saturday, 7:30 a.m. to restaurant closing. Baked goods are available at the restaurant next door after bakery closes.

208 College just south of Eighth Street in downtown Holland. Plenty of parking off Ninth. (313) 392-6883.

Till Midnight, downtown Holland's first creative, late-night restaurant, was known from the start for the wonderful breadbaskets that come with each meal. Now it has spawned a nifty little bakery next door, with an expanded selection of outstanding breads. Most are made with simple sour doughs because baker Eddie Parach has found that the slow-fermentation breadmaking process used in making traditional European rye breads allows bakers to create far more variations on the same theme.

Parach first started making bread on weekends on a kibbutz, then worked as a baker to earn his B.A. in piano performance at Western Michigan University. "I baked the American way: fill the dough full of yeast and run with it," he says, "until I put two and two together." Talking to a French baker, he came to realize that the slow-fermentation, sour-starter process that takes as long as 24 to 48 hours for the first rising actually lets the breadmaker achieve the biggest variety of flavors and textures of bread by manipulating the basics. Interestingly, this variety is won with the simplest of ingredients — just flour, water, salt, and a little yeast in the starter. The sourdough method results in the kinds of bread he likes the most — those with a chewy crust and a firm, close-grained interior texture that comes from having less carbon dioxide, which makes smaller gas bubbles when the bread rises. Furthermore, by varying the temperatures of the water and flour, he found he could affect the flavor of the yeast mold in the starter, and thus the flavor of the bread.

Till Midnight's sourdough breads are mostly tangy, extremely flavorful breads, not unpleasantly heavy but with lots of body. They look beautiful in their varied golden brown crusts made shiny with steam. On the other hand, French bread ($2 for a large loaf) and baguettes are light inside with a hard crust because they're made with a blend of pastry flour and bread flour that approximates the softer flours of Europe. Breads baked daily usually include light rye, whole wheat raisin, oat bread, and a dark rye pumpernickel, plain or with raisins. Most loaves are 23 to 26 ounces and cost $2.50 plain. Romano cheese and fresh herbs are added for a special $3.50 loaf.

On Saturdays more kinds of breads are baked for the weekend: a tangy San Francisco-style sourdough ($2.50 a loaf), to which fennel, raisin-fennel, and rosemary-garlic may be added; seven grain; various onion breads; and brioche. That golden butter-egg yeast bread represents everything Parach has come to detest — too much fat, for a fluffy texture and rich but boring taste. (For more on sour or lean breads, Jewish style, see page 225.)

JACKSON

23 European Bakery

Sunday 6 a.m.-12:30 p.m. Monday and Tuesday 7 a.m.-6 p.m. Wednesday (a no-baking day) 8 a.m.-noon. Thursday and Friday 6-6. Saturday (no baking) 8 a.m.-noon.

622 Page at Sweet, on Jackson's east side. From I-94 east of downtown and the Cooper St. exit, take the Elm Ave. exit. Go south on Elm, crossing Michigan Ave. In about 8 short blocks, you'll come to Page. Turn right. Bakery is in about a block, just west of the Polish National Alliance. It's attached to a small house and easy to miss. (517) 787-5726.

Jackson's east side developed around the big yards and repair shops of the Michigan Central Railroad, Michigan's transportation powerhouse until the Age of the Automobile. So when Anthony Niesluchowski came from Poland to the U.S. in the first part of the 20th century, it wasn't surprising that he first came to Detroit's booming Polish enclave of Hamtramck and then got a railroad job in Jackson. There he decided to make use of his baker's skills and start a bakery on Page Avenue, right by the rail yards, to supply Polish railroad workers with the bread they'd known at home.

Today, 80 years later, the streetcar and stores that served the Polish neighborhood are long gone, and the neighborhood itself is finally dwindling. But the European Bakery remains, run by Niesluchowski's daughter, Gert Ludwig, son-in-law Tom McCann, and Tom's four children. In a town with a great gulf between east side and west side, demand for its fresh-baked breads is one of the very few things that draws country-clubbers from south of Sharp Park to over here to the working-class east side. The dark rye or pumpernickel is the best-selling bread; there's also a black rye with caraway, a light rye, and crusty Vienna bread. (Dough for Vienna bread is also used in hard rolls.) The rye breads are made from sour starter for good flavor, baked in a coal-fired brick oven the size of a small room, and steamed for an excellent crust. They don't rise two or three times — the ultimate in developing the fullest flavor. But for $1 a one-pound loaf ($2 for the two-pound loaf), you can't have everything. All things considered, this is very good bread, well worth the trouble of finding the obscure bakery itself. (It's also sold elsewhere, but not delivered fresh daily; call to inquire.)

Babkas and paczki round out the Old World specialties. Among Poles in Jackson, authentic paczkis should not have jelly fillings; here they are available in their familiar jelly doughnut guise, or unfilled, each 35¢. The eggy, buttery light coffeecake crown known as babka (from the word for grandmother) is filled with raisins and fruit. It sells for $2.75. Other sweet rolls have been mostly discontinued. Croissants (80¢, filled with strawberry, cherry, blueberry, or cream cheese) are the major exception.

24 Hinkley Bakery

Wednesday-Saturday 5:15 a.m.- 3 p.m.

South of downtown Jackson at 700 S. Blackstone at Wilkins. Blackstone is one-way going north, so the bakery can be hard to get to. From I-94: take West Ave. (Business 127 and M-50) into town. Continue south of Michigan Ave. (M-50 and 127 go east into downtown) 4-5 blocks to Morrell, go east onto Morrell for several blocks, then, after you've passed First, turn left onto Blackstone. Bakery is in two blocks. (517) 782-1122.

Hinkley's Bakery in Jackson is one of many good bakeries tucked away in older urban neighborhoods. By keeping overhead low, such bakeries can stay profitable without assuming the risk of more expensive space.

Once you understand old and extremely settled towns like Jackson, you *expect* to find a fair number of hidden treasures tucked away in hard-to-find areas, with hardly a sign out front. In places with few outsiders or newcomers, signs are hardly necessary; word of mouth is the only advertising needed. It's not all that surprising that Jackson has not one but two old-time bakeries. Space here is cheap, customers loyal, and it's not hard for several generations of bakers to have a steady, profitable, controllable small business by doing much of the work themselves. Though his name's not German, fourth-generation owner-baker Brian Hinkley puts himself and his father and partner Jack squarely in the conservative German tradition of most of his ancestors. (It's amazing how often the oldest family businesses you're likely to run into are German.)

Morning sweet rolls are the heart of Hinkley's business, though even here healthier options like muffins are gaining ground. But fritters (55¢) are what Hinkley's is known for — big, sugary, fried affairs, made from scratch, with lots of apples or walnuts. The walnuts are a nice contrast to all that sugar. Brian Hinkley is fussy about the nuts he buys; the pecans in his popular 10-inch coffee cake ($2.90) come straight from Georgia growers, so they're sure to be the latest crop.

Hinkley's also sells a full line of cookies, made without preservatives. But the bread is what many people make a special trip for — especially the white salt-rising bread, leavened with a fermented flour-water mixture instead of yeast for a tangy, interesting flavor. At $1 for a one-pound loaf, it has become so popular that it's baked daily.

Other breads include rye, Italian, and Vienna breads baked direct on the ancient oven's stone hearth and steamed for chewy crusts. White, whole wheat, and oat bran breads are all baked in pans. All are $1 a loaf.

KALAMAZOO

25 Boonzaayer Bakery

Tuesday through Friday 8-5:30, Saturday 8-2.
2111 South Burdick, about a mile south of downtown and 3 lights past the Crosstown Parkway at Burdick near Alcott. From I-94, take North Westnedge exit, in about 2 miles make a right (east) onto Inkster to Burdick, turn left (north). Bakery is on right in 1/4 mile. (616) 343-3001.

Sometimes it looks as if the Dutch baking tradition — quality ingredients, with lots of flavorful butter and special attention paid to cookies — has died out in West Michigan, the very center of Dutch-American culture — despite its huge Dutch-American populations. Michigan's Dutch have been remarkably enthusiastic about large-scale mass marketing systems, from Amway to shopping strips, Meijer stores, Russ's and Arnie's popular bakery restaurants. So it's a welcome relief for food-lovers to learn of Boonzaayer's, a small pastry shop that upholds the high-quality Dutch tradition.

Owner-baker Karel Boonzayer grew up in a family of bakers and graduated from a highly regarded Dutch bakery school. Strong principles direct his philosophy of business, baking, and life. Be honest toward God and man. Give and you shall receive. Use the best ingredients and people will expect more and get more. "Our business is an extension of our own being; we give quality, service, and self," he says.

All this means baking from scratch, often with ingredients from the Netherlands and Germany. Many cakes and items are mainly made to order for freshness, but most days you can expect to find quite a range of European pastries with lots of whipped cream: tortes, mocha slices, Napoleons, and molded Bavarians ($1.10 in many flavors). Marzipan figures are made on the premises in fanciful shapes. Butter tea cookies in many kinds are $3.50 a half-pound bag; Danish coffee cakes (apple, caramel, cinnamon, and blueberry, with real butter, of course) are also $3.50 the half pound. Not all recipes are traditional European, but the holidays do bring an extra number of European specialties.

Boonzaayer's is in an old turn-of-the-century neighborhood that was still neat as a pin when Karel Boonzayer located here 30 years ago. Now most of its Dutch residents have moved to suburban Portage, but they return here for special-occasion cakes and desserts. There's a single table, more for planning wedding cakes than for snacks. Good warm-weather places to sit and enjoy pastries and carryout coffee are about 5 minutes away, at downtown's Kalamazoo Mall (the nation's first, it has outdoor tables) or nearby Bronson Park, landscaped to show off the colorful annuals grown here in the Bedding Plant Capital of America. Ask for directions.

26 Rykse's Restaurant and Bakery

Monday-Saturday 6:30 a.m.-9 p.m.

West of Kalamazoo, at 5924 West Stadium on the commercial strip in Oshtemo, just west of U.S. 131. From I-94, take U.S. 131 north to the Stadium exit (exit 36B). Go west 1/2 mile on Stadium. Just west of DeNooyer Chevrolet. (616) 372-3838.

Increasingly, good bakeries and independent, family-run restaurants go hand in hand. Good, fresh breads — in sandwiches, breadbaskets, and breakfast toast — and good desserts and morning pastries distinguish them from chain competitors. The restaurant is able to introduce its bakery's goods to diners who become retail customers.

That's how it works at Rykse's. The large yet cozy place on a new suburban strip between Kalamazoo and Paw Paw looks like another up-to-date mainstream restaurant chain. Actually, it's a hands-on family operation, and all the recipes are based on those Helen Rykse used in cooking for her husband and five children. This is American home cooking if every American home had a mom who was a good cook and concerned about her family's health. It's more in the style of the Better Homes and Gardens cookbook (Helen's favorite) than Fanny Farmer or James Beard.

Helen has modified favorite recipes by cutting back on sweetening and fat. Everything is made from scratch, and you can taste the difference. Even cherry pies start from a 30-pound package of frozen cherries.

Breads are yeast breads but much more substantial than the typical American fluffy yeast breads. Each loaf, made in a standard loaf pan, weighs in at two pounds, not one. Oatmeal, whole wheat, multigrain, raisin, and cinnamon twist breads are baked daily; most are from $1.50 to $2 a loaf. White bread dough reappears as dinner rolls and sub buns.

But the star and signature item is a terrific cinnamon roll — tightly coiled with a delicious brown sugar filling that becomes a crunchy crust on top. The effect is satisfyingly gooey and rich with only seven grams of fat. It's 95¢ for the big, six-inch version, 50¢ for a half size, and $1.15 with pecans in the crust. When the Rykse family began planning the restaurant, after Gene Rykse took early retirement following the Bell Telephone breakup, sons and partners Mark and Nate urged him to help them start a family home-cooking restaurant using their mother as the chief food consultant. Her cinnamon rolls were to be their trademark. Nate had been a management trainee at Wendy's but didn't like fast food. Mark had been injured as a construction worker.

The eastern terminus of the delightful Kal-Haven Trail through western Michigan's fruit belt is just a mile from here; a cinnamon roll would be a welcome addition to any bike ride. Call (616) 637-2788 for a trail map. The drive west from Rykse's along the Red Arrow Highway to Paw Paw and beyond also offers an interesting look at orchards and old towns.

27 Sarkozy Bakery

Tuesday-Friday 7-6, Saturday 7-3.

335 North Burdick one door down from Kalamazoo Street. From I-94 westbound from Battle Creek, take business route 94 into town. It becomes Kalamazoo. When you see the Old Kent Bank branch or the train station, look for an on-street parking place. From I-94 eastbound from Chicago or Paw Paw, take business route 94 into town. You turn onto U.S. 131 for a short way, then take Stadium Dr. to downtown. At Main, turn right (east); look for a parking place as you pass Rose. (616) 342-1952.

A good bakery has the potential for accomplishing all sorts of things beyond producing tasty, healthy basic food and treats. In an increasingly fragmented society, it can serve as a common ground linking a great variety of people on a daily basis, even to the point where they sit down and talk over a cup of coffee. With a minimum of investment aside from a baker's hard work and long hours, a bakery can also create a sense of community and help stabilize downtowns and older neighborhoods.

By these standards, Kalamazoo's Sarkozy Bakery has got to be Michigan's consummate bakery. In 1979 Ken and Judy Sarkozy had just given up the academic life and decided that, of any place within a three-hour drive of friends and family in southeast Michigan, Kalamazoo offered the best promise for developing a well-balanced, community-based business and way of life. They were pondering the specifics of a start-up business when a blizzard occurred. Their pantry and Julia Child's *Mastering the Art of French Cooking* yielded a simple but memorable meal: pea soup, red wine, and delicious French bread. It occurred to them, "Hey, we could sell this!"

Today the Sarkozy Bakery's delicious European-style breads, plus morning sweet rolls, cookies, and muffins, and cakes, attract food-lovers from all over Kalamazoo and its far-flung suburbs to downtown's north side — an area a fair number of locals don't visit, due to a blend of ignorant timidity and racism.

The door handles are bronze replicas of bread loaves, donated by an artist friend. Above them, a small sign says, "We accept food stamps." The exterior sign is most tasteful, the music played is usually classical, and neatly framed milling and baking memorabilia (another donation) decorate bare brick walls. The place would seem arty if it weren't so friendly. At inside tables, having coffee and juice, you're likely to find an assortment of people commonly branded yuppies, hippies, street people, academics, establishment types, and just plain folks, of all ages and colors, just like the staff. Every Saturday morning from around 8:30 to 11:30, an eclectic bunch of regulars gather at Table One to enjoy kaiser rolls hot out of the oven and discuss issues of the day. Other customers are invited to join in. Postcards are addressed to Table One. One year when the dishwasher, hot water heater, and furnace broke down at the same time, a $550 deposit from Table One was placed into the bakery's checking account.

☞ EXACT PRICES have been given to provide the best possible relative price comparisons. **It is expected**, of course, that **prices will increase** over the life of this book.

The Sarkozy Bakery in Kalamazoo is as much about everyday camaraderie as it is about good eating. Staff and customers supply blackboard "Judy sez" comments (upper right) next to a caricature of white-coiffed owner-baker Judy Sarkozy. Here she chats with a customer. This day in May was designated "Lilac and dogwood adoration day."

Breads here reflect the diverse ethnic bakeries remembered by Ken Sarkozy in his childhood home of Dearborn, and by Judy from Flint. Everything here is made from scratch and baked in a 90-year-old brick oven that forces bakers to pay attention to experience and intuition because it has no thermostat. Breads made with sour starters include rye, pumpernickel, and a crusty Sicilian loaf, all $1.95 for a 24-ounce loaf; Julia Child's French bread is $1.30 a load. The American style of bread (lighter breads made with yeast, fat, and sweetener, with a big crumb structure) are also important here. The oatmeal loaf (22 ounces for $1.70) is the bakery's biggest seller.

In all, almost a hundred kinds of baked goods are made here. Staples of the morning coffee crowd are danish cheese crowns (60¢) and paczki (50¢, plain or raspberry-filled). They're lighter than jelly doughnuts, though rich and more delicate. For light lunches, there's foccaccia, that recently trendy herbed flat bread, fresh fruit, muffins, carrot cake, and cookies (30¢) for dessert. Popular favorites are oatmeal-raisin and oatmeal bars with raspberry or apricot filling. Judy Sarkozy enjoys the delicate almond cookie with an unusual flavor.

Holidays feature traditional treats, sometimes made from family recipes of staff and customers. Lent brings Irish soda bread; for Easter, there's Josephine's Italian Anise Bread — "incredible," Judy calls it, beautiful and light, with luscious ingredients, including wine and butter. Ken's Czech mother contributed the recipe for *kalacs* (rolls filled with walnuts or poppyseed), available between Christmas and Easter. Fried dough angel wings, dusted with powdered sugar — they're called *chruscik* in Hungarian — are baked for all holidays.

Two nice nearby options for takeout eating are the tables on the Kalamazoo Mall, two blocks south (it was the first malled main street in the U.S.) and beautiful Bronson Park, replete with a great deal of sculpture and bedding plants. (Kalamazoo is, in fact, the bedding plant capital of America.)

LANSING

28   Hearthstone Community Bakery

Monday-Thursday 7:30 a.m.-10 p.m., Friday 7:30-midnight, Saturday 9 a.m.-midnight, Sunday 11-9.

2003 East Michigan at Fairview in Lansing, 1/2 mile east of the capitol in a one-block 1920s retail strip. (517) 485-8600.

This friendly, sunny little bakery and vegetarian cafe began as the Wolfmoon Co-op Bakery. After its dissolution, a single owner bought the equipment and runs it as a community bakery with considerable input from the nearby alternative community it serves. (The surrounding neighborhood of auto boom bungalows is a popular and inexpensive place to live.) This is an interesting area for browsing, even on Sunday, because of the pleasant Wolfmoon food co-op next door, along with an interesting variety of stores selling used books and comics, women's books, vintage clothing and furniture, and outdoors store, and more.

Breads ($1.39-$2 for a pound or a little more) and rolls are mostly made only with whole wheat flour, and the only sweeteners are honey and molasses. Many items are dairy-free and egg-free. It's tasty — crumbly rather than chewy and crusty. (No steam is used while baking.) Popular varieties are whole wheat, rye, 12-grain, three-seed, and two breads hand-formed on sheets rather than pans: a yeastless sourdough that rises overnight, and a French bread.

Additional baked goods include a Danish made with safflower oil and ricotta and cottage cheese, various fruit bars, sweet rolls, and cookies. Particular favorites: the Ultimate Cookie (a rich mix of chocolate, raisins, nuts, and more for $1), bran-oat muffins (79¢), and calzone pocket meals in various vegetable/cheese combinations ($3). Bakery customers can sit down to eat and drink coffee. Friday and Saturday evenings Hearthstone becomes a coffee house for folk and women's music respectively. Potter Park, a pleasant, shady spot on the Red Cedar River with a nifty small zoo, isn't too far away for a takeout picnic. Go west on Michigan to Pennsylvania, then south across the river to the park.

29 Dusty's Cellar

Monday-Saturday 7:30 a.m.-9 p.m., Sunday 7:30 a.m.-6 p.m.
In Okemos, the booming suburb east of East Lansing, on Grand River just east of Marsh Road and the Okemos Mall. In The Galleria, the second strip center east of Marsh. (517) 349-5150.

From a demographic and consumer point of view, Lansing is a cross-section of the broad and varied middle of American society, without too much at either end. For particular consumers, its lack of great wealth and sophistication can be an irritating weakness. When journalist and PR man Dusty Rhodes returned from living in Europe, he couldn't find the food and wine he'd come to love and expect. So he started a wine bar and bakery-gourmet store that have now expanded into a casual restaurant.

French breads and croissants are the specialty here, and the prices are reasonable. The breads are $1 for a long, skinny baguette, $1.50 for a sandwich-size Parisian loaf. Croissants are 80¢, or $1 filled with raspberry, apple, or chocolate. Farmer's bread in whole wheat, rye, or pumpernickel is $1.60 for a one-pound round loaf. All breads are steamed while baking for a hard crust. Tortes ($1-$2 a slice) and individual French pastries are also made here.

Now that Rhodes has open an inn in a manorial Eaton Rapids estate, his son Matt runs the Okemos store. Food service begins at 10:30. Before that, customers can seat themselves and have coffee and baked goods on the premises.

MIDLAND

30 Hamilton's Pastry Shop

Monday-Saturday 6 a.m.-6 p.m.

*117 E. Main in downtown Midland. From I-75, take U.S. 10 to Midland, follow signs of Business Route 10 to downtown. As you approach the center of town, go left onto Ashman; in 3 blocks turn left onto Main. Bakery is in first block. (517) 832-8190. A **second location** is a coffee shop in Eastlawn Plaza, 925 Saginaw Road, open daily except Sunday 7-5.*

When Peggy and Ray Hamilton bought this full-line bakery in 1968, they adopted its recipes and from-scratch methods, which they continue to use today. That means the Danish dough is made the labor-intensive but authentic way, rolled, brushed with butter, folded upon itself, then refrigerated and rolled again, three times in a two-day period. That makes for a light, flaky crust. Danish (60¢ each, also in coffeecake size) are filled with cream cheese, almond, pecan, or butterscotch-walnut, or seven fruit fillings.

Muffins (50¢), sunflower bread and a multi-grain bread ($1.30 a loaf), cookies — there's a lot here that, combined with fruit and cheese, would make a fine picnic on the pretty park behind downtown, where three rivers come together. Ask for directions. And every leisurely visit to Midland should include a stop at the beautiful Dow Gardens, west of downtown on Business Route 10. Planned in the American spirit according to principles of Japanese and Chinese landscape design, it uses only plants well suited to Midland's climate. Dow Chemical's founder started the garden in his back yard to show how logged-over Midland could be transformed through intelligent landscaping. Over the years, its designers worked to create an environment that's interesting and attractive at every season of the year — and they succeeded brilliantly. For more about it and Midland, consult *Hunts' Highlights of Michigan.*

☞ EXACT PRICES have been given to provide the best possible relative price comparisons. **It is expected**, of course, that **prices will increase** over the life of this book.

MUSKEGON AREA

31 Mike's Bread

Tuesday-Friday 8-5, Saturday 8-3. (616) 726-2954.
1095 Third at Houston in downtown Muskegon, one block east on Third from the corner of Third and Webster, where Hackley Park faces the Hackley Public Library and Muskegon Museum of Art. (Entrance and parking lot are on Houston.) From I-96, take Seaway downtown and turn east onto Third.

A little like a French patisserie, a little like a co-op with glass jars of spices for sale, this cheerful bakery and coffee shop is tucked away — like a number of surprising places in the old lumbering and industrial town of Muskegon. A low office building isn't where you'd expect to find a bakery and coffee shop whose flyer claims, "The world's best bread is made right here *in Muskegon!*" And that's not a lot of hype. Whole grain yeast breads, which Mike Canter specializes in, are notoriously difficult, all too often heavy, crumbly leaden bricks. His are chewy, light, and satisfying. Many breads are made with concern for nutritional balance, but to eat them, you'd think good eating was the paramount consideration. Mike's Apple Raisin has black molasses, bran, dried fruit, and whole wheat, while five-grain's combined grains makes for more protein. Pumpernickel rye is coarsely ground, with bran, sweetened with molasses, honey, and corn-barley malt. In its crusty hard roll form, it's terrific.

In addition to European-style breads, characteristically made without fat, and yeast breads, Mike's offers tasty cookies and fruit bars, muffins (the carrot-raisin muffin is especially delicious), and cakes, and occasional extras of party cakes, mousses, and tortes his wife, Darma, bakes for catering jobs. She will prepare picnics to order for a minimum of 5 people or so, with quiches or croissants, rolls, and desserts. Prices for bread loaves range from $1.50 to $2.25, while muffins and large cookies are 75¢.

This is a friendly place, with three booths where you can have coffee or a light lunch. Don't be surprised if other customers strike up a conversation with you.

32 Robinson's Bakery

Monday-Friday 6 a.m.-5 p.m., Saturday to 3.
In Whitehall, on 1019 South Mears. From U.S. 31, take the

*Business Route 31 exit into town. The main downtown intersection
before 31 turns and descends to the lake is Mears. Go south on
Mears about a mile. Bakery is in a residential area. (616) 894-5979.*

Despite the English name, Robinson's is a Swedish bakery featuring limpa bread (a light rye flavored with fennel, anise, and orange; baked Wednesdays); terrific sourdough rye and pumpernickel, chewy, crusty, and robust, made the slow-rise way; a substantial, multigrain Whole Earth bread and many other breads; and
a big assortment of Danish-style coffee cakes and sweet rolls,
made with butter.

In old logging towns like Whitehall, there are often sizable Swedish populations. Resorters are another appreciative customer
base for Robinson's.

Everything here is baked from scratch, even doughnuts. Cookies include Swedish Dreams and cinnamon diamonds as well as
most all the old and new American standards. Prices are remarkable; it's well worth a stop if you're heading home, to fill your
freezer with good bread.

Half a dozen tables are largely patronized by regulars who come
in for coffee, morning pastries, and the newspaper.

PAW PAW

33 Grain Dance Bakery and Paw Paw Food Co-op

Monday-Saturday 8 a.m.-6 p.m.
*243 East Michigan Ave. in downtown Paw Paw. Michigan Ave. is
also the Red Arrow Highway. The bakery is just east of the courthouse. From I-94, take M-40 into town, turn right onto Michigan
Ave. (616) 657-5934.*

Natural foods co-ops and bakeries don't only exist in college
towns. In rural areas like Paw Paw, such stores have to reach out
beyond their natural constituencies, which brings them closer to
the broader, more inclusive spirit of agrarian co-operatives of the
past. Unfortunately, that happy phenomenon is far more prevalent
in Wisconsin and Minnesota, with their Scandinavian co-op traditions, than in Michigan.

Right in downtown Paw Paw, this appealing little storefront
houses a natural foods co-op store and bakery. Most everything is
organically grown, including the whole wheat flour in the whole
wheat and oatmeal breads. (Both are about 1 1/2 pound and cost

$1.89.) Spelt, a wheat substitute for people allergic to wheat, is the third bread baked here. Stuffed bagels ($1.59-$1.89) are another specialty — plump little pizza, vegetable, burrito, and sauerkraut/cheese sandwiches. What with homemade cinnamon rolls, muffins, and juices, and cheese from the deli case, this is a fine picnic stop. Ask for directions to nearby Maple Isle, Paw Paw's delightful island park.

PETOSKEY/HARBOR SPRINGS AREA

34 Dutch Oven

Tuesday-Saturday 6:45 a.m.-5:30 p.m.
On U.S. 31 in the center of Alanson, about 11 miles east of both Petoskey and Harbor Springs. (616) 548-2231.

By all accounts, the best bakery in the Petoskey-Harbor Springs area, and the only one worth going out of the way for, is the Dutch Oven in the unpretentious little town of Alanson, on the Inland Waterway east of Petoskey. The Dutch Oven is a hands-on family business that has remained small deliberately. Its roots are in the old European baking tradition based on quality ingredients and a craftsmanlike attitude to manual work, using no preservatives, no mixes, and few short cuts. Co-owner and baker Rudolf Burgherr was trained in his native Switzerland. He gets up at 1 a.m. to do the day's baking along with his assistants. (The Dutch Oven name goes back 50 years, predating the Burgherrs by a quarter-century. The name comes from the rotating oven, not the nationality of the original bakers.)

Pastries, special-order cakes, desserts, and popular gift items like cinnamon bread and Christmas plum puddings form the basis of the Dutch Oven's reputation. The cakes are "always perfect," says Laurie Smith, innkeeper at Stafford's Bay View Inn, which orders cakes and desserts from the Dutch Oven. A New York producer of soap operas orders 350 loaves of cinnamon bread as holiday gifts for business associates. It's a spiral loaf, rolled in butter and cinnamon sugar, meant to be sliced thick, and perhaps grilled in butter. A 26-ounce loaf is $3. Tiger Paws ($5 for a 10-ounce box) are small, two bite affairs of homemade almond paste with a creamy chocolate filling. Another delectable little dessert is the Milander Square (75¢), a 3-inch shortbread square, spread with raspberry jam and dipped in chocolate. Yet another unusual specialty is Biber — cookies made of gingerbread dough and homemade almond paste, embossed with old handmade molds.

Last year the Dutch Oven started making a hard-crust European rye bread ($1.60 a loaf), made the traditional way with sour starter and three risings. Muffins are another popular lower-calorie item. Either could form the basis of easy picnic lunches to enjoy at Petoskey State Park or the far less crowded Thorne-Swift Nature Preserve and Beach, on Lower Shore Drive 4 miles west of Harbor Springs. (Just don't bring glass containers to Thorne-Swift.)

The Dutch Oven is also a simple, 12-table cafe serving sandwiches, soups, and baked goods until 5:15. And it is a yarn shop — one of the best in Michigan, says Mary Burgherr, Rudolf's wife and partner, who runs it.

35 Stafford's Bay View Inn

Open daily breakfast, lunch and dinner from Mother's Day through fall color season. Open for Sunday brunch year-round.

On the north side of U.S. 31 at the intersection of Woodland Ave. in Bay View, a mile northeast of Petoskey. (616) 347-2771.

The high rents and short seasons of most resort areas don't encourage good bakeries, which are nurtured by cheap space and a steady year-round customer base, not by a captive summer market willing to pay top dollar for mediocre stuff in the right place. That probably explains the paucity of good bakeries in the affluent Grand Traverse/Little Traverse areas. If you're willing to pay more and call ahead to insure availability, Stafford's five restaurants are your best bet in Harbor Springs, Petoskey, Boyne City, Bay View, and Charlevoix, especially if it's Sunday or Monday and the Dutch Oven in Alanson is closed.

Stafford's bakery and commissary is in Stafford Smith's original restaurant in the Bay View Inn, a centerpiece of the Methodist summer colony that set the model for later Northern Michigan resorts when it was organized in 1875. (For more on Bay View and the area, see *Hunts' Highlights of Michigan*.) Deliveries are made twice daily to the other restaurants. Baked goods, soups, pastas, and deli items are all available to go, if orders are called in advance.

French bread, made with two risings and steamed for a more fully developed flavor and good crust, is $4.50 a one-pound loaf. People also talk about the good foccaccia (flat garlic-herb bread,

$3.50 a one-pound piece) and the sweet nut breads — date, banana, and zucchini-carrot, all $8 for a big 3 1/2-pound loaf. Pies and carrot cakes (each $14) are also available carry-out; pre-orders are advised.

36 Stafford's Perry Hotel

Open breakfast, lunch and dinner year-round.
In Petoskey's Gaslight District on Bay at Lewis. Park at the foot of Bay Street or between Bay and Lake just east of the tracks. (616) 347-2516.

See Stafford's Bay View Inn. The pretty little park along the train tracks just south of the hotel is a delightful place for a take-out snack; so is Bayfront Park, reached via a tunnel beneath busy U.S. 31.

37 Stafford's Pier

Open daily 11:30-11 from Mother's Day through color season. Open for dinner January through March. Call for Nov. and April hours.
In downtown Harbor Springs, 102 Bay at the harbor. (616) 526-6201.

See Stafford's Bay View Inn. Benches are by the marina and in Zorn Park, on the waterfront a little west from here.

PORT HURON

38 French's Bakery

Monday-Saturday 6 a.m.-6 p.m., Sunday 8 a.m.-2 p.m.
1041 Griswold at southwest of downtown Port Huron, south of the Black River bridge. From I-94 take exit 271 into Port Huron. (From I-69 this same exit is called 199.) You will be on Business Route 69, which becomes Oak. Take it to 11th Street and go left. Griswold is in one block, going the other way.

A supplier of flour to bakeries recommends French's as one of the better all-around bakeries in Michigan. It's known for breads — rye, salt-rising, pumpernickel, and a banana-nut bread. They sell for a remarkable 69¢ to $1.25 a loaf. Pastries include cream horns, turnovers, and Napoleons. Since Henry Stefanski and his sons bought French's ten years ago, they have added two restaurant-bakeries in malls.

Beef pasties ($2.29) can be heated to eat at tables in the bakery — or, for one of the most exciting water views in Michigan, get back onto Oak, follow Business Route 69 east to where it joins Business Route I-94. Take them north through downtown and to Pinegrove Park. It offers an outstanding view of freighter traffic, a floating lightship, the Bluewater Bridge, and the opposite shore of Canada's Chemical Valley. At night, it's a stunning, somewhat ominous-looking fairyland of lights. The site of Thomas Edison's home, now commemorated with an interpretive marker, is near the lightship.

SAGINAW AREA

39 Maria Elena's Bakery

Monday-Friday 8:30-6, Saturday 7:30-6, Sunday 7:30-2.
In Carrollton, across the Saginaw River from Saginaw's north end. At 512 Shattuck, about a block east of Michigan Ave. From I-675, take Exit 3 (Davenport and State streets), turn immediately north onto Michigan, go north less than a mile, turn right. Bakery is in a block. From Fashion Square Mall, go south about 1 1/4 or 1 1/2 miles on Bay Road (M-84) to Shattuck, then left on Shattuck about 1 1/4 miles. (517) 753-5388.

If you enjoy something slightly sweet with coffee or milk, but if greasy doughnuts or over-rich coffee cakes turn you off, a trip to a Mexican bakery may be well worth your while. Mexican sweet breads are light but not vacuously puffy, simple, and not too sweet. They come in many attractive shapes that look terrific together on a serving plate. They are meant to be eaten at breakfast, after meals, and as snacks.

Despite Michigan's considerable Chicano population, the state has only a very few Mexican bakeries. Saginaw has a bakery and a tortilla factor to serve the community that goes back to the 1920s and 1930s, recruited from Texas to work on railroads and in Saginaw Valley sugar beet refineries.

Maria Elena's is in a retail strip in Carrollton, north across the Saginaw River from Saginaw's north end. It's only takeout, and Sunday is its biggest day. Empanadas (golden-brown turnovers) come with pumpkin, strawberry, or cherry filling. They and most other sweet rolls are only 30¢. (See page 231 for a complete description of traditional Mexican pastries.) On the non-sweet side,

Zehnder's may be best known as the restaurant with the chicken dinners, but it also has a fine, elaborately equipped bakery in the basement. You can watch bakers at work through a window.

ready-to-eat tamales are $5 a dozen.

It's an easy drive to Saginaw's beautiful riverside park complex, south on Michigan to the first or second arterial street over the river, then turning right almost immediately onto Washington. About two miles south of downtown on Washington at Rust, there are picnic tables at Hoyt Park (next door to the children's zoo). Across the way, off Ezra Rust Boulevard and behind the Japanese Tea House, you can also drive across to Ojibway Island in the Saginaw River and picnic there, or picnic at the Anderson Wave Pool on the south side of Ezra Rust. Call (517) 759-1648 for more on the summer tea ceremonies at the Tea House.

SOUTH HAVEN

40 *Golden Brown Bakery*

Monday through Saturday 6-5:30.

421 Phoenix in downtown South Haven. From U.S. 31 take the main South Haven exit into town along Phoenix. Bakery is in last block before Lake Michigan. (616) 637-3418.

Founded in 1938, this successful resort-town bakery keeps up with changing food trends and now wins good comments in the area for its dense, satisfying 6-grain bread ($1.59 a one-pound loaf) and even heavier 3-seed bread ($3.79 a two-pound loaf). Both consist mainly of wheat flour. The six grains are barley, oatmeal, cornmeal, crushed rye, millet, and sesame; the three seeds, poppyseed, sesame, and raisins, are on the crust and inside, too. In all, some 20 kinds of bread, all raised with yeast, are made, though not every day.

Other favorite items are cheese danish (70¢) and lots of things featuring South Haven's leading fruit crop, blueberries. They're fresh in season, and held frozen for use throughout the year in oversize blueberry muffins (80¢), coffee cakes ($4 for 22 ounces), and more.

The cafeteria here serves soups, salads, and entrees as well as baked goods and sandwiches. It closes at 3 p.m.

TECUMSEH/ADRIAN AREA

41 Lev's Bakery

Tuesday-Friday 4:30 a.m.-5:30 p.m., Saturday to 3 p.m.
124 Chicago Boulevard (M-50) in downtown Tecumseh. From U.S. 23 at Dundee, take M-50 west to Tecumseh. (517) 423-2948.

Leverett Dejonghe opens up at 4:30 a.m. for workers on the early shift at the Saline Ford plant. Lev's is a ritual stop for sweet rolls (creamy-filled long johns are especially popular) and coffee — 3,000 cups a week, more than any restaurant in town, according to Lev. He began working here in 1952, bought it 14 years later, and now runs it with his son. Parents mail cookies around the world to adult children who fondly remember Lev's.

Lev makes his own fillings for the fruit pies he bakes, and for coconut, banana, lemon, and chocolate meringue ($4.25-$4.80). He cooks his own custard for custard-filled rolls topped with chocolate ($4.20 a dozen) and for German custards, with icing like that in German chocolate cake. German soft pretzels are a Saturday specialty. Customers wait for his dense salt-rising bread; it comes out of the oven at 10 o'clock Friday morning.

☛ EXACT PRICES have been given to provide the best possible relative price comparisons. **It is expected**, of course, that **prices will increase** over the life of this book.

TRAVERSE CITY AREA

42 Grand Traverse Bagel Factory

Monday-Friday 7:30-5:30, Saturday to 4.

1327 South Airport Road (Hwy. 620) on the southeast side of Traverse City, in Hillside Plaza retail strip just west of Garfield Road and the airport on the north side of the road. From U.S. 131/M-37 coming into town from the south, take Hwy. 620 east.
(616) 947-0337.

The best bread you can buy in the Grand Traverse area is, surprisingly, from a bagel factory. Filling a big bread gap in this affluent area, it branched out from bagels into lean breads (made from scratch without fat or oil, or any preservatives, either) baked in a hearth oven and steamed for a good, chewy crust. Sourdough-flavored white, cracked wheat, two kinds of rye, French and Italian breads, plus hot dog and burger buns, are baked fresh daily except Sunday, then distributed to stores around town (Max Bauer's and Prevo's markets in Traverse City and groceries in almost all the resort towns on the Leelanau Peninsula) and sold here at the retail store. Most of it is $1.40 for a 20-ounce loaf.

Bagels are still made, too: plain, sesame, poppyseed, garlic, onion, and salt, plus cinnamon-raisin in either bagel or stick form. They're 30¢ each, or $2.75 a dozen.

43 Manitou Farm Market and Bakery

Open from early May through October. Daily 8-6, to 7 in July and August.

On the west side of the Leelanau Peninsula, on M-22 about 4 miles south of Leland and 1 1/2 miles south of the intersection with Hwy. 204. In front of Good Harbor Vineyards. (616) 256-9165.

Leland, Northport, and Suttons Bay all have small bakeries that seem to change hands frequently. Of all that charming peninsula's bakeries, we've had the best reports about the one in this beautiful seasonal farm market owned by David and Martha Schaub. David grows the vegetables sold here, and Martha is in charge of preparing food for the bakery and deli, and making a line of jams, jellies, and chutneys. (Everybody up here tries to diversify to tide them through the winter; the Schaubs also grow and sell Christmas trees.)

Over a dozen kinds of pan breads sell for $1.45 to $1.55 for a one-pound loaf: oatmeal, light rye, sourdough, cinnamon, Swedish rye, natural grain, and more. Despite the names, these breads are American-style, raised with yeast for a lighter crumb. Among the quick breads ($3.,25) a rhubarb nut bread has been very popular. With pies, cakes, cookies, and a deli department featuring a much-praised potato salad, this makes a convenient picnic stop. The beautiful beach nearby at Good Harbor Bay is among the least heavily used in the Sleeping Bear National Lakeshore.

44 Northern Delights

Open year round. Restaurant hours usually Monday-Saturday 11-8 (bakery opens earlier). From July 4 through Labor Day, open daily 8 a.m.-10 p.m.

In Benzonia, at the top of the hill, on U.S. 31 just south of M-115. (616) 882-9631.

High principles and good food distinguish Northern Delights from the typical resort-area eatery. Benzonia is a little off the tourist track, up the hill and away from the water. The wholegrain bakery is an adjunct of a cheerful, spare little restaurant that serves lunch and dinner year-round, and breakfast during the summer season. Breads are mostly yeast breads baked in loaf pans, 1 1/2 pounds and $2 a loaf. There are three-seed bread (poppyseed, sunflower, and sesame), seven-grain, French and Swedish rye (these two are made without the hard crust that comes from steaming), cracked wheat, oat bran, and cinnamon-raisin.

As for the principles — baked goods are made without sugar (honey, molasses, and maple syrup are used instead). They use organic flours to support organic growers. And they are prepared in ways that recycle and have minimal impact on the environment. Other bakery products include various muffins (85¢), big $1 cookies, and a pecan-honey butter-cinnamon sweet roll (85¢).

A block away, the large central park of Benzonia has picnic tables. This was once the campus of a Congregational college intended to be an Oberlin of the North Woods. Bruce Catton's father came there to teach after it had become a college-prep high school; Benzonia is the setting for the famous American historian's engaging, provocative memoir and Michigan history, *Waiting for the Morning Train*. Ask at the bakery for the current hours of the interesting Benzonia historical museum down the street.

UPPER PENINSULA

MANISTIQUE AREA

1 Dreamland Motel and Restaurant

*20 miles east of Manistique and 2 miles west of Blaney Park on U.S. 2. **Open** daily May through November, 7 a.m.-9 p.m. (906) 283-3122.*

To make it in the U.P., it helps to be flexible and diversified. It's not at all surprising, for instance, to buy books at a gas station/motel/cafe. The Dreamland Motel and Restaurant is also a small bakery, where Jim and Ellen Troxler make well-recommended bread (white and rye, $2 a loaf), pasties ($2.50 to go), fresh doughnuts, and four kinds of pie from scratch — strawberry, blackberry, blueberry, and coconut-banana cream ($1.50 a slice). Only the apple pie uses canned filling.

TRENARY

2 Trenary Home Bakery

*In the center of Trenary on M-67, a mile north of U.S. 41 between Escanaba, Munising, and Marquette. Trenary is 20 miles north of the head of Little Bay de Noc, where U.S. 41 turns north from Lake Michigan. **Open** Monday-Saturday 5 a.m.-4 p.m. or so. (906) 446-3330.*

Next to the bank in the center of tiny Trenary, the Trenary Home Bakery does a big business, mostly wholesale, baking buns for subs and brats, and breads geared to local tastes shaped by the Upper Peninsula's many ethnic groups. There's a sour rye bread that rises overnight (it's $1.55 for a one-pound loaf), a round 24-ounce limpa rye bread (lightly flavored in the Swedish way with orange, fennel, and cardamom; $1.80), and Italian bread ($1.35).

But its claim to fame rests on Trenary toast. Dried overnight after the cinnamon and butter has been baked on, this rye bread toast has a shelf life of at least six months, without preservatives. It's not just cinnamon toast, the owner points out; there's a secret ingredient or two — quite possibly including cardamom. The toast is typically dunked in coffee or milk. Like hardtack, which also

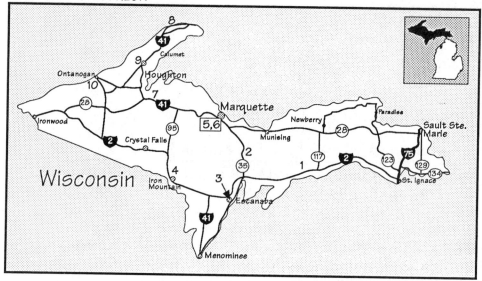

KEY

7 U.P. Bakeries,, pp. 281-288

12 Federal Highway

140 State Highway

⊗ ▦ City or town

Bakeries in Michigan's
UPPER PENINSULA

used to be made here, it's perfect for taking to hunting and fishing camps without spoiling. Brown paper bags of Trenary toast ($2.15 plus shipping) are sent UPS all over the U.S. to homesick Yoopers. The area's weak economy sends natives out into the wider world en masse, but strong regional ties are kept alive by vacations (it seems three-fourths of the vacationers you meet on the Keweenaw have roots there) and even Yooper clubs.

ESCANABA

3 Swedish Pantry

819 Ludington Street in downtown Escanaba, between the two theaters. **Open** *9 a.m.-7:30 p.m. in summer; call to confirm winter hours. (906) 786-9606. Winter hours may be a little shorter.*

Some of the warmest and best restaurants are based not on food trends or exotic vacation experiences but on memories of mother's cooking, tried and true recipes passed down over generations and fine-tuned over time to the tastes of the immediate family. That's the story at the Swedish Pantry restaurant and bakery, where Betty Maycunich bakes the way her mother did, from scratch. She grew up during the Depression, when cooking with basic ingredients not convenience mixes was rewarded by important savings as well as better results.

The oatmeal bread, white bread, and Swedish limpa bread (rye lightly flavored with cardamom and orange) made here are dense and substantial. Made in a typical loaf pan, they weigh two pounds rather than the usual one or one and a half. All are $2.25. Other bakery products include four kinds of normal-size muffins a day (55¢ each; two are always fresh blueberry and bran); cookies; Scandinavian braided coffee bread, flavored with cardamom and iced, with almonds; and two homemade desserts. Pies like raspberry supreme or rhubarb custard are $1.95 a slice. Other desserts may be bread pudding with rum or custard sauce; fresh apple dumpling in pastry with sauce.

The bakery is run as an extension of the restaurant; to be sure of getting what you want, come by noon or call in your order. Some visitors buy a dozen loaves of bread at a time to take home and freeze.

IRON MOUNTAIN

4 Schinderle's Italian Maid Bake Shoppe

On the north side of Iron Mountain on U.S. 2 (Stephenson Hwy.) by the Chapin pit, next to Hardee's. **Open** *daily except Tuesday 7:30 a.m.-6 p.m. Monday is a no-baking thrift day. (906) 774-0366.*

Italians were one of the most numerous ethnic groups to immigrate to the Upper Peninsula's mining regions during the great mining boom just after the turn of the century. In this sparsely populated region you can find good ethnic bakeries that normally are found only in big cities.

Though the Schinderle family that now owns this bakery is not entirely Italian, there are plenty of Italian customers to keep it authentic. The baking is done in an old soapstone oven at the original bakery in an old residential neighborhood; the highway location is retail only.

Twelve kinds of bread include crusty Italian sourdough ($1.39), a softer Vienna bread, and a round limpa rye bread for the many area Swedes. Cornetti (six for $1.89) are hard rolls shaped like a fat, puffy cross with equal arms — a shape that creates more crust and is perfect for breaking off and dunking in soup, salad oil, or gravies.

The white, chewy sourdough is used in burger buns that won't fall apart. There are also biscotti (toasted bread to dunk in wine), garlic bread, cannoli stuffed with whipped cream, ricotta, cherries, and chocolate chips ($1.49), and pizzelli (45¢), flower-shaped anise-flavored cookies made two at a time on a waffle iron by the owner's elderly mother.

A full line of sweet rolls (45¢) and Danish (55¢) are also available. "Everything is big," says the owner. "This shop doesn't do anything little."

MARQUETTE

5 Angeli's Bakery-Deli

In Marquette at 119 West Baraga. As you enter town from the south on U.S. 41/Front St., Baraga is the street just after the Chamber of Commerce and the RR tracks. Turn left; bakery is right there. **Open** *Monday-Saturday 7 a.m.-6 p.m. (906) 226-7335.*

Marquette has lost most of its Italians to neighboring Ishpeming and Negaunee, but it still has Angeli's Bakery. Italian specialties baked here from scratch include the cross-shaped crusty rolls called cornetti (see page 283; here they're 40¢ each), big, football-shaped loaves of Vienna bread ($1.39 for 1 1/2 pounds), and 18-inch loaves of Italian bread (also $1.39). Fried sweet rolls are made here, but Angeli's doesn't go in for desserts — it's more of a deli, with breads to go with salads and meat and cheese in subs. And there are also the inevitable pasties.

You can sit down at a table or take out food to beautiful Presque Isle Park, about 10 minutes away.

6 Babycakes

In downtown Marquette at 223 West Washington (Bus. Route 41), across from the old city hall. Open Monday-Friday 6 a.m.-6 p.m., Saturday 7 a.m.-5:30 p.m. (906) 226-7744.

Up in the U.P., where the trends and trappings of contemporary consumer culture seem far away in time and space, it can occasionally be a welcome thing to come upon a spot like Babycakes that serves, say, cappucino and muffins. In Marquette (population 22,000), the largest urban area in the U.P., Babycakes is a popular café where you can have espresso or cappucino and any of 12 kinds of big muffins a day from a repertoire of some 80 varieties; they're 85¢ each. Of several kinds of bread, favorites include a honey-whole wheat ($1.75), cashew date, onion-dill, and a somewhat heavier sourdough rye ($2).

L'ANSE

7 Hilltop Restaurant & Motel

*Just southeast of L'Anse on U.S. 41. **Open** daily year-round. From mid-May through deer season: 6 a.m.-8 p.m. Otherwise: 7-7. (906) 524-7858.*

Because of their flavor and size, the Hilltop's spiral cinnamon rolls enjoy a formidable fame and name recognition throughout the Upper Peninsula and beyond. Made with apple and brown sugar filling, they weigh in at a pound and stand some five inches high — quite a value for $1.25. "On a normal day we make 40 to 50 dozen, but we have made up to 250 dozen in a day," says owner Judy Jaeger with pride, figures readily at hand. "We use seven to nine tons of flour a month, and up to 500 pounds of powdered sugar for the frosting." These and other rolls are baked throughout the day, so they're fresh when you get them. College students from nearby Michigan Tech and Northern Michigan buy them in quantity, as do tourists, and the restaurant will mail them UPS upon request. Jaeger sees their success as a just reward for her insistence on baking from scratch in this age of frozen dough and mixes.

Jaeger's own favorite is the big 60¢ dinner roll — the equivalent of seven pieces of bread. Pies are made with fresh fruit in season (out of season some prepared fillings may be used). Muffins come in many flavors — cranberry-apple, banana-nut, and more. Raised doughnuts are also made from scratch, as are all the items on the salad bar, from salad dressing to vegetable soup to pickled fish, if you come for a meal. But visitors are always welcome just to come for coffee and a roll.

HOUGHTON/KEWEENAW

8 The Jampot

On M-26 between Eagle River and Eagle Harbor, by Jacob's Falls where Jacob's Creek enters Great Sand Bay. **Open** *daily in season (May through fall color in early October). No phone. Mailing address: The Society of St. John, Star Route 1, Box 226, Eagle Harbor, MI 49950.*

If you want a pretty good bakery with a bustling, coffee-sipping scene of locals and tourists, go to Johnson's Bakery and Restaurant on U.S. 41 near the east end of Copper Harbor. But for baked goods served up in sweet simplicity of the most picturesque order, the tiny Jampot by Jacob's Falls, overlooking the Great Sand Bay of Lake Superior, would be very hard to match. Tucked into the piney hillside, with the rushing falls well within earshot, it's a memorably quaint little spot without being in the least bit fussy. The mood is like that of a tearoom from an earlier, gentler, smaller-scale era of tourism. And M-26 between Phoenix and Copper Harbor is one of the most unaffectedly beautiful drives anywhere, with the steep forest on one hand, on the other Lake Superior (alternately rocky like Maine or sandy-beached), and frequent delightful waterfalls beckoning you to take a short walk back into the woods, carpeted in pine needles. If it were on either coast, it would be famous and overcrowded. Here, so far away from population centers there's remarkably little traffic even in season.

To this idyllic spot two monks (yes, monks — complete with hooded brown robes) have withdrawn from the world and their native city of far-away Detroit. They bake very good muffins, breads, cookies, brownies, and giant chocolate chip cookies, along with rich cakes, largely sold mail-order. And they make jams and butters from a big variety of local berries — apple-plum butter, wild billberry, strawberry, and more.

The muffins ($1.50) are huge — one makes a good lunch. The pumpkin muffin, full of raisins and nuts and iced with lemon frosting, wins raves for its flavor and texture. The cakes — things like walnut ginger cake, lemon pound cake, Jamaican Black Cake — are quite elaborate and costly. Take the Abbey Cake (four pounds, $30), described as "the perennial favorite. Rich, moist, and chewy, with dark raisins and walnuts in a molasses batter, it

Brother Peter in front of The Jampot bakery, on picturesque M-26 by Jacob's Falls. Just one muffin from The Jampot makes a satisfying lunch.

is generously laced with bourbon and will keep and improve for years." And at $4 to $7, the jams and jellies aren't cheap, either. Order forms are sent in back of a newsletter filled with prayers, scripture, meditations, and reflections about life (spiritual and everyday) at the two monks' Keweenaw home. An excerpt: "When we hear the comment at the Jampot, 'Well, you certainly do live in God's country,' we are likely to respond, 'Everywhere is God's country.' If we are feeling talkative, we may also add, 'But it is easier to see Him in some places than in others.'"

There's nothing to drink here, and there really isn't a grocery store in Eagle Harbor, the next stop on the drive along M-26 up to Copper Harbor. You're well advised to take coffee or juice (ask for directions to the big supermarket in Calumet) and picnic in one of the two delightful little parks overlooking Lake Superior between Eagle Harbor and Copper Harbor.

9 Suomi Home Bakery & Restaurant

In downtown Houghton at 54 North Huron. (It's a covered street, to keep it snow-free in winter.) From Business U.S. 41 downtown, turn down toward the channel. **Open** *Monday-Friday 6-6, Saturday to 5, Sunday 7 to 2. (906) 482-3220.*

More of a restaurant than a bakery, this antiseptically plain, super-friendly place, where coffee is constantly refilled, is known for Finnish specialties. It bakes pies ($1.30 a slice), white and whole wheat breads, cookies, rolls, and pasties. The Upper Peninsula's signature food, pasties were actually brought by Cornish miners, not by Finns, but rutabagas are a Scandinavian introduction.) *Nisu* is a Finnish bread that's soft and sweet, flavored with cardamom, sometimes with fruit mixed in. Nisu makes a good French toast. And the *pannukakku*, a custardy, oven-baked pancake ($2.85), is outstanding with raspberry sauce. No wonder breakfast is served all day here!

ONTONOGAN

10 Syl's Restaurant & Bakery

In downtown Ontonogan at 713 River. **Open** *daily 5:30 a.m.-10 p.m. (906) 884-2522.*

Syl's pies earn it a mention among the U.P.'s noteworthy bakeries. Over 20 years ago, Syl Laitola took over this place, planning to run a short-order restaurant. "But it kinda got bigger," she says. White and whole wheat bread ($1.50 a loaf) are baked from scratch, as are all the pies except cherry, which uses canned filling. Blueberries, raspberries, rhubarb, and apple pies ($1.35 a slice) all start out as fresh fruit prepared on the premises. Syl's pasties ($2.50 to go) are also highly regarded.

The restaurant's long hours (5:30 a.m. to 10 p.m. daily) make this a convenient place to pick up takeout food for anyone going to the Porcupine Mountains State Park.

☛ EXACT PRICES have been given to provide the best possible relative price comparisons. **It is expected**, of course, that **prices will increase** over the life of this book.
